Voices

into

Choices

Acting on the Voice of the Customer

Center for Quality of Management

Gary Burchill

Christina Hepner Brodie

Voices *into* Choices
Acting on the Voice of the Customer

Oriel Inc. 3800 Regent Street P.O. Box 5445 Madison WI 53705-0445 USA
Phone: 800-669-8326 (U.S. only) or 608-238-8134 Fax: 608-238-2908
First Printing June 1997

Development Team

Center for Quality of Management

Gary Burchill
Author

Christina Hepner Brodie
Author

Toby Woll
Subject Matter Expert
Executive Director

Joiner Associates Incorporated

Casey Garhart
Instructional Designer
and Developer

Jan Harris
Desktop Publisher

Alicia Kratzer
Graphic Designer

Dale Mann
Illustrator

Dawn Olson
Desktop Publisher

Vickie Peters
Production

Elizabeth Ragsdale
Editor

Sue Reynard
Contributing Writer

Carol Roberts
Indexer

Jennifer Schilling
Copyeditor/Proofreader

Angela Schoeneck
Project Leader and
Marketing

Franny VanNevel
Contributing Writer

ISBN 1-884731-13-9

Foreword

Joiner Associates Incorporated and the Center for Quality of Management (CQM) are enthusiastic about collaborating to combine our areas of expertise in *Voices into Choices: Acting on the Voice of the Customer*. This book embodies the core philosophy of each organization—the development of resources and methods that enable customers to achieve and sustain excellence, and the spirit of organizations benefiting from mutual learning.

For the past seven years, CQM has been offering its member organizations educational programs, advising services, research initiatives, and networking activities to address the three areas critical to long-term success: planning, operations, and managing change. Now, in the spirit of mutual learning, CQM has recently opened its courses and other services to nonmembers as well. For over 13 years, Joiner has been helping organizations attain high quality standards, understand their customers, build customer and employee loyalty, and achieve business success.

Through its work with member organizations, CQM has developed and refined a process for collecting, analyzing, and acting on the Voice of the Customer. In order to share this knowledge with others, a collaboration was formed with Joiner, a company that believes in developing resources and methods to allow individuals and organizations to Unleash the Potential™ that lies within.

We hope our book will help you understand your customers' needs and translate their voices into tangible results for your organization.

Pat Zander, CEO
Oriel Incorporated
formerly Joiner Associates

Toby Woll, Executive Director
Center for Quality of Management

Acknowledgements

The creation of this book reaches far beyond the development team. A special tribute is due to Professor Shoji Shiba who first introduced the authors and the Center for Quality of Management members to the methods and skills that form the foundation of the FOCUS process. Thanks are also due to Dave Walden from Bolt, Baranek and Newman and to three CQM founding member companies: Analog Devices, Inc.; Bolt, Baranek and Newman; and Bose Corporation. They were instrumental in the initial development of Concept Engineering™, the method from which so many of the learnings in the FOCUS process are derived. And finally, we wish to acknowledge the many CQM member organizations whose work and learnings from using the process helped create *Voices into Choices: Acting on the Voice of the Customer.*

ADAC Laboratories

Alegro Microsystems

American Power Conversion Corporation

Analog Devices, Inc.

Analysis & Technology, Inc.

Bose Corporation

BTU International

Castellini Company

Champagne/LaFayette Communications

ChoiceCare

Communications and Power Industries

Center for Quality of Management

Digital Equipment Corporation

Energy Systems Industries, Inc.

Federal Reserve Bank of Boston

Fluke Corporation

Grason-Stadler/Welch Allyn

The Health Alliance of Greater Cincinnati

Hewlett-Packard Company

Hillerich & Bradsby Company

Honeywell Centra A.G.

Ingersoll Rand Company

ITT Barton

L.L. Bean, Inc.

Lily Transportation Inc.

LTX Corporation

Massachusetts Institute of Technology–Industrial Liaison Program

MARKEM Corporation

Mercury Computer Systems

Millipore Microelectronics Division

Naval Undersea Warfare Center, Newport

Nortel Technologies, Inc.

PictureTel

Polaroid Corporation

Procter & Gamble Company

Sippican, Inc.

Synetics/SAIC

Synopsys, Inc.

Teradyne, Inc.

Titleist and Foot-Joy Worldwide

Varian Associates

Volvo Car Corporation

W.R. Grace

Throughout the development of this book, many people have made contributions and have volunteered numerous hours of time. Some have reviewed our writing; groups have allowed us to come in and observe them working with the FOCUS process; and others have critiqued our ideas about book titles, layout and format, and reviewed early cover design concepts. We feel all of these reviews and subsequent feedback have made this a better book than we could have developed on our own. Thank you to everyone who has made a contribution. A special thank you to our reader panel who spent numerous hours reviewing our writing and providing feedback on our ideas. We couldn't have done it as well without you!

The Association for Manufacturing Technology

Charlotte Bell
Wisconsin Educational Communications Board

Richard J. Blotz
Ohmeda, Medical Systems Division

Regine Buchanan
The American Health Quality Association

James A. Evans
Union Camp Corp.

Mark P. Finster
Professor, School of Business University of Wisconsin-Madison

Sonya Hall
ChoiceCare

Brent A. Kedzierski
Blue Cross and Blue Shield of Maryland, Inc.

William H. Lawton
Professor, Simon Graduate School of Buisness, University of Rochester

Kevin Little
Informing Ecological Design

Jim Marteney
John S. Barnes

Mary Radue
Matousek & Associates

Doug Scott
Ohmeda, Medical Systems Division

Diane C. Shen
Center for Quality of Management

Andrew Simon
TU Electric

Terry Sullivan
Ohmeda, Medical Systems Division

Brent Sussman
Sears, Roebuck & Company

Dave Walden
Center for Quality of Management

Marnel Winns
Community Medical Center
An affiliate of Saint Barnabas Health Care System

Book Structure

This book is divided into an introduction and five sections, each representing one phase in the FOCUS process. There are also two appendices: the first provides an At-A-Glance summary of the FOCUS steps and the second describes additional resources.

The information has been organized to help you work through the process in a step-by-step fashion. However, we have also tried to accommodate readers who want to move around in the book, or use it as a reference, by including overviews and summaries of the work.

Each of the five main sections in the book follows a similar structure and flow.

Section Outline

Out of FOCUS: These fables illustrate what can go wrong when the steps in a phase are skipped or are done poorly. While none of the stories is true in the literal sense, they are all based on incidents that occurred in companies before people there started using the FOCUS process.

FOCUS Outline: This outline provides a complete list of the steps in the FOCUS process and illustrates where the section falls in the overall flow.

Overview: These pages set the stage for the section. They describe the type of work you will be doing, the benefits of the work, and the time required for each step. The list of Questions You Will Be Answering may be thought of as an advance organizer for the section, or as objectives for learning. They can also be used as a check when you are done.

Steps: Each phase is made up of several steps, which comprise the actual work involved in this process. Like the sections, these steps also follow a similar structure and flow (discussed on page *viii*).

Section Summary: Each section concludes with a summary of what you should have completed and a look at what is yet to come.

Step Outline

The Big Picture: This page provides a "map" of each step describing necessary prework, time and logistics, supplies, and the outcomes of your efforts.

Description: This is usually a single paragraph describing the work in the step.

Benefits: This paragraph describes what you will gain by completing the step.

Getting Your Bearings: These paragraphs help connect each step with both the work that has gone before and the work that is yet to come.

How to...: The bulk of each step is made up of a series of substeps which describe specific activities.

Step Check: At the end of each step a checklist enables you to make certain that you have accomplished what you need to in order to continue successfully.

Example of the start of a step

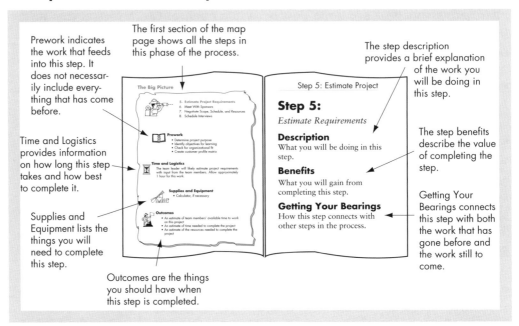

General Layout

In addition to the structure of the sections and steps, many common elements are repeated throughout the book. These include

- Background information
- "How to" information
- Checklists
- Sidebar boxes
- Tips
- Examples
- Case studies

Basic layout of the pages

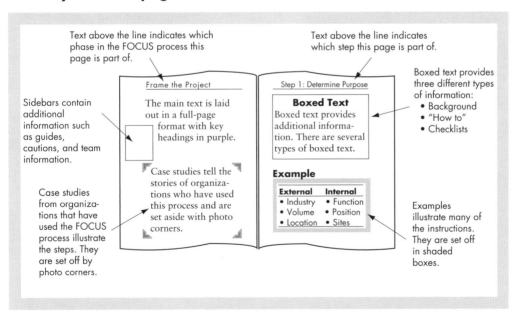

There are three basic types of full-page boxed text. The different formats used for each type will help you differentiate them.

Background Information

This boxed text is designed to provide readers with a little more depth or breadth of information than the basic text.

Going As an Explorer

This text provides additional information about what it means to be an "explorer" during the interview process. Some people may find this information more valuable than others, so it is set apart.

"How To" Information

Whereas Background Information is often more theoretical, this boxed text is practical in nature and provides specific information on how to accomplish various tasks, procedures, and exercises.

What Every Notetaker Should Know

This text provides basic tips and instructions to help team members take notes during the interviews. The key is to capture the customers' language without editing or interpreting.

Checklists

Checklists provide specific checks for an activity or a procedure. They are designed to serve as practical tools for team members as they work through the steps of the FOCUS process.

Supply Checklist

Supplies needed

- ❏ Interview schedule
- ❏ Interview guide
- ❏ Observation guide
- ❏ Notetaking pads
- ❏ Pens or pencils

Sidebar boxes and tips help provide guidance along the way. There are three types of sidebar boxes: Team boxes, Caution boxes, and Guide boxes. These boxes highlight key points that may be helpful to you as you work through the steps in the process.

The Team Icon

This box contains information that is of particular importance for teams. Sometimes it describes methods for the team to use in working together; other times it describes ways in which work can be divided among team members.

 If you are working as a team, the work in Step 2 can be divided among team members. However, the work in Steps 1, 3, and 4 should be done as a whole group.

The Caution Icon

This box contains warnings of potential pitfalls teams can stumble into if they are not careful. It often alerts you to unexpected outcomes of skipping a part of the process or doing a less than thorough job.

 People who fail to check their statements for scope often end up bogged down in unwieldy projects because their purpose statement is too broad.

The Guide Icon

This box provides a variety of information to guide you. It covers such things as alternate paths, answers to questions that may arise, and advice for when your project doesn't quite seem to fit with the general step descriptions.

 Remember that you will build multiple perspectives by interviewing different people—you don't have to cover every issue with each person.

The Tip Icon

 Tips are helpful hints that are connected to a specific substep or action in the process. They will help you stay on the path throughout your exploration.

TABLE OF CONTENTS

Understand the Voices .188

Select Action 356

Case In Point 407

Appendix A 409

Appendix B 415

Index 421

Case Studies

Product Redesign

Program Management

Scientific Imaging

Web Site Development

Acting on the Voice of the Customer

Market leaders compete against their rivals to be first to market with cutting-edge products; they also continuously challenge their own last best effort. What about you? What can you do to improve your organization's products or services? How can you identify and fulfill your customers' needs? How can you ensure that the changes you make to processes and policies are meaningful improvements? The information you need in order to focus your efforts is available—it is in the voices of your customers.

The FOCUS Difference

Much has been written about listening to your customers; few of these sources tell you how to gather information from them firsthand and put it to optimum use. *Voices into Choices* offers you the FOCUS process—a proven methodology to help you ground your actions using your customers' perspectives. This Voice of the Customer approach teaches you, step-by-step, how to: effectively conduct in-depth customer interviews, capture customer voices verbatim, produce data that is capsulized in language, not numbers, and transform that data into a blueprint for action. The FOCUS process gives you confidence that future relevant business decisions are customer-driven, not influenced by personal or organizational bias or based strictly on instinct or technical expertise.

> **Defining "Customer"**
>
> Customers are usually defined as external individuals or organizations who purchase or use your products or services. Many Voice of the Customer projects use the term just this way. Customers sometimes also include internal "customers" or constituents, external experts, lead thinkers, and others who do not actually use your products or services. Throughout this book, "customer" means anyone whose interests you represent or whose perspective can add value to your exploration and understanding.

The FOCUS process consists of 20 steps divided into five phases:

Frame the Project. Articulate the boundaries of the issue you want to explore and plan the project.

Organize Resources. Determine the appropriate balance of scope, schedule, and resources needed to do the work and schedule the interviews.

Collect Data. Interview a diverse sample of people who represent key viewpoints on the issue.

Understand the Voices. Analyze statements collected during the interviews to gain insight about important areas of concern or opportunity.

Select Action. Generate and choose specific actions that will address the concerns or take advantage of the opportunity.

The FOCUS Process Gets Results

Projects benefitting from the FOCUS process typically fall into one of three categories:

1. Clarifying a suspected problem or weakness

Explorations of this nature often begin with someone sensing that something is wrong with what is happening now. The FOCUS process builds a rich, detailed understanding that illuminates the structure of a problem or the location of weaknesses; that understanding becomes the basis for generating solutions for action which are responsive to customer needs.

Project Issue: Every summer the Federal Reserve Bank of Boston endured an arduous budgeting cycle that consumed extraordinary resources of staff and time. Staff often worked into the evening, came in on weekends, and no one could take a vacation until the process was complete. Carl Madsen, the Manager of Management and Planning, sensed that these symptoms were evidence that the budget process could be better.

FOCUS Solution: As the team leader, he invited experienced budget analysts from other departments to join the project team. They divided into pairs and interviewed a variety of internal budget process participants, from the chief operating officer on down. The team used these customer voices to understand the full range of problems and to build a new structure for the budget cycle. Now, business plans, not budget caps, drive the budget process. Each department plans its resources for its own business plan, shifting funds among functions as needed. Now during budget time, overtime is minimal, and vacations are again an option.

2. Defining an opportunity

Explorations in this category seek to discover opportunities that exist around unmet customer needs or expectations. These explorations start with a clear intent to understand explicit customer needs before creating new or improved capabilities. If appropriate, the customer voices collected can be used to create a list of customer requirements that become the basis for a design effort.

Project Issue: Hillerich & Bradsby, maker of well-known Louisville Slugger® bats, had once been a market leader in its PowerBilt Golf Division. After ignoring changes in the golf club industry, PowerBilt now faced a drastically diminished market share. Division leaders believed that redesigning the infrastructure would make them more efficient and help stave off their losses. When they introduced their proposed organizational structure to their sales force they learned that their customers, the retail stores, believed the company lacked viable products. Clearly structural changes would not be enough. The leaders had been trying to solve the wrong problem!

FOCUS Solution: John Hillerich, the new General Manager of PowerBilt, invited respected leaders from marketing, engineering, and production to join him in interviewing 15 retailers—a few satisfied ones, but also customers they had lost, and some they never had. Then, responding to their voices, in less than one year, the team created and delivered two new lines of golf clubs and radically changed the programs and services they offered their retailers.

> *"We learned about FOCUS just in time; had we not completed this project and changed immediately and radically, we would have faced dire consequences. When we started getting comments like, 'You've got the best programs in the industry' and 'This year you've done your homework', we realized that we had finally started to listen and to recognize what was really important to customers rather than acting on what we thought was important. We learned from our customers exactly what we needed to do and because of the consensus the process generated, we were able to align on a course of action and implement it immediately."*
>
> John Hillerich, General Manager
> PowerBilt Golf Division

3. Understanding a complex or strategic issue

Explorations in this category seek to build groundwork for thinking about a complex or strategic issue. A question like, "Does our current way of thinking about our business make us blind to either threats or opportunities?" may be the impetus for such an initiative. Results may lead to the discovery of a weakness or an opportunity, but more often the findings will lead to insight that shapes decision making or influences a shift in the organization's strategy.*

Project Issue: Polaroid Corporation was considering a new product to complement emerging technology in the field of mammography. Because the development would require significant investment, it became apparent to Roy Miller, the Director of New Product Development, that he needed to better understand the dynamics of the changes occurring in this market.

*See Appendix B for more information on the Interactive Planning Method for Strategic Planning.

FOCUS Solution: Instead of relying only on the usual industry experts who would have encouraged the product's development, the director decided to use the FOCUS process to take a 360° look at the issue. He invited a colleague to join him in interviewing leaders from several relevant fields, including academic researchers, insurance company managers, federal regulatory representatives, and radiologists. These diverse customer voices provided a different answer: while technology was expected to change, the change would happen gradually. This insight allowed the company time to experiment, pace their product development investments, and position themselves to play a role when the time is right.

"It's not what it costs to complete the FOCUS process, it's what it would have cost NOT to do the project."

Dave Walden, Vice President
Bolt, Baranek and Newman

These few examples begin to illustrate the countless ways the FOCUS process can be used by all organizations to listen to their customers—both externally and internally—to understand their voices and then move to action in response. Projects have been completed by teams and by individuals, by commercial and non-profit organizations, for issues that were relatively simple and others that were quite complex. Whatever the scope, these projects share important elements:

- All involved wide-ranging or strategically important issues.

- Issues needed further clarity before management could decide on the appropriate course of action.

- Useful data was difficult to obtain. Most project leaders tried to peer into the future where no factual, quantifiable data exists, making it necessary to rely on anecdotes or descriptions of individuals' experiences.

- People from diverse organizational levels often participated in the efforts, and executives or senior managers were either actively involved or sponsored the efforts.

Voices into Choices Moves You to Action

The process outlined in this book is designed to help you use the voices of your customers to gain clarity and insight on an issue that is important to you and your organization. The FOCUS process allows you to gain this insight by structuring purposeful opportunities for divergent and convergent thinking—that is, you broaden your view to consider numerous possibilities and then focus your decision making in order to move toward action that will get you results.

Is FOCUS for You?

Description

This section helps you assess whether the FOCUS process is appropriate for your issue. While it is valuable in a wide variety of situations, this approach may not always suit your current purpose. If you decide the FOCUS process is for you, you will then go on to assess the need for sponsorship and identify who should be involved.

Benefits

By investing time now you will determine if understanding your customers' needs and opinions is important to your current endeavor, and if using the FOCUS process is the best way for you to proceed.

Getting Your Bearings

Voice of the Customer projects begin in different ways. Sometimes a senior manager identifies a need and hands off the project to another manager or team, or an executive sees a need to tackle a challenging issue and initiates a project. Often, when individuals learn about the FOCUS process, they discover a new way of approaching something already on their agenda.

Using the FOCUS process is often most beneficial when you have only a vague sense of a problem or opportunity. By clarifying your issue through this process, you may then be able to use traditional problem-solving tools.

How to Determine If FOCUS Is for You

A. Clarify the issue

In order to decide if this is the right process, you need to start by clarifying a core issue. The FOCUS process is most successful in situations where you need to do one of the following:

- Gain insight about a suspected problem or weakness

- Define an opportunity around a new or existing product, service, policy, or procedure

- Understand a complex or strategic issue

To clarify your issue, write a phrase or sentence that you think captures the essence of the issue you want to explore. A good way to get started is to begin with "How to…" or "What is/are…."

Examples of issue statements

- How to improve the auditing process and its results
- How to understand the communication needs of constituent groups before improving our electronic communications
- What are the barriers preventing collaboration between Information Systems and Sales and Service?
- What are the needs of all of the different departments relative to the new facility?
- What are the diverse needs for pharmacy services across four very different merging hospitals?
- How do we get active participation of managers in the TQM implementation?
- What are the key factors driving changes in mammography?
- What prevents the reorganization from succeeding?

B. Decide if the FOCUS process is appropriate

Although the FOCUS process can be adapted to a wide range of circumstances, it is not the right approach for every purpose. To help you determine whether the FOCUS process is appropriate, ask the following question:

> "Will understanding the issue from the customers' point of view help me and my organization make better decisions?"

Review the following checklist to see if your project shares any of these characteristics.

Is FOCUS for You?

❏ The targeted issue is fuzzy or ill-defined. More clarity is needed before a decision can be made about what course of action is best.

❏ The subject of the issue is one in which you need to clarify problems, anticipate needs, or see into the future.

❏ The subject of exploration may have important implications with potential for significant impact.

❏ The results would benefit from multifunctional participation, alignment, or ownership.

If you answered yes to the initial question and your project has one of the above characteristics, then the FOCUS process is for you.

Do not try to force your project to fit this methodology if you realize your project will not benefit from customer input or does not share any of the above characteristics. You may have a clearly defined problem that requires more traditional reactive problem-solving tools,* or your issue may really require a decision based on cost, convenience, and other criteria important to your organization that are not driven by customer input.

---

*See Appendix B for more information on 7-Step Problem Solving Method.

IS FOCUS FOR YOU?

C. Decide who should be involved

Voice of the Customer projects are generally cross-functional in nature, and therefore will potentially involve people from diverse areas and levels within an organization. The key to successful projects is to involve everyone from the beginning all the way through to the end of the project. There are three possible categories of involvement:*

- Team members are responsible for doing the project work and should participate in each step of the FOCUS process. The most effective teams are typically groups of no more than eight people who represent a useful mix of perspectives.

 Sponsors can be valuable to a Voice of the Customer project in a number of ways. They can

- Influence the amount of time allocated to the project
- Approve major budget expenses
- Help make contact with customers
- Work across organizational boundaries
- Help deal with issues that arise during the project
- Decide whether actions the team recommends get implemented

- Sponsors are generally managers or executives within an organization who have the authority to allocate resources, approve budgets, work across organizational boundaries, and the like. The team will have periodic check meetings with them on the progress of the project. Often, the person who initially identified the issue for exploration will be a sponsor. Depending on the composition of the team and the structure of your organization, securing sponsorship may or may not be necessary. If you have the authority to allocate time and resources, and implement results, you may not need a sponsor.

- Stakeholders are people who will be affected by the project or who can influence it, but who do not need to be involved in every step. Typically, they need to be kept informed about the progress of the work.

*See Appendix B, *The Team*® *Handbook Second Edition*, for more information on team roles.

Participation Fosters Ownership

Everyone benefits when the people responsible for the project work are involved in all stages of the process—from the early thinking and planning stages through execution and follow-up action. This is important because

- Decisions made in the early stages shape the purpose and intent of the project as a whole

- Team members who engage directly with customers, and see firsthand what issues they deal with, routinely return with invaluable gut-level understanding for which there is no substitute

- As the team works together over the life of the project, they learn from each other's experience, complement each other's skills, and come to appreciate each other's roles in the organization

- Effective implementation is more likely when the people being asked to administer the changes have a hand in developing the changes

The benefits of involving others in the FOCUS process also show up in many small ways that have a cumulative effect extending beyond the project.

"At the conclusion of our first project I didn't think I learned anything new, but then over the next two years during implementation the folks from the other functions now knew what I knew; there was less contention, we were always on the same page. Then when I participated in a second project and it happened again, I became a believer!"

Lois O'Halloran
Polaroid Corporation

When determining who should be involved in the project, think broadly about likely areas within your organization that will be affected by the project work and people whose expertise or influence could help the project. Some questions to answer as you think about who to involve include the following:

- What internal functions, departments, or processes will be affected by this project? Are any of these areas outside my own level of authority?

- What expertise will be needed for the project?

- What external relationships may be affected by this project (such as customers or suppliers)?

- Who will be responsible for approving and acting on the recommendations?

- Who needs to approve team members' participation?

- Who needs to authorize budget expenses?

- What informal leaders within the organization does this project need support from?

- Who could possibly derail this project?

After you have come up with a list of people to involve, determine which category of participant they fall into: team member, sponsor, or stakeholder.

D. Meet with project participants

If you need sponsorship, set up a meeting to get the project started. Share information on how this project came about within the organization and what you hope to accomplish. You will also talk about who you would like to include as team members, especially if you need your sponsor to approve allocation of time to this project. Appendix A will help you understand the types of activities in each phase of the process, and the time required to complete the work.

Later, in Organize Resources, you will again meet with your sponsors to provide them with much more detail about the project's scope and your expected timeline.

Next, invite those people you have identified as potential team members to meet. You will want to share with them information on how this project came about, what you hope to accomplish, and their roles. Having already met with the project sponsors, you will be able to assure them that their involvement and the associated commitment of time has been approved by the appropriate persons.

If you have stakeholders, it is a good idea to bring them up-to-date on the project, its intent, and how you envision their involvement.

The following case studies show who was included in two different projects.

Case Study: Pharmacy Merger (Part 1 of 1)

When four hospitals were joining to create a health care alliance, the pharmacy and other support functions were slated to merge for efficiency. To plan the change, someone needed to understand the customers' diverse needs so that they could design a new structure that would excel in service, quality, and financial performance. For the pharmacy merger, it was clear that administrators, pharmacists, budget analysts, and members of the medical and nursing staffs had roles to play. Making the distinction between the roles of team member and stakeholder helped the team leader decide who to invite to participate on the project team. Because of the diversity of the groups who would be affected by the merger, the final team included 14 members. This was an unusually large team but everyone agreed that the complexity of the project required this level of involvement.

Team Members	Sponsors	Stakeholders
Team Leader, Alliance VP	Board of Directors	Staff of pharmacy
Directors of Pharmacy (4)	Organizational	departments
Assistant Pharmacy	Effectiveness Committee	Patient Service
Directors (3)		representatives
Information Systems		General employees
Representative		Physicians
Human Resources		Nursing staff
Representative		Deans of College
Financial Analyst		Pharmacy
Purchasing Representative		Vendors
School of Pharmacy		Hospital administrators
Representative		Alliance executives
Public Relations		Patients
Representative		Patient families

Case Study: Budget Process (Part 1 of 1)

A manufacturing company had gone through a major restructuring, changing from an organization with a strong central structure to one with a decentralized divisional structure. As part of creating a five-year plan, the Chief Financial Officer (CFO) wanted to understand aspects of the budget process that could be made easier for the Divisional General Managers and what information they needed that they were not getting.

The team included only the CFO and one member of his staff to help conduct interviews.

Team Members	Sponsor	Stakeholders
CFO Staff Member	None, CFO has authority	Other Executives

If you decide that any additional people or groups need to be included in any steps of the FOCUS process, invite them to participate now, before the work of Frame the Project begins.

Section Summary

You have now determined if using the FOCUS process is appropriate for the issue you want to explore. If you plan to continue, you should have completed the following:

❏ Written an issue statement

❏ Determined if understanding the issue from the customers' point of view will help you make a better decision

❏ Identified and met with a sponsor, if necessary

❏ Identified and met with potential team members

❏ Identified and communicated the project's intent with stakeholders

Looking ahead...

It is now time to move on to the first phase of the FOCUS process, Frame the Project. You will determine the purpose of the project, what you want to learn, the types of customers to interview, and what questions to ask.

Out of FOCUS

A company was exploring the market for a possible new product in the health care field. To gain information from customers, the project team scheduled interviews with a variety of people at a major medical center. Three team members were to participate in the visit, but due to illness, the team leader was unable to attend. Prior to the trip the team had not formally discussed the purpose of the visit, or what they hoped to learn. They knew only that they needed to talk with their customers.

As might be expected, the two remaining team members each had a different perspective on the purpose of the trip, as did their customers at the medical center. Without an interview guide, the team members filtered what they heard through their own sets of biases and the interviewees led the discussions in their own directions.

After an exhausting trip, the team members met again only to realize they had little information that was really useful for their project. In addition, they had a group of influential customers who were thoroughly confused about what to expect as an outcome of this visit.

FRAME the Project

SECTION CONTENTS

FRAME

F

FRAME THE PROJECT

1. Determine Purpose
2. Review Existing Data
3. Create Customer Profile Matrix
4. Create Interview Guide

O

ORGANIZE RESOURCES

5. Estimate Project Requirements
6. Meet With Sponsors
7. Negotiate Scope, Schedule, and Resources
8. Schedule Interviews

C

COLLECT DATA

9. Prepare for Visits
10. Polish Your Skills
11. Finalize Preparations
12. Conduct Interviews
13. Follow Up

U

UNDERSTAND THE VOICES

14. Check Your Direction
15. Focus Your Data Analysis
16. Structure the Data
17. Determine Key Areas to Address

S

SELECT ACTION

18. Generate Ideas
19. Evaluate Ideas and Create a Complete Solution
20. Develop an Action Plan

Overview

If you start an exploration without pausing to clarify its boundaries, you might invest significant effort and get little in return. You could look in the wrong places or ask the wrong kinds of questions, ending up with information that is not pertinent. Time spent in this first phase of the FOCUS process can have a big payoff down the road.

Before the project begins, you or someone else in your organization will have identified an issue that requires the Voice of the Customer and assembled a team of people who will need to be involved. Now is the time for the project team to collectively frame the issue in greater detail.

FRAME

What You Gain by Framing the Project

- A clear purpose statement that is achievable but still reaches beyond traditional boundaries

- The inclusion of diverse perspectives that will assure a 360° view of your issue

- Alignment of the project with your organization's goals

- A clear direction for the rest of the project

Questions You Will Be Answering

- Why are we doing this work?

- What do we want to learn from the interviews?

- How does the project fit with other work being done by the organization?

- What do we already know that will help us be successful?

- What types of customers should we interview to get diverse perspectives?

- What should we ask in order to learn what we need to know?

Logistics

The four steps of Frame the Project can take anywhere from 4 to 8 hours, depending on the complexity of your project.

In Step 1, Determine Purpose, you will zero in on what you want to accomplish. By taking time to do this work at the beginning, you minimize the likelihood of having to retrace your path later.

 If you are working as a team, the work in Step 2 can be divided among team members. However, the work in Steps 1, 3, and 4 should be done as a whole group.

Step 2, Review Existing Data, will begin during this phase and probably continue throughout your project.

Step 3, Create Customer Profile Matrix, and Step 4, Create Interview Guide, are critical precursors to collecting data. These steps will provide much of the information you will need to confirm the scope, schedule, and resources for the project in the next phase, Organize Resources.

The following table shows how long this work typically takes.

Step	Estimated Time
Step 1: Determine Purpose	1 – 3 hours
Step 2: Review Existing Data	From several hours to several days, spread over time
Step 3: Create Customer Profile Matrix	1 – 4 hours
Step 4: Create Interview Guide	1 – 2 hours

The Big Picture

1. **Determine Purpose**
2. Review Existing Data
3. Create Customer Profile Matrix
4. Create Interview Guide

Prework

- Clarify your core issue
- Identify sponsor, if appropriate
- Identify team members
- Identify stakeholders

Time and Logistics

Determining the project's purpose can usually be completed in 1 – 3 hours. Teams will often choose to complete the work in Frame the Project in a single meeting, lasting up to a whole day.

Supplies and Equipment

- Flipchart
- Flipchart markers
- 3" x 3" self-stick notes
- Black and red pens for each participant

Outcomes

- Written purpose statement
- List of objectives for learning
- Confirmation of organizational fit

Step 1:

Determine Purpose

Description

In Step 1, you will create a purpose statement that identifies what you are doing and why, as well as objectives for learning that identify what you hope to learn from your customers when you collect data. You will also check to make sure the project fits with the goals of the organization.

Benefits

Having a purpose statement and objectives for learning helps ensure that everyone starts out with the same destination in mind and stays on track as the project moves forward. The check for organizational fit guards against wasted time and energy on a project that is not aligned with the goals of the organization.

Getting Your Bearings

Before you begin the FOCUS process, you should know what the project is about in general terms and who will be on the team. Now it is time to start thinking in more detail about what you want to accomplish.

At this point you are laying the foundation for the project. You will come back to your purpose statement frequently during the FOCUS process: when you confirm your scope, schedule, and resources; interview your customers; analyze your data; and select the actions to take as a result of your data analysis. Everything revolves around the purpose.

FRAME

You will use the objectives for learning when generating questions for the interview guide. Clearly writing your project purpose and objectives for learning will make it easier to assess the project's value for the organization.

How to Determine Your Purpose

A. Create a purpose statement

Now that the team is together, it is important to create a purpose statement from the project's original issue statement. This statement should make explicit what you intend to explore and why. Having a succinct statement not only helps align the team so everyone is heading in the same direction, but also helps you communicate with managers and other employees not on the team.

A purpose statement should identify a problem or question you want to understand better, not a solution. If you phrase a purpose statement as a solution, you limit your exploration by biasing the questions you ask and filtering what you are open to hearing.

> If you are working as a team, divide the team into subgroups and ask each to create a purpose statement. After writing all the statements on a flipchart, have the whole group collaborate on crafting a final statement.

The first part of the statement should reflect what it is about the customers' world you hope to understand better, and the second part should link this work with your organization's desired business results.

A useful format for writing a purpose statement is:

- To explore _____ in order to _____.

- To discover _____ in order to _____.

- To learn _____ in order to _____.

The following examples of purpose statements identify both what you want to accomplish and why.

Examples of good purpose statements

- To learn what the shared concerns are among utilities, local citizens, and regulatory agencies in order to develop better policies for placement of power plants
- To discover the nature of the shift from analog to digital technology in the medical field so we can determine the pace of our investment in digital products
- To understand which problems might be diagnosed remotely in order to develop support tools for service providers

The following table shows how an ineffective purpose statement can be improved.

Examples of improving a poor purpose statement

Purpose Statement Iterations	Commentary
1. To learn how to improve our document management system	Statement does not tell what the team wants to learn from their constituents during the interviews or what the desired result is.
2. To understand what functions need to be part of an improved document management system in order for people to do their work more efficiently	In the next iteration the second part of the statement now tells what "improve" means for the organization, but the first part is solution-oriented. There is an assumption that the solution will include new functions.
3. To understand how people in the company create and use documents in order to create a document management system that will enable people to do their work more efficiently	This is the best statement of the three. The first part now tells what the team wants to learn, rather than what they think the solution will be.

FRAME

Ladder of Abstraction

The ladder of abstraction concept helps people comprehend how abstract or specific a given issue, voice, or comment is.[1] At the bottom of the ladder, language expresses facts or objective descriptions that carry the same meaning to different individuals. As language moves up the ladder it becomes more conceptual.

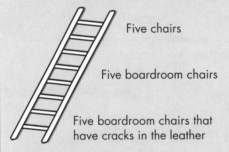

Five chairs

Five boardroom chairs

Five boardroom chairs that have cracks in the leather

In the example above, "five chairs" initially sounds fairly specific, but it isn't clear if they are office chairs, dining room chairs, or dentist chairs. Moving down the ladder the description becomes more specific. As a discussion develops about the chairs, the language could move back up the ladder to talk about "boardroom furniture" or higher still to "office furniture."

The ladder of abstraction is a fundamental frame for thinking about language that is relevant throughout the FOCUS process. The following story illustrates how we often think and speak in high-level abstractions, but can provide detail if pushed.

Carlos was part of a team to interview employees about their workspace needs because the company was building a new facility. One of the interviewees, Casey, said at first she wanted "lots of space so it would feel roomy..." Carlos probed for detail and Casey said, "I don't want to feel cramped when I have all my equipment here. People drop by my office all the time, so they need a place to sit." Carlos probed more and heard, "I need desk space for a computer, monitor, and keyboard, and three racks for file folders, plus space for an extra chair, two bookcases, and a vertical file cabinet..."

Lots of space; roomy

Don't want to feel cramped...need room for visitors...

Need room for computer equipment, file folder holders, extra chair...

When collecting the voices of customers, if only highly abstract language is captured, its ambiguity may prevent understanding of the issue due to the various meanings of abstract words. Later in the process you will move up the ladder as you look for common themes and concepts among different interview notes.

---

[1] S.I. Hayakawa and Alan R. Hayakawa, *Language in Thought and Action*, 5th ed. (NY: Harcourt Brace Jovanovich, 1990).

B. Check your purpose statement

After choosing the statement that you think best captures what you want to accomplish, check to make sure it is not solution-oriented. Avoid phrases that begin with "to implement," "to create," "to change," "to revise," or "to reengineer."

Next check the statement for scope. You want a purpose statement that is broad enough to let you open your eyes to new ways of thinking, but specific enough to prevent you from getting distracted by side issues.

To check the scope, use the ladder of abstraction.

- First rephrase the statement moving up one rung on the ladder, that is, one level broader than where you started.

- Rephrase the statement again, moving down one rung on the ladder, that is, one level narrower than where you started.

- Choose the level which seems appropriate for your project.

 People who fail to check their statements for scope often end up bogged down in unwieldy projects because their statement is too broad. Or they can miss important opportunities that lie just beyond the question at hand because their statement is too narrow.

FRAME

Examples of checking scope

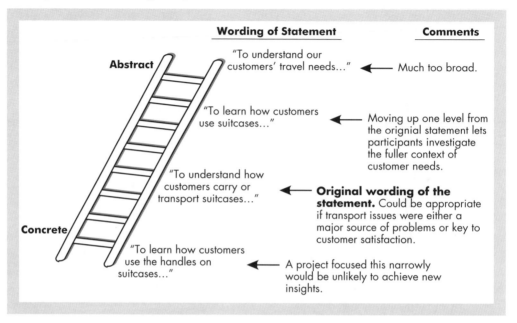

	Wording of Statement	Comments
Abstract	"To understand our customers' travel needs…"	Much too broad.
	"To learn how customers use suitcases…"	Moving up one level from the orignial statement lets participants investigate the fuller context of customer needs.
	"To understand how customers carry or transport suitcases…"	**Original wording of the statement.** Could be appropriate if transport issues were either a major source of problems or key to customer satisfaction.
Concrete	"To learn how customers use the handles on suitcases…"	A project focused this narrowly would be unlikely to achieve new insights.

When you are in agreement that the first part of your purpose statement describes what aspect of your customers' world you want to explore, the second part articulates for what business result, and your scope is at the right level of abstraction, you are ready to move forward.

> *Do not spend hours trying to craft a statement that is perfectly worded. The goal is to define the scope of your exploration as clearly as possible.*

The following case study describes how a project team used the ladder of abstraction to check the scope of their purpose statement.

FRAME

Case Study: Employee Benefits (Part 1 of 6)

A project team was started by a company that was faced with rising benefits costs. Before they started making changes, they wanted to better understand employees' needs. Their issue statement was "How to better understand what kind of benefits our employees want and need." First, the project team created a purpose statement:

"To understand employee benefit needs in order to provide an optimal benefit package at reasonable company expense."

Then they used the ladder of abstraction to check the scope of the purpose statement.

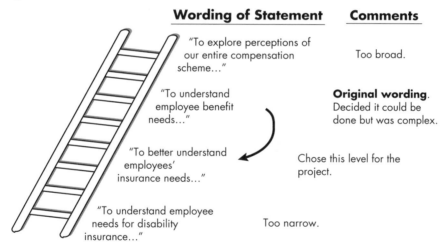

Wording of Statement	Comments
"To explore perceptions of our entire compensation scheme..."	Too broad.
"To understand employee benefit needs..."	**Original wording.** Decided it could be done but was complex.
"To better understand employees' insurance needs..."	Chose this level for the project.
"To understand employee needs for disability insurance..."	Too narrow.

As a result of this check, the team revised their purpose statement. They decided that although they could examine all benefits, the complexity of the issues would make data collection, analysis, and action impractical in the given time frame. Also, the insurance parts of the benefits package were showing the greatest cost increases, an indication that they might be the best areas to change. Disability insurance, while very expensive, did not make sense as a subject for exploration because it was not used by most employees. If disability insurance was a concern, it would still come out at the higher level of abstraction.

C. Identify your objectives for learning

Each person on the team should work individually. Working silently ensures that all team members have an equal voice.

Based on your purpose, identify your objectives for learning—these capture what you hope to learn as a result of visiting customers. To help you stay clear about the exploratory nature of your venture, begin your objectives with phrases such as "To learn ___," "To discover ___," or "To understand ___."

Print each objective on a self-stick note in black. Take time to identify everything you would like to explore. Later you will organize all of your objectives more succinctly.

The following are some examples of well-written objectives for learning.

Examples of objectives for learning

- To discover our customers' values regarding health care
- To understand the criteria customers use in the purchase process
- To understand what's not working in getting products to market
- To understand what support our customers need
- To discover the company's image in the eyes of our customers
- To learn the process for creating an industry standard

The following table shows how ineffective objectives for learning can be improved.

Examples of improving ineffective objectives for learning

Objective for Learning	Problem	Improved Objective
To discover the criteria people use to choose and to switch dentists	An "and" usually means there are really two objectives.	This should become two separate objectives, one for choosing dentists and the other for switching dentists.
To evaluate the barriers to implementation of the reorganization	"Evaluate" is not an exploratory word.	This could become "To understand the barriers to implementation of the reorganization."
To learn what stereo components potential customers want in a home theater system	The language is focused on stereo components. It needs to be broader.	This could become "To learn what components of a home theater system are most important to potential customers."

D. Sort your objectives for learning into clusters

Have everyone place their self-stick notes on a wall, table, or flipchart. People have likely written some similar statements of what they want to learn from interviews. As a group, cluster similar statements, eliminating duplicates. Statements may remain alone if they do not fit into a cluster.

E. Write a summary label for each cluster

After you have clustered all of the objectives for learning, write a label in red that best summarizes the theme or essence of each cluster. Use the same language as in the original notes ("to learn," "to discover").

When you are satisfied with your clusters of objectives for learning, compile them into one document. You will refer to them later when drafting the interview questions.

This next case study describes how a company used the clustering process to compile a list of objectives for learning.

Case Study: Document Management (Part 1 of 9)

A company set up a team to learn about its employee needs for creating, storing, and retrieving documents so that they could improve the document management system. Team members wrote down what they wanted to learn on separate self-stick notes. One person put up the first note, and team members with similar ideas added their notes. Then someone put up a new idea, and the process continued until all notes were posted and clustered. Some clusters had four or five notes; others had only one. When everyone was satisfied with the clusters, the team wrote a label in red for each cluster that summarized its theme or idea.

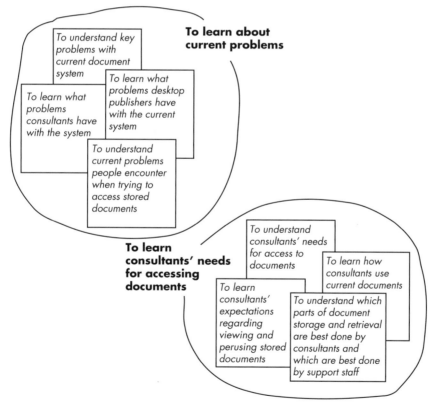

When the team had completed all of the clusters and labels, they compiled the following list of objectives and subobjectives.

Continued...

FRAME

To learn about current problems

- To understand key problems with current document system
- To understand current problems people encounter when trying to access stored documents
- To learn what problems consultants have with the system
- To learn what problems desktop publishers have with the current system

To learn consultants' needs for accessing documents

- To learn how consultants use current documents
- To understand consultants' needs for access to documents
- To learn expectations of consultants re: viewing, perusing previously stored materials
- To understand which parts of document storage and retrieval are best done by consultants and which are best done by support staff

F. Check for organizational fit

Projects should be aligned with at least one important organizational goal in order to justify the time and resources needed. If you discover the project does not fit well with organizational goals or you are unsure how it fits, meet with your sponsors to discuss your findings. If the scope is outside your area of authority, check with appropriate management. They may be able to modify the project goals to align with organizational goals, or they may discover that organizational goals overlook an important issue represented by your effort. They also may decide to drop the project altogether.

The following checklist reflects common ways a Voice of the Customer project can support organizational goals. You may have other criteria not reflected here.

Organizational Fit Checklist

❑ This project ties in with the following organizational goals:_____

❑ This project will help us understand and counteract competitive threats

❑ This project fits with leadership's commitment to understand employee concerns before making decisions that affect employees

❑ This project will help us identify opportunities for extensions to our product lines

❑ This project will help fulfill goals to introduce X new products a year

❑ This project requires information from customers to make a good business decision

❑ This project helps us look into the future to understand changes under way in the customer environment

❑ This project allows us to understand a new trend first-hand before finalizing our strategy

❑ This project helps us to understand the problems with our current department, work unit, or organizational structure

FRAME

The following case study describes what can happen if a team fails to check for organizational fit.

Case Study: New Markets (Part 1 of 1)

A team was looking for ways to move into a new market area. Team members interviewed customers about their experiences with similar products, their problems, and their proposed solutions. The team then analyzed the data and created a set of customer requirements. After months of hard work, they went to management with what they believed was an exciting breakthrough solution—a whole new technical approach.

However, they had skipped one step in the process—checking for organizational fit. Management took one look at their recommendations and said, "No. We do not want to be on the cutting edge here. We do not have time to develop a new technology. We need to start with a product that will let us use our existing technology to get into this market within the next year. Later, we can worry about improving our offerings with cutting-edge technology."

The team's work was not wasted because they had learned a lot from their interviews and site visits, and much of their work was used in later products. However, because they had not solved the company's current problem, they had to backtrack and create different solutions.

Some teams are not so lucky. When a lack of organizational fit is discovered after weeks or months of effort, the project is simply dropped, and time and resources have been wasted.

Step 1 Check

Check to make sure your boundaries are clear. You should have

- ❏ A clear, agreed-upon purpose statement

- ❏ A list of objectives for learning

- ❏ A common understanding of how the project fits with the organization's goals

FRAME

The Big Picture

1. Determine Purpose
2. **Review Existing Data**
3. Create Customer Profile Matrix
4. Create Interview Guide

Prework

- Determine project purpose
- Identify objectives for learning

Time and Logistics

How much time you spend reviewing data will depend on the nature of the project and your data resources. You will want to do some up front data review before deciding on customers to visit. It is possible that you will also review various data sources throughout the life of this project. This work can be divided among team members.

Supplies and Equipment

- Highlighting markers, if necessary

Outcomes

- Relevant sources of information
- Perspectives on the project that you cannot get from interviews alone
- Information to help you select which customers to visit

FRAME

Step 2:

Review Existing Data

Description

Before you start gathering new data from your customers, you should review existing sources of information in order to gain a broader understanding of your issue. Most organizations have data about their customers, the performance of their products or services in the marketplace, and employee attitudes toward certain issues. This information captures the history your organization has with an issue, including what efforts have already been undertaken. You may also want to gather information from outside your organization to learn what others in your industry are doing related to this issue.

Benefits

Reviewing data helps you gain a 360° perspective of your issue. In addition, understanding related work helps prevent duplicate efforts.

Getting Your Bearings

In order to decide whom to interview, and later analyze what you hear in the interviews, it is valuable to understand the greater context of your issue. This includes both the history your organization has with the issue as well as what is happening throughout your industry. Initially, you may need to review data to help you decide the types of customers you should be interviewing. However, you will probably find it valuable to continue your research efforts throughout the life of your project.

How to Find Existing Data

The type of information that will be relevant depends on the nature of your project. Basically, you are looking for any data, reports, or articles that address areas related to your project. Start by asking people working on the project and those in relevant departments such as marketing, sales, or engineering about sources of existing information on the issue at hand. Some likely sources of information are shown in the following table.*

Examples of information sources

External Sources	Internal Sources
• Customer complaint data	• Benchmarking studies
• Engineering or technical specifications for the product or service	• Company policies
• Market research reports	• Employee surveys
• Customer surveys	• Suggestion systems
• Customer profiles	• Customer profiles
• Industry benchmarking data	• Internal publications
• Competitor assessments	
• Journals	

*See Appendix B, *Plain & Simple*® series, for more information on how to analyze data.

The next table shows sources of information that would be appropriate for specific projects. Some of this information will help the team decide what types of people to interview and later, perhaps, specific individuals to interview. Other information will help guide team members as they conduct their interviews and observations. And all of it will help provide a fuller frame of reference as the team analyzes the data they collect.

> Some Voice of the Customer projects cross organizational boundaries. If you are going outside your department for information, make sure the people you contact understand what you are doing, how their information can help you, and how your project may affect them.

Examples of project data sources

Purpose Statement	Sources of Information
To discover customer needs in document photography in order to propose alternatives for improved hardware	• Customer complaint data • Data compiled during original product development effort • Engineering and technical records • Customer profiles developed by sales or marketing
To better understand employees' insurance needs in order to provide an optimal benefit package at reasonable company expense	• Employee surveys • Employee suggestions • Labor contract negotiation records • Industry reports on trends in insurance benefits

FRAME

If you involve different team members in this work, it is important to plan how you will collect and share the information. As individuals explore different avenues for learning you want to make sure you avoid duplication. This is especially important when you call upon others in your organization for assistance. You also need to make sure you have methods in place for people to share what they learn with the whole group. Some of the kinds of detailed information you may learn are shown in the following table.

What your data may show

External Sources	Internal Sources
• Buying patterns among customer groups	• Differences in viewpoints regarding a department, function, or job
• Characteristics that distinguish key customer groups	• Previous solutions and results
• Specific customer needs identified in previous work	• Results of a relevant company survey

The next case study describes how a company gathered background information for its project.

Case Study: Scientific Imaging (Part 1 of 1)

A company that creates scientific imaging film felt it was losing market share to new technologies. It wanted to use the FOCUS process to better understand its customers' work and needs. But first it wanted to get a better understanding of the marketplace in general.

The team leader started by surveying 25 of the company's top customers to learn how they used the company's product, the extent to which they used the product, and whether they were adopting or planning to adopt new technologies and why.

Marketing members on the team also researched the new competitors. Where possible, they learned the size of the company and the amount of annual sales in the imaging technology market. To learn as much as possible about their competitors' products, they compiled a list of products, features, and prices. Finally, they reviewed an industry report on current market conditions and future trends.

This background information was valuable throughout the rest of the FOCUS process—as the team identified whom to interview, developed interview and observation guides, and analyzed their findings.

Step 2 Check

Check to make sure you have gathered background information for your project. You should have

- ❑ A list of relevant sources of information that provide a variety of perspectives

- ❑ Information to help you select which customers to visit

- ❑ A plan for completing the research

The Big Picture

1. Determine Purpose
2. Review Existing Data
3. **Create Customer Profile Matrix**
4. Create Interview Guide

Prework

- Determine project purpose
- Identify objectives for learning
- Review existing data

Time and Logistics

Creating a customer profile matrix can be the most time-consuming work in Frame the Project.

If interview segments are easy to identify, you may be able to complete this step in less than one hour. However, in some cases it may be more difficult to identify segments and the work can take from 1 – 4 hours.

Supplies and Equipment

- Flipchart paper
- Flipchart markers
- 3" x 5" self-stick notes
- Tape or pushpins

Outcomes

- Customer profile matrix
- 15 – 20 profiles of the types of people you want to interview

FRAME

Step 3:

Create Customer Profile Matrix

Description

In this step you will think about how you can fulfill your objectives for learning. Your goal is to think about how you are going to get relevant information while thinking broadly about your issue. You will identify the characteristics of the people you want to interview so you can be sure you are exploring your issue from every angle.

Benefits

One of the most powerful aspects of the FOCUS process is the ability to discover common concerns or needs among different groups. You will take advantage of this power by creating a customer profile matrix, a tool that helps make sure you interview diverse people.

Getting Your Bearings

The check for organizational fit has determined that it is worthwhile for the organization to expend resources to explore the issue or problem at hand. Now you will create target profiles that will ensure you include diverse viewpoints in your interviews. This broad perspective is essential when analyzing your interview data and deciding what actions to take based on the data.

360° Perspective

Targeting representative, diverse perspectives illustrates an important principle of the FOCUS process: the 360° perspective. The illustration on the left represents what you as an individual can see of an issue from your single vantage point.

In order to gain a 360° perspective it is necessary to to look at your subject of exploration from diverse points of view, as shown in the illustration on the right.

One of the key factors contributing to the success of Voice of the Customer projects using the FOCUS process is that teams think carefully about how to gain multiple perspectives. In doing so they see the issue in the broader context.

Single Perspective

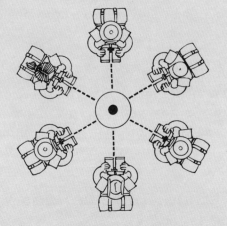

360° Perspective

How to Create a Customer Profile Matrix

A. Create a list of traditional segments

Generate a list of traditional ways to segment the customer groups that may have valuable input. Use the relevant data you gathered to spark ideas about which segments are most important to your group or organization. As shown in the following table, these are often familiar categories.

 Designate one person to capture ideas on 3" x 5" self-stick notes. Different marker colors may help distinguish differences in customer types. Organize the notes on the left side of a large matrix in a way that makes sense to the team. Some categories may be subcategories of others. You may decide at the end of the brainstorming process that some categories are less important or not useful.

Examples of traditional customer segments

External Projects	Internal Projects
• Type of industry or sector	• Functions, departments, or divisions: sales, customer service, financial services, engineering, human resources, shipping, research and development, manufacturing
• Large volume vs. medium or low volume users or purchasers	
• Type of product application	
• Location in customer chain: distributor, purchaser, user	• Chain of command: senior manager, mid-manager, supervisor, line
• Geographic location: region of the country; continent; urban vs. suburban	• Users of different parts of an internal process
• Economic group	• Sites: manufacturing plants, distribution centers, regional offices
• Gender	

FRAME

What Is a Customer Profile Matrix?

ZA customer profile matrix helps you map out different combinations of characteristics important to your study. One advantage of using this tool is that it helps you get a 360° perspective of your issue. Instead of randomly selecting customers to visit (or visiting your favorites), a profile matrix helps ensure diversity among your interviewees.

As shown below, the key feature of a profile matrix is that it integrates traditional ways of thinking about who your customers are (left side of the matrix) with nontraditional categories (top of matrix).

Traditional segments help you identify people or groups that are economically or operationally important to your organization. Nontraditional segments help you identify particular characteristics of the types of people within the traditional categories who may offer unique or insightful views on the subject. By looking for combinations of traditional and nontraditional characteristics, you will increase the chances of creating a 360° perspective.

Nontraditional Segments

		Lead Users	Satisfied Customers	Dissatisfied Customers	Former Customers	Customers We Never Had
Traditional Segments	Customers of Product Line A					
	Customers of Product Line B					
	Customers of Product Line C					
	Customers of Product Line D					

Write each traditional segment on a self-stick note and arrange the notes on the left side of a flipchart.

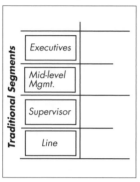
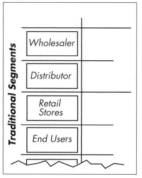
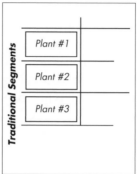

The following two case studies describe different ways of segmenting customers.

Case Study: Career Center Customers (Part 1 of 1)

A career center wanted to learn how to better serve its customers. As team members discussed how they traditionally thought about their customers, they came up with two different ways they could create segments. One way was by looking at the groups who used their services:

Youth	Under-educated adults
Physically/mentally disabled	Veterans
Refugees/homeless	Dislocated workers

However, they could also look at segments in terms of the different programs they offered. Then they came up with:

Specific Skill Training	Basic Education Skill Training
Job Placement	Counseling and Assessment
Job Search	

Both approaches to segmentation were ways they traditionally thought about their customers. The next step was to decide which approach would help them understand their issue best. They chose to look at the groups being served. If, however, the team had decided both types of segmentation were equally important, they could have used a nesting approach, as described in the next case study.

Case Study: On-Time Delivery (Part 1 of 1)

A company wanted to learn what aspects of on-time delivery were most important to their customers. Team members discussed how they traditionally thought about their customers—by product line. They also thought it might be important to distinguish between high volume customers and medium volume customers. In the end, they decided to look at both types of segmentation—product line and volume. These are shown on the left side of the following customer profile matrix.

Customers of Product Line A	High Vol.					
	Med. Vol.					
Customers of Product Line B	High Vol.					
	Med. Vol.					
Customers of Product Line C	High Vol.					
	Med. Vol.					
Customers of Product Line D	High Vol.					
	Med. Vol.					

Traditional Segments

B. Create a list of nontraditional segments

Next, generate a list of nontraditional ways to segment customers. These characteristics will give you additional perspectives on the world of your customers. You may have already come up with some of these characteristics when generating your list of traditional segments. The idea here is to find new ways to look at each of your traditional segments to get a richer perspective. Some nontraditional categories frequently used are shown in the following table.

Examples of nontraditional customer segments

External Projects	Internal Projects
• Lead users or thinkers • Happy customers • Demanding customers • Dissatisfied customers • Former customers • Customers you never had • Leading researchers, both academic and corporate	• People who have worked at solving your issue • People who have shown resistance to your issue • Outspoken or demanding employees • Conformers • Opinion leaders • Official leaders • Natural leaders/influencers

Print each nontraditional segment on a self-stick note and arrange them across the top of your matrix.

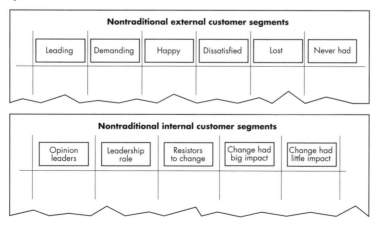

What Is a Lead User?

When exploring needs related to a product or service, one important nontraditional segment is lead users.[2] These are people at the forefront of the market.

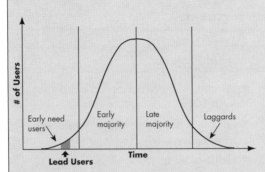

Lead users are a useful group to interview for the following reasons:

- They have a high need for the capability your product or service provides. That is why they are among the first to try it and to test its limits.

- Their needs often foreshadow the general demand of others in the market.

- They have probably taken available products or services beyond their intended limits. For instance, they might have jury-rigged a product to perform functions it was not designed to perform.

- Because lead users typically have thought a lot about their needs and how products or services do and do not meet those needs, they often have solutions either in theory or in practice.

---

[2]Eric von Hippel, "Lead Users: A Source of Novel Product Concepts," *Management Science* 32:7, 1986.

FRAME

Getting a Richer 360° Perspective

The purpose of the customer profile matrix is to identify a relatively small set of customers who provide the fullest possible perspective of the issue you are exploring.

Figure 1 shows how traditional segments can provide a 360° view of the issue. Each segment has one perspective; together they provide a 360° view. This view, however, is flat and two-dimensional.

In Figure 2 each traditional segment has corresponding slices that represent nontraditional segments. Each traditional segment includes lead users, dissatisfied customers, customers you lost, and customers you never had. Others could also be included. Whatever nontraditional segments you select, they provide a fuller, three-dimensional view.

If you identify only traditional segments, it is quite possible you will find some lead users or dissatisfied customers to interview. It is less likely you will identify former customers or customers you never had. By formally identifying nontraditional characteristics, you make sure you will get the diverse perspectives you seek.

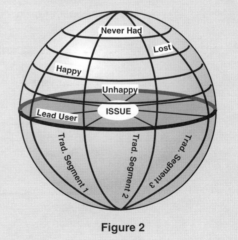

Figure 2

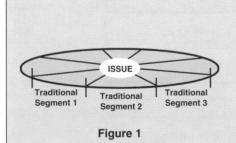

Figure 1

This next case study shows how one team created its customer profile matrix.

Case Study: New Photographic Film (Part 1 of 2)

Before developing a new photographic film that could be used to create passport and other documentation photographs, a company wanted to understand their overseas customers' problems with film.

First the project team decided to interview customers in both Europe and Asia to account for cultural differences. Next, they needed to consider differences in climate, so they divided each continent into north and south and selected a representative country in each segment. They also needed to distinguish between decision makers (shop owners) and film users (shopkeepers). They also made a note to be sure to include both high volume and medium volume shops as they scheduled interviews. The following customer profile matrix shows the traditional segments they identified.

Traditional Segments			
Asia	Northern: South Korea	Shop Owners	
		Shopkeepers	
	Southern: Malaysia	Shop Owners	
		Shopkeepers	
Europe	Northern: Germany	Shop Owners	
		Shopkeepers	
	Southern: Spain	Shop Owners	
		Shopkeepers	

Continued...

Next, they looked at nontraditional characteristics. They chose lead users as a segment because they wanted to identify customers who had used their film in new ways or who had experimented with it to try to get it to do what they wanted. Because they were also interested in interviewing customers whose needs they were not currently meeting, they included dissatisfied customers, customers they once had but lost, and customers they never had. The final profile matrix follows.

			Nontraditional Segments			
			Lead Users	Dissatisfied Customers	Cust. Had but Lost	Customers Never Had
Asia	Northern: South Korea	Shop Owners				
		Shopkeepers				
	Southern: Malaysia	Shop Owners				
		Shopkeepers				
Europe	Northern: Germany	Shop Owners				
		Shopkeepers				
	Southern: Spain	Shop Owners				
		Shopkeepers				

(row group label at far left: Traditional Segments)

Note: Include high and medium volume film shops in the interview mix.

 A profile matrix with 20 to 30 cells is usually large enough to allow you to thoroughly understand your customers' needs.

FRAME

C. Choose which segment combinations to interview

Choosing the right types of people to interview is partly art, partly science. Use your judgment to identify 15 to 20 types of customers who represent a cross-section of the customers described in the profile matrix. Research indicates about 95% of the useful information comes from the first 15 to 20 interviews.[3]

When trying to determine which categories to visit, review your project purpose, your objectives for learning, and the data you have gathered. Try to match your goals with the characteristics of the matrix.

Although you will be interviewing only a subset of your potential customers, remember that each individual is intended to be a representative of all the members of both their traditional and nontraditional segments. Your discussions with each of the people you select will be detailed and substantive. What you learn from your selected subset will symbolize the issues and needs of the broader group.

---

[3]Abbie Griffin and John R. Hauser, "The Voice of the Customer," *Marketing Science* Vol. 12, No. 1, (Winter 1993):1-27.

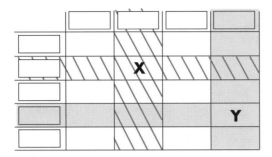

Each cell is representative of both its row and column.

One guideline is to have three or four interviews in the cells you consider to be most important and fewer, if any, interviews in the other cells. If you suspect the segments might have very different needs—such as needs for a product that might be used in both hospitals and oil refineries—then it is a good idea to interview at least ten customers per segment (i.e., the total for a particular row or set of rows, not per cell).[4]

To make your job easier, check for combinations of characteristics that do not exist in real life or that represent a minor piece of the big picture and therefore need not be included in the exploration. Also check to see if existing research might represent the viewpoint of a particular cell.

 Your budget, deadlines, and proximity to your customers will also influence how many interviews you can include.

[4]E.F. McQuarrie, *Customer Visits: Building a Better Market Focus* (Newbury Park, CA: Sage, 1993).

FRAME

The following case study describes how the team from the photographic film company chose their interviews.

Case Study: New Photographic Film (Part 2 of 2)

The film company team ended up with 32 cells. They wanted to keep the interviews fairly evenly divided between Europe and Asia, between northern and southern climates, and between shopkeepers and shop owners. They also tried to make sure they had at least four to five interviews in each of their nontraditional categories. Because they thought their segments might have very different needs, they decided on a minimum of ten interviews per continent.

The following profile matrix shows their final selections.

Nontraditional Segments

Traditional Segments				Lead Users	Dissatisfied Customers	Cust. Had but Lost	Customers Never Had
Asia	Northern: South Korea	Shop Owners			1		1
		Shopkeepers		2		2	
	Southern: Malaysia	Shop Owners		1			2
		Shopkeepers				1	
Europe	Northern: Germany	Shop Owners				1	
		Shopkeepers		1	2		1
	Southern: Spain	Shop Owners		2		2	
		Shopkeepers					1

Step 3 Check

Check to make sure your customer segments provide a 360° perspective of your issue. You should have

- ❏ A matrix that represents both traditional and nontraditional characteristics of potential interviewees

- ❏ At least 15 – 20 profiles of the types of people you want to interview

FRAME

The Big Picture

1. Determine Purpose
2. Review Existing Data
3. Create Customer Profile Matrix
4. **Create Interview Guide**

Prework

- Determine project purpose
- Identify objectives for learning
- Create customer profile matrix

Time and Logistics

Creating an interview guide usually takes about 1 – 2 hours, but may take longer if you decide to do multiple guides. This work often is completed in the same meeting in which you determine the project purpose and create the customer profile matrix.

Supplies and Equipment

- Copy of objectives for learning
- Flipchart
- Flipchart markers
- 3" x 3" self-stick notes
- Black and red pens for each participant

Outcomes

- Introduction for your interviews
- One or more interview guides
- Observation guides

FRAME

Step 4:

Create Interview Guide

Description

Coming face-to-face with your customers is an exciting opportunity. With little effort, you can probably generate dozens of questions to ask them, such as "What do you think about _____? What do you like about it? Not like? How does it affect your work?" The point of the visits is to purposefully explore your customers' world. Here you will generate the main questions you want to ask, as well as prompts for follow-up questions and a guide for your observations.

Benefits

Having interview and observation guides helps ensure that you cover all of the important issues, gather the most critical information, and stay on track during your interview visits. In addition, the information you obtain will be of higher quality and more useful when analyzing your findings.

Getting Your Bearings

All of the work to this point has been done to set a solid foundation and to make the project as successful as possible. To add to the likelihood of success, you want to go into interviews prepared with questions that will help you obtain useful, relevant information. The interview and observation guides are tools to help you do this.

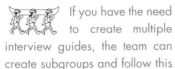 If you have the need to create multiple interview guides, the team can create subgroups and follow this process in parallel.

In most Voice of the Customer projects you will develop a single interview guide. However, if you will be interviewing groups that have widely differing needs or that represent different kinds of information needed for the project, you may need more than one guide.

Taking time now to prepare good questions will enhance the quality of your interviews. They will go more smoothly and you will have a better chance of not straying too far from course.

Four Basic Dimensions of Questioning

During your interviews you will want to get a 360° view of your customers' world. Imagine yourself at the center of a circle, looking out at the world around you, and ask questions that will allow you to stand in their shoes and elicit a 360° perspective of what they see from that vantage point. The following four areas of exploration will help you do this.

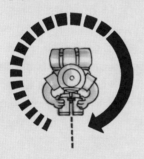

Images: Getting images fixed in your mind that represent the customers' experience is one of the more powerful vehicles of the FOCUS process. If at all possible, arrange to watch your customers in their workplace. If you cannot observe them directly, ask them to describe using your product or service, or encountering the policy, strategy, or process you are studying. These images will become mental snapshots that create a context for what the customer tells you—a critical element in helping you interpret properly what the customer is saying.*

Past breakdowns and weaknesses: Asking people about the problems they have encountered around your issue gives you a good glimpse into their past experiences.

Their responses will reflect needs or capabilities that are not met, frustrations stemming from weaknesses or gaps in current processes, policies, or training, and indirectly their standards for judging what is of value.

Current considerations: Asking interviewees about current considerations may open up new avenues of exploration. Further, exploring what comes to mind when they are preparing to choose or use the process, product, service, or policy under consideration provides clues as to how they make decisions related to the issue.

Future enhancements: Asking people what changes they would like to see in the future or what an ideal situation would look like is a good way to surface their likes, desires, wishes, and needs. Often underneath a solution they offer is a need they are solving the best way they know. Sometimes there are latent or unexpressed needs that you may be able to address in ways they have not considered.

*See Appendix B for more information on Concept Engineering™, which provides a more rigorous approach to using images.

FRAME

FRAME

How to Create an Interview Guide

A. Develop open-ended questions

Before you begin generating questions, review your project purpose statement and objectives for learning. Remember, Voice of the Customer projects are designed to explore the world from perspectives other than your own. For this reason, the interview questions should be open-ended; you do not want to impose your perspectives on the answers.

Individually, team members should generate all of the questions they would like to have answered in the interviews. In black, print each question on a separate self-stick note. Think about questions that relate to each of the groups identified in your profile matrix. Be sure to include questions that will encourage people to describe their environment in detail. These descriptions lead to visual images of the environment that will enable you to recreate their context. After generating the interview questions, review them to make sure the wording is open-ended.

The following are some examples of good image questions.

Examples of image questions

- If I were to follow you through your hospital routine, what problems would I see you encounter?

- Describe what you went through the last time you used this process.

- If I were to videotape you setting up your new home theater, what scenes would I capture?

- If I were to listen in on a phone conversation of you requesting service for your computer, what would I hear?

- Describe an incident when that happened to you.

Interview Question Checklist

❏ Questions are open-ended—they have unlimited potential answers. Avoid questions that have only a few possible answers, such as yes or no; A, B, or C; etc.

❏ Questions give no clue to the interviewee about what the "right" answers might be.

❏ "What" and "How" questions are included. They focus on events: "What problems have you experienced?" "How does that help you?"

❏ "Could" questions are included. They are perceived as nonthreatening and open: "Could you tell me more about … ?"

❏ "Why" questions are used sparingly. Although they can help you understand motivation, they can also sound like criticism: "Why do you do that?" They can also make an interview feel like an interrogation: "Why…? Why…? Why…?"

❏ "Are," "Do," and "Can" questions are avoided. They are most often limiting questions that may get only a yes or no answer. Poor question: "Are you happy with the way the product performs?" Better question: "Describe how the product performs."

FRAME

The following table shows how some interview questions were improved.

Examples of improving interview questions

Question	Problem	Improvement
Do you enjoy your job?	Not open-ended	What do you enjoy most about your job?
Do you ever use the lathe?	Not open-ended	Tell me about the equipment you use.
Why is that frustrating for you?	Might sound like criticism	Tell me more about the frustration you're describing.
Would it be easier for you to use the remote control if the buttons were larger?	Assumes a solution	What problems do you have using the remote control? What would help?

You will generate more questions than can be answered in an hour or hour-and-a-half interview. Therefore, the next step is to select what questions to include. You will then structure these questions in your interview guide to make it easy to gather key information.

B. Cluster questions

Now you are ready to organize the questions into related groups.

- Select one self-stick note from the set of questions and place it on a flipchart or wall. If you are working with a team, read the question aloud.

- Gather notes that capture similar or related thoughts.

- Select another self-stick note and repeat the process until most questions are grouped; some may not fit in a group and will stand alone.

C. Write summary questions

For each cluster, write a question in red on a self-stick note that summarizes the theme. The summary question should capture only what is common among the clustered notes, not describe everything covered by them.

> *Keep the original questions with the summary question written in red. You will need them later in this process. Some of them may become the follow-up probes.*

Review your questions to be sure you cover the four dimensions of questioning: images, past weaknesses, current considerations, and future enhancements. Then check to be sure you have questions that cover your objectives for learning.

FRAME

D. Identify five or six key questions

If you have more than five or six clusters, scan the questions in red to see if some are similar enough to group again. If you identify any new clusters, write summary questions for them, preferably in a third color of ink. Grouping and summarizing is complete when you have only five or six clusters, with a summary question for each cluster. These questions will be the basis for the interview guide.

 Some summary questions may be relevant to all the groups you intend to interview, but others may only pertain to a particular profile segment. In that case, you may end up with more than five or six key questions overall. Remember, when appropriate you can use different interview guides with different groups.

E. Organize the questions

Your interview guide will be just that—a guide. Because you are asking open-ended questions you will never know exactly what direction an interview will follow. You will follow the lead of the person you are interviewing. To help make sure you get the information you need, it is usually beneficial to include prompts or follow-up questions along with your key summary questions.

Taking each summary question one at a time, look over the original questions in the cluster to determine if some of them might be follow-up questions or prompts. Next, add any other prompts or follow-up questions that seem relevant. These questions can then serve both as probes for additional information and as quick checklists to help you make sure important aspects of each summary question have been covered.

A good way to begin an interview is to lead off with questions designed to evoke images about the environment or about the firsthand experience of the individual. This gets people "out of their heads" and into their more visceral experiences. However, if you plan to observe the workplace, you may want to start with questions about past experiences instead. This helps get people grounded in their core issues. If you begin with past experiences, it may make sense to then move from past to the present to the future, interspersing image-oriented questions throughout.

The following case study describes how the document management team organized their questions.

Case Study: Document Management (Part 2 of 9)

The company wanted to learn about its employees' needs for creating, storing, and retrieving documents so it could improve the document management system. To prepare for the interviews, each team member wrote down questions that came to mind. The team ended up with a list of 35 open-ended questions, each written on a self-stick note.

To reduce the number of questions for their interview guide, they chose one question from the group and put it on a flipchart. They then looked for similar questions. As groupings started to coalesce, team members moved the notes from cluster to cluster. Everyone took part.

The following illustration shows some of the groups the team came up with. Although the team had only one question about anticipated changes, they thought it was an important question, so it stood alone.

Continued...

FRAME

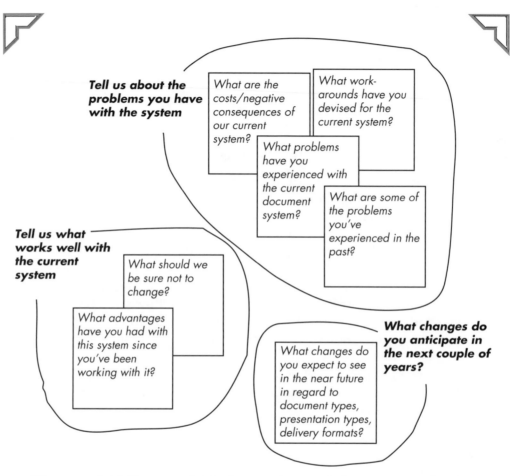

The team initially created 12 clusters. Some of these contained only a single question. The group decided some single questions were not important enough to include, whereas they left others as a cluster of one. A few clusters were combined into even broader themes.

Next the team looked back at the original clusters to identify relevant prompts and follow-up questions. Some prompts were taken exactly as they had been written, some were revised, and some new ones were added, as shown on the following page.

Continued...

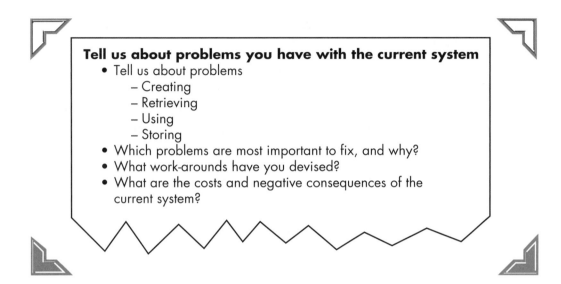

Tell us about problems you have with the current system
- Tell us about problems
  - Creating
  - Retrieving
  - Using
  - Storing
- Which problems are most important to fix, and why?
- What work-arounds have you devised?
- What are the costs and negative consequences of the current system?

FRAME

F. Write an interview introduction

Even experienced interviewers find it helps to have written notes that remind them of points to cover at the start of an interview. Taking time to write a brief standard introduction can help you capture key messages the team wants to get across. The introduction should

- Provide an opportunity for introductions if they are needed

- Describe the purpose of the interview briefly

- Explain the interview process (how long it will take, how notes will be captured, etc.)

- Tell the interviewee what you will do with the data

- Provide the interviewee with an opportunity to discuss the degree of confidentiality

- If necessary, confirm permission to use technical devices (e.g., tape recorder, computer, video camera)

The following is the introduction from the interview guide that the document management team used.

Case Study: Document Management (Part 3 of 9)

Members of the document management team who did not have experience interviewing wanted a very detailed introduction written out. Although they did not rely on reading the introduction at the start of each interview, it provided them with a sense of security. They knew what to include and if they did become tongue-tied they could always fall back on their "script."

Interview Guide Introduction:

As you probably know, a few weeks ago we formed a team to study and improve the way documents are created and shared. We want to understand the ways people create, store, and access documents including the problems they have so that we can identify a system that comes as close as possible to meeting everyone's needs. The team thought you would have a unique perspective that could help us and we want to thank you for taking the time to speak with us.

In the interview we hope to cover the five key topics listed on the page I gave you ahead of time, but we'd like to keep the discussion open-ended and let you talk about whatever is on your mind related to this issue. We were hoping to spend about an hour with you today. Is that still all right?

Do you have any questions?... [Introduce the team members and explain their roles.]

G. Lay out the interview guide

Interview guides can be organized in various ways. You may find it easiest to simply list the questions and follow-up prompts in what seems to be the most logical sequence. However, since it is just a guide, you may find it more helpful to take the questions out of a linear sequence. This discussion map may help remind you to ask the questions in whatever order seems most appropriate as you follow the lead of your interviewees. Use whatever physical organization seems most comfortable for the individuals on the interview teams.

The last case study in this section presents the document management team's final interview guide.

Case Study: Document Management (Part 4 of 9)

The document management team decided to lay out their interview guide as a discussion map. That way they could easily move from one question to another. They also put the word "Images" in the center of their map to remind them to look for images of their customers' environment throughout the interview.

The diagram on the next page shows what the team's final interview guide looked like.

Continued...

How do you use the current system?
- Tell us about the last few times.
- How do you create documents?
- How do you find them?
- What do you do with them?
- Where saved?
- How coded?
- How are hard copies filed?

Tell us about problems you have with the current system.
- Tell us about problems
  - Creating
  - Retrieving
  - Using
  - Storing
- Which most important to fix? Why?
- Any work-arounds?
- Any costs and negative consequences?

Tell us what works well with the current system.
- What not to change
- What advantages now

IMAGES

Describe what you see as an ideal system.
- What would it look like?
- How would you interact with it?
- Any other systems you've seen or heard about?

What changes do you anticipate in the next couple of years?
- Include changes in
  - Technology
  - Your work
  - Document types
  - Presentation types
  - Delivery formats
  - Client demands/expectations

FRAME

H. Create observation guide

Even if you don't have a formal observation period scheduled, you can still keep your eyes open everywhere you go. As with an interview guide, having some key areas you want to pay attention to during observation will ensure that important areas are not overlooked.

- What do you want to know about the physical environment? Possibilities include lighting, temperature, humidity, cleanliness, types of equipment, amount of clutter, noise, etc.

- What do you want to observe in the use of your product, service, or process? Possibilities include ease of use, points of frustration, places where the user is doing things differently than intended, work-arounds being used, whether instructions are posted, etc.

- What do you want to notice about the emotional environment? Are people friendly? curious? rushing about? relaxed? nervous?

The observation guide is not meant to be a strict checklist, but a list you can quickly review prior to your interviews. Many times you make observations you are not aware of. By reviewing your observation guide after the interview you can note additional observations.

FRAME

FRAME

Step 4 Check

Check to make sure your interview and observation guides are complete. You should have

- ❏ Five or six open-ended summary questions
- ❏ Several prompts or follow-up questions for each summary question
- ❏ A standard introduction
- ❏ Separate interview guide, if needed, for different customer groups
- ❏ An observation guide, if appropriate

Section Summary

You have now worked through the first phase of the FOCUS process, Frame the Project. You should have completed the following:

- ❏ Written a purpose statement
- ❏ Identified your objectives for learning
- ❏ Checked the project for fit with organizational goals
- ❏ Reviewed existing relevant data
- ❏ Created a customer profile matrix
- ❏ Chosen which customer segments to interview
- ❏ Created an interview guide
- ❏ Created an observation guide

Looking ahead...

Now it is time to move on to the second phase of the FOCUS process, Organize Resources. You will identify resources you will need to carry out the interviews and analyze the data.

FRAME

Out of FOCUS

A company wanted to learn how its customers were using new technologies so the company could better position itself in the market. It set up a team to conduct interviews and analyze the results. After meeting with their sponsor to make sure their purpose statement was aligned with organizational goals, the team proceeded with the interviews on their own.

In an effort to be thorough, they decided to interview a wide range of customers across the country and in Europe. As they proceeded, they realized they needed to devote more time than they had initially estimated. Several team members adjusted their schedules so they could devote more time to the project, and the team recruited two new members.

As the team prepared for the interviews, they decided it would also be helpful to understand what technologies might be entering the marketplace over the next few years. To gain this information, they added researchers and leading edge companies to their interview matrix.

After they completed six interviews, their supervisors and sponsor began to review time sheets and budget reports. The project scope was not at all what they had expected. The sponsor called a team meeting to discuss what was going on. She had assumed the team understood they could only spend 25% of their time on this project and they could not add members to the team. Further, she had expected them to conduct most of their interviews within a day's drive of their offices. Resources were limited. The team, on the other hand, had defined the project scope much more broadly and assumed they could expend whatever resources were necessary to do a thorough job. They also thought that because they had already begun, they should be allowed to finish, although they were willing to eliminate the interviews in Europe. Management, however, decided enough damage had been done and canceled the project. The company would go back to telephone surveys instead.

ORGANIZE
Resources

SECTION CONTENTS

ORGANIZE

F

FRAME THE PROJECT
1. Determine Purpose
2. Review Existing Data
3. Create Customer Profile Matrix
4. Create Interview Guide

O

ORGANIZE RESOURCES
5. Estimate Project Requirements
6. Meet With Sponsors
7. Negotiate Scope, Schedule, and Resources
8. Schedule Interviews

C

COLLECT DATA
9. Prepare for Visits
10. Polish Your Skills
11. Finalize Preparations
12. Conduct Interviews
13. Follow Up

U

UNDERSTAND THE VOICES
14. Check Your Direction
15. Focus Your Data Analysis
16. Structure the Data
17. Determine Key Areas to Address

S

SELECT ACTION
18. Generate Ideas
19. Evaluate Ideas and Create a Complete Solution
20. Develop an Action Plan

Overview

All projects require some expenditure of resources and time. Therefore, they also require careful planning, scheduling, and budgeting to be successful. Explorers who start out without knowing what resources they need, what resources are available, and what support they can expect will likely find themselves in trouble before their journey is complete. The larger and more complex the expedition, the riskier it is to start without this knowledge.

The interplay of your scope, schedule, and resources is important to discuss with your sponsor. When the scope of a project falls outside your boundaries of authority, it is particularly important to have clear communication with and support from your sponsor. Without that support you run the risk of not completing the project or not having the final recommendations implemented.

ORGANIZE

What You Gain by Organizing Resources

- Explicit understanding of the time commitment required of you and others

- Consensus about scope, schedule, and resources

- Support from management

- Completed interview schedule and designated interview teams

Questions You Will Be Answering

- What resources do we need to get the project work done?

- Do we have agreement from our sponsor on the scope, schedule, and resources?

- Is the project still in line with broader organizational issues and goals?

- Whom will we be interviewing?

Logistics

Much of the work in Organize Resources may be done by the team leader with input from others or in subsets of the team. These steps can be completed over the course of one week.

In Step 5, Estimate Project Requirements, the team leader will estimate the project requirements with input from the team members on their availability and, possibly, customers to contact.

While it may be valuable to involve the entire team in Step 6, Meet With Sponsors, it is not necessary if this means delaying the meeting. The meeting with sponsors also includes Step 7, Negotiate Scope, Schedule, and Resources.

> If you are working with a team, you may want to involve at least some members in Step 6. It is also good to involve the entire team in identifying and contacting people who fit the profile matrix. However, much of this work can be done individually, rather than in full team meetings.

Step 8, Schedule Visits, can take varying amounts of time, depending on how easy it is to identify the right people, arrange interviews, and confirm times.

The following table shows how long this work typically takes.

Step	Estimated Time
Step 5: Estimate Project Requirements	1 hour or less
Step 6: Meet With Sponsors	1 2 hours
Step 7: Negotiate Scope, Schedule, and Resources	30 minutes or less
Step 8: Schedule Interviews	From a few hours for straightforward, internal projects to 8 hours spread over time for an external project in which you do not know the people

ORGANIZE

The Big Picture

5. Estimate Project Requirements
6. Meet With Sponsors
7. Negotiate Scope, Schedule, and Resources
8. Schedule Interviews

Prework

- Determine project purpose
- Identify objectives for learning
- Check for organizational fit
- Create customer profile matrix

Time and Logistics

The team leader will likely estimate project requirements with input from the team members. Allow approximately 1 hour for this work.

Supplies and Equipment

- Calculator, if necessary

Outcomes

- An estimate of team members' available time to work on this project
- An estimate of time needed to complete the project
- An estimate of the resources needed to complete the project

Step 5:

Estimate Project Requirements

Description

To put together a realistic plan and timeline for your project, you need to have an idea of what resources you will need. In the FOCUS process, resources include people, time, and money, with time being the single most important resource. This step includes a planning worksheet to help you estimate your project requirements.

Benefits

Estimating your project requirements will provide you with planning information needed for the discussion with your sponsor on scope, schedule, and resources.

Getting Your Bearings

You have done a lot of work to identify the scope of your project, what you want to learn, and the types of customers you want to visit. Now you will begin to put together some details regarding the schedule and resources needed to do the work. Realistic plans that are supported by your organization will contribute to the overall success of your work.

ORGANIZE

How to Estimate Project Requirements

A. Anticipate overall time requirements

Before you can create a project plan, you need to have some idea of how long the work will take. The table on the next page outlines the phases of the FOCUS process and includes time estimates and activities for each phase. This outline will help you get an overall sense of how much time will be required to work through the FOCUS process.

B. Complete project requirements worksheet

The project requirements worksheet on page 90 will help you estimate the resources you need to do the work, including how much time it will take to gather your data and complete the project. This information will be used in your discussion with sponsors when negotiating scope, schedule, and resources (Step 7).

ORGANIZE

FOCUS process time outline

Process Phase	Type of Activities	Time Estimates
FRAME the Project	1 to 3 team meetings Meeting with sponsor Research by individual team members	4 – 8 hours plus time to review existing data
ORGANIZE Resources	Work by team leader and/or members Meeting(s) with sponsor Phone calls to potential interviewees	4 hours to several days
COLLECT Data	1 to 2 team meetings Work by team leader and/or members Skill practice in small groups Interviews by team members	1 – 2 hours 1 – 2 hours 2 – 4 hours Approximately 3 hours per interview plus travel time
UNDERSTAND the Voices	Individual work by team members Several team meetings The time spent to Understand the Voices will vary depending on which of three paths for analysis you choose	1+ hour per interview **Targeted Path**: 6 – 8 hours **Requirements Path**: 15 – 18 hours **Systems Path**: 24 – 36 hours
SELECT Action	2 to 4 team meetings Research by individual team members	1 – 7 days

ORGANIZE

For a more detailed overview of the FOCUS process, see pages 409 to 413 in Appendix A.

Project Requirements Worksheet

General information   **Requirements**

Targeted completion date (if any) . . . . _____

How many people are on the team? . . . . _____

What percentage of their time can they
devote to this project? . . . . _____

How many interviews will be conducted? . . . . _____

Estimate of time to complete the project

How much time will it take to contact interviewees? . . . . _____

- If you know everyone personally, this will be easy

- If you have good leads, this will require a moderate
  amount of effort

- If you are going to have to track down appropriate
  people, this will be time-consuming

How long will it take to do the interviews? (in hours) . . . . _____
(Allow 3 hours plus travel time for each interview)

How long will it take to complete all the interviews? (in weeks) . . _____
(This is elapsed time, not the time for the actual interviews)

How much time will it take to analyze the interview data? . . . . . _____
(See the chart on page 89)

Estimate of resources needed to complete the project
(This includes the cost of people's time)

How many people will be scheduling interviews? . . . . _____

How many people will be conducting interviews? . . . . _____

How many trips will be taken? (total trips) . . . . _____

      Local _____   National _____

      Regional _____   International _____

Estimated cost for transportation to interviews . . . . _____

Estimated cost for accommodations . . . . _____

Estimated cost for food . . . . _____

Continued...

ORGANIZE

Project Requirements Worksheet (cont.)

Estimate of resources (cont.)   **Requirements**

How many person hours will it take to complete the interviews? _____

(#I x #P x (Lt + Tt)) = total FTE (full time equivalency) to complete interviews

  #I = Number of interviews
  #P = Number of team members at each interview
  Lt = Length of each interview + debriefing (generally 3 hours each)
  Tt = Average time needed to travel to and from interviews

  For example:

    15 interviews (#I)
    2 team members per interview (#P)
    3 hours per interview (Lt)
    4 hours average travel time to and from interviews (Tt)
    (15 x 2 x (3 + 4)) = 210 person hours, or about 5 weeks FTE

How much time will it take to get interview transcripts
typed? (optional) . . . . _____

- If you are transcribing audio tapes, allow 4 hours of transcription for each interview hour

- If individuals are typing up handwritten notes, time will vary depending on their typing ability

Optional incidental costs . . . . _____

- Thank-you gifts
- Hiring someone to transcribe interview tapes
- Tape recorders, batteries, tapes
- Cameras, film, developing

Project requirements summary

Projected number of people . . . . _____

Projected length of project . . . . _____

Projected number of person hours . . . . _____

Projected budget . . . . _____

ORGANIZE

The following case study shows how a team used the worksheet to better understand their project requirements.

Case Study: Document Management (Part 5 of 9)

The document management team used the worksheet to determine how much time their project would take and what resources would be needed to finish. Since this was an internal project, it was clear that their biggest resource would be time.

General information	Requirements
Targeted completion date (if any)	November 1
How many people are on the team?	7
What percentage of their time can they devote to this project?	10%
How many interviews will be conducted?	16

Estimate of time to complete the project

How much time will it take to contact interviewees? . . . . 2 days

  • If you know everyone personally, this will be easy

  • If you have good leads, this will require a moderate amount of effort

  • If you are going to have to track down appropriate people, this will be time-consuming

How long will it take to do the interviews? (in hours) . . . . 48 hours
(Allow 3 hours plus travel time for each interview)

How long will it take to complete all the interviews? (in weeks) . . 3 weeks
(This is elapsed time, not the time for the actual interviews)

How much time will it take to analyze the interview data? . . . . . 36 hours
(See the chart on page 89)

The team was not surprised with the amount of time needed to complete the interviews. The total of 48 hours would be divided among the team members and spread out across three weeks. Everyone agreed they could do this without interfering excessively with their regular work. This was important since it had been assumed that they could complete this project in relatively short weekly meetings.

Continued…

When they looked at the amount of time it would take to analyze the data, however, the team became concerned. About half of this time involved work that could be done individually, but the rest of it would need to be done in team meetings. If they could only meet four hours a week it would take five weeks. They knew they would have to discuss this with their sponsor.

Using the information from the project requirements worksheet, they created the following Gantt chart to take with them to the meeting with their sponsor.

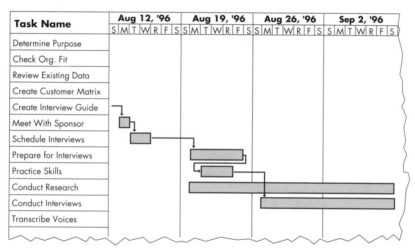

Task Name	Aug 12, '96							Aug 19, '96							Aug 26, '96							Sep 2, '96						
	S	M	T	W	R	F	S	S	M	T	W	R	F	S	S	M	T	W	R	F	S	S	M	T	W	R	F	S
Determine Purpose																												
Check Org. Fit																												
Review Existing Data																												
Create Customer Matrix																												
Create Interview Guide																												
Meet With Sponsor																												
Schedule Interviews																												
Prepare for Interviews																												
Practice Skills																												
Conduct Research																												
Conduct Interviews																												
Transcribe Voices																												

Step 5 Check

Check to make sure you have a good idea of what it will take to complete your project. You should have

- ❏ An estimate of team members' available time to work on this project
- ❏ An estimate of time needed to complete the project
- ❏ An estimate of the resources needed to complete the project

The Big Picture

5. Estimate Project Requirements
6. **Meet With Sponsors**
7. Negotiate Scope, Schedule, and Resources
8. Schedule Interviews

Prework

- Determine project purpose
- Identify objectives for learning
- Check for organizational fit
- Create customer profile matrix
- Complete project requirements worksheet

Time and Logistics

Allow 1 – 2 hours to make sure you have enough time to discuss all of your agenda items. If the entire team cannot participate in the meeting, the team leader and one or two team members may represent the group. Step 7, Negotiate Scope, Schedule, and Resources, is part of this meeting with sponsors.

Supplies and Equipment

- Copy of project purpose statement
- Copy of objectives for learning
- Copy of customer profile matrix
- Copy of project requirements worksheet
- Copy of scope, schedule, and resources grid (see Step 7)

Outcomes

- Agreement on organizational fit
- Agreement on scope, schedule, and resources
- Schedule of future checkpoints with your sponsor

Step 6:

Meet With Sponsors

Description

Some Voice of the Customer projects do not have a formal sponsor, but the majority do. In this step you will meet with your sponsor to share the scope of the project, what you want to learn, what types of customers you plan to visit, and what you see as the project requirements. Keeping clear, open channels of communication with your sponsor is important because he or she will help you secure necessary resources including funding.

Before completing your preparations for the meeting with your sponsor, it is important that you read ahead to Step 7, Negotiate Scope, Schedule, and Resources, as this is an integral part of the meeting.

Benefits

You will get the project off to the right start by communicating your learnings to date about the scope of your project, what you want to learn, what types of customers you plan to visit, and what resources you expect it will take to do the work. This information will help your sponsor understand the decisions made so far.

ORGANIZE

Getting Your Bearings

Now that the project team has completed important preliminary work, it is time to include the project sponsor. Because sponsors play a key role in the success of the project and its connection to the organization, it is important for the team and sponsor to work well together. The sponsor's knowledge of the project and understanding of the decisions made so far may benefit you down the road if you need them to smooth the way for an interview or run organizational interference regarding the project's work. Sponsor support is especially critical when it comes time for the organization to act on the team's recommendations.

How to Meet With Sponsors

A. Compile project information

Everything you have done so far has prepared you for this check meeting with your sponsors. You should be able to discuss the following:

- Project purpose statement
- Objectives for learning
- Names of team members (if appropriate)
- Names of sponsors and stakeholders (if appropriate)
- Results of your check for organizational fit
- Customer profile matrix
- Project requirements worksheet

> In this meeting with sponsors you should also discuss the scope, schedule, and resources. Read ahead to Step 7 to get a better understanding of how this discussion should progress. Agreement on the scope, schedule, and resources is key to setting realistic expectations for the project and developing shared understanding among the team members.

ORGANIZE

B. Generate questions for sponsors

In the previous steps, you may have discovered areas of concern and raised questions you cannot answer. To make sure you get the information needed from your sponsor, write down your questions and take them to the meeting. Here are some typical questions:

- What expectations do you have of us?
- What resources are available to us?
- How will the results of this project be used?
- How does the project fit in with other efforts under way?
- How soon do you expect us to finish?
- Relative to other assignments, how much time can we devote to this work?
- What is the budget for the project?
- Do you have specific types of people in mind who should or should not be interviewed?

C. Arrange meeting with sponsors

Create an agenda with time estimates for the topics you want to cover in this meeting. Contact your sponsor and set a time to meet. Your agenda, which should be sent to all participants ahead of time, should include opportunities to update the sponsor on your work, get answers to the team's questions, and set times for future checkpoints.* Your agenda may contain the following items:

- Introduce all participants
- Review the project's purpose statement and objectives for learning
- Review the check for organizational fit
- Review the customer profile matrix
- Discuss the project as a whole
- Discuss the scope, schedule, and resources (Step 7)
- Agree on the overall timeline, budget, scope, and resources
- Review and, if necessary, adjust the team membership
- Schedule future checkpoints
- Evaluate the meeting

 If your team has a regularly scheduled meeting and the timing is appropriate, you may choose to invite the sponsor to this meeting rather than schedule a separate meeting.

*See Appendix B, *The Team® Handbook Second Edition*, for more information on effective meetings.

D. Hold meeting with sponsors

This meeting is important because it allows all involved to calibrate the scope of the project and see the path ahead. Work through the agenda at the meeting and be sure to provide ample opportunity for discussions between your team and the sponsor regarding project boundaries, limitations, and so on. The following case study shows how the document management team prepared to meet with their sponsor and how they conducted the meeting.

Case Study: Document Management (Part 6 of 9)

The document management team members initially thought their purpose would be to look at how people used, and would like to use, training and other presentation documents. However, when they checked this purpose statement on the ladder of abstraction, they decided to move up a rung and include all the documents used by the company. In the meeting with their sponsor, the team wanted to make sure the scope of the issue was not too broad. They also wanted to make sure they could bring in outside expertise to help develop a new system once they had identified people's needs. They created the following agenda for the meeting with their sponsor:

Document Management Team Meeting Agenda

Time	Topic	Person Responsible
10 min.	Discuss revised purpose statement	Dave
5 min.	Review objectives for learning and profile matrix	Sue
5 min.	Discuss organizational fit	Dave, Barbara
15 min.	Review project work to date	Whole group
10 min.	Confirm ability to hire outside expertise as needed	Sue, Barbara
30 min.	Reach agreement on overall timeline, budget, scope, and resources	Whole group
10 min.	Schedule future checkpoints and agree on methods of communication	Dave, Barbara
5 min.	Evaluate meeting	Whole group

Continued...

ORGANIZE

The meeting went well and even ended earlier than anticipated. The team's sponsor was impressed by the amount of work the team had done and the clarity of their thinking. Most topics needed little discussion.

The sponsor agreed with their revised purpose statement. In fact, she felt it fit even better with the organization's plans and strategies than had the original purpose statement. The team was also given authority to hire outside expertise as needed. At the end of the meeting, the sponsor felt comfortable with the team's direction, and the team was motivated by their sponsor's recognition of their work so far and the autonomy they would be afforded as they moved forward.

E. Establish future checkpoints

Maintaining contact with your sponsor throughout the course of a Voice of the Customer project can be critical to your success. Ongoing checks will help keep the team aligned with organizational goals and your sponsor informed and involved. Even with the best planning in these early stages, you may need to correct your course. That is the nature of an exploration. As things change, it is important that your sponsor stay informed; no one likes surprises.*

Natural checkpoints include when you move from one phase of the FOCUS process to another and when major documents are completed. Typical checkpoints are as follows:

- When customer interviews have been completed. (If something totally surprising has been learned that might change the course of the work, then check in with your sponsors.)

- After the data have been analyzed.

- When conclusions have been reached.

- Before the recommended actions begin.

- After the recommended actions have been implemented.

---

*See Appendix B, *The Team® Handbook Second Edition*, for more information on meetings with sponsors.

Step 6 Check

Check to make sure you covered the important points of discussion with your sponsor. You should have

- ❑ Agreement on the organizational fit of the project

- ❑ Agreement on the scope of the project, the resources available to do the work, and the project schedule

- ❑ A schedule of future checkpoints with your sponsor

ORGANIZE

The Big Picture

5. Estimate Project Requirements
6. Meet With Sponsors
7. **Negotiate Scope, Schedule, and Resources**
8. Schedule Interviews

Prework

- Determine project purpose
- Identify objectives for learning
- Check for organizational fit
- Create customer profile matrix
- Complete project requirements worksheet

Time and Logistics

Allow 30 minutes for the discussion and negotiation of scope, schedule, and resources during your meeting with sponsors (Step 6). The content is treated separately here in detail due to its importance and relevance throughout the project.

Supplies and Equipment

- Copy of project purpose statement
- Copy of objectives for learning
- Copy of customer profile matrix
- Copy of project requirements worksheet

Outcomes

- Agreement on how to balance scope, schedule, and resources

Step 7:

Negotiate Scope, Schedule, and Resources

Description

In this step the project team and sponsor will use a grid to reach agreement on the scope of the project, the schedule, and the resources needed to do the work. The key in this step is to find a balance between what you want to accomplish and what resources are available.

Benefits

This discussion with your sponsor is a good way to gain a common understanding of the project and to correct any false assumptions. This work creates a win/win situation. The sponsor has the opportunity to learn about the work done to date on the project and make some choices about scope, schedule, and resources in relation to future work on the project. The project team gets a clear understanding of the project parameters as well as what resources they have at their disposal.

Getting Your Bearings

Having sketched out what commitments will be necessary for the project, you will now determine how to balance the scope, schedule, and resources. This is usually done as part of the meeting with your sponsors (Step 6). Later, as you learn more about the work that needs to be done, you may have to renegotiate the balance. Before you begin to work through this step, examine the following grid, which you will use to balance the scope, schedule, and resources.

ORGANIZE

Scope, Schedule, and Resources

The scope, schedule, and resources grid is a planning tool. The project team and sponsor should review the grid when an element changes. Similar to a hanging mobile, as soon as any element in the grid moves, the other elements shift to maintain the balance.

The objective is to put three Xs in the grid so that each column and each row has only one X. In other words, you need to decide which aspect of the project is fixed, which is set, and which is accepted. Use the following definitions.

- Fixed: This element is dictated by need or circumstance; it is the least flexible.

- Set: This element is set at a particular level by agreement.

- Accepted: This element is set at whatever level will make the fixed and set elements possible.

The scope, schedule, and resources grid is an especially helpful tool when it appears that more than one element is fixed. As the team and sponsor discuss where to place the Xs they are often challenged to think creatively in order to reach agreement. The outcome is that they usually can discover some flexibility in an element that seemed to be fixed.

The scope, schedule, and resources grid can help teams and sponsors see the implications of a change to one of the elements. For example, if a person is taken off the project or if conflicts with other ongoing work affect the time people can spend on the project, the balance between the scope, schedule, and resources has to be adjusted.

	Scope	Schedule	Resources
Fixed			
Set			
Accepted			

How to Negotiate Scope, Schedule, and Resources

A. Determine which element is fixed

Review your project requirements worksheet with your sponsor. Based on the information at hand, determine which element is fixed—scope, schedule, or resources—and what about the element is fixed. For example:

- If you have a firm deadline, put an X in the Schedule column of the Fixed row.

- If all of the issues defined by the project boundaries absolutely must be addressed, put an X in the Scope column of the Fixed row.

- If the number of people working on the project has been set and the amount of time they can spend is inflexible, put an X in the Resources column of the Fixed row.

Example of identifying the fixed element

Management groups at a large facility frequently found themselves clashing with each other over who had responsibility for issues. Senior management started a Voice of the Customer project to realign the responsibility of all the management teams and individual managers. When the project team and sponsor met, they first checked to see which of the project elements was least flexible.

- The **resources** were **fixed**: The project participants could spend no more than six hours a week on the effort.

	Scope	Schedule	Resources
Fixed			X 6 hrs./week
Set			
Accepted			

ORGANIZE

Be sure to note in the grid the explanation for the Fixed element, such as a list of issues for Scope, a due date for Schedule, or the number of person hours for Resources.

B. Determine which element is set

After reviewing the project requirements worksheet, decide which of the remaining two elements has the least flexibility. Put an X in that column of the Set row. Also note an explanation for this element as well.

Example of identifying the set element

When the team and their sponsor agreed that resources were fixed, they looked to see which of the remaining elements was least flexible.

- The **schedule** was **set**: Senior management wanted results for a board meeting at the beginning of the next quarter and were willing to be flexible on scope in order to meet this deadline.

	Scope	Schedule	Resources
Fixed			**X** 6 hrs./week
Set		**X** Board meeting beginning next quarter	
Accepted			

C. Determine which element is accepted

Put an X in the Accepted row of the remaining element. This is the element that must be accepted by the sponsor and project team to achieve the fixed and set aspects.

- If Scope is accepted, decide which issues must be addressed and which will be covered only if Schedule and Resources allow.

- If Schedule is accepted, set a due date that seems reasonable, based on your decision about Scope and Resources.

- If Resources is accepted, decide how many people you need for how long to cover the issues defined by the Scope within the agreed-upon Schedule.

Example of identifying the accepted element

Finally, the team and their sponsor checked to make sure the last element, scope, could be most flexible.

- The **scope** was **accepted**: The team estimated what they could accomplish by the board meeting, and this was accepted as sufficient by everyone involved.

	Scope	Schedule	Resources
Fixed			X 6 hrs./week
Set		X Board meeting beginning next quarter	
Accepted	X Adjusted what they could accomplish		

Example of balancing scope, schedule, and resources

A leading outdoor clothing manufacturer wanted to better understand consumer trends so it could maintain its market position. The team that was formed to do the interviews met with their sponsor and created a scope, schedule, and resources grid that looked like this:

	Scope	Schedule	Resources
Fixed		**X** New product out 4th quarter next year	
Set	**X** 20 interviews in diverse parts of country		
Accepted			**X** Provided necessary resources to meet scope

- The **schedule** was **fixed**: It was critical to the organization to get new products to market on time. It needed to have the new product out by the fourth quarter of the next year.

- The **scope** was **set**: To meet this schedule, the team met with their sponsor to negotiate how much they needed to accomplish and what resources would be available. The group agreed on the desired scope, and management agreed to provide the necessary resources to meet the scope and schedule.

- The **resources** were **accepted**: The sponsor and the team accepted the level of resources they believed it would take to get the task completed in the time available.

However, as the project unfolded, the team discovered they could not meet their deadlines at the set scope and with the accepted resources; they would have to renegotiate their scope, schedule, and resources.

The case study on the next page shows how the document management team negotiated their scope, schedule, and resources.

Case Study: Document Management (Part 7 of 9)

The document management team discussed the project's scope, schedule, and resources during their meeting with their sponsor. Initially, they had thought that their resources were fixed. But after estimating their project requirements they wanted to negotiate this with their sponsor. It was clear that if they were limited to seven people trying to fit this project in around their regular work, either the scope or schedule would have to change.

When their sponsor saw their project requirements worksheet and Gantt chart, she understood the situation. In her mind the project's scope was more critical than maintaining fixed resources, so the group determined that scope was fixed. The company had to have a new, and more robust, document management system. The team filled in the first row on their scope, schedule, and resources grid.

	Scope	Schedule	Resources
Fixed	**X** must recommend complete system		
Set			
Accepted			

Next, they discussed which of the two remaining categories had the least flexibility: schedule or resources. Nothing seemed to be driving a specific schedule. Although their document management system was outdated, they were still able to get work done. Resources, on the other hand, were less flexible. They put their second X under Resources.

	Scope	Schedule	Resources
Fixed	**X** must recommend complete system		
Set			**X** 7 people, part-time
Accepted			

Continued...

ORGANIZE

Using the Gantt chart they had created from their project requirements worksheet, the team estimated that if they could spend several large blocks of time together to analyze their data they could complete the project in less than three months. This was acceptable to their sponsor as long as they did not enlarge their team. They completed their grid with the final X under Schedule.

	Scope	Schedule	Resources
Fixed	**X** must recommend complete system		
Set			**X** 7 people, part-time
Accepted		**X** 3 months	

By using their project requirements worksheet to negotiate the project's scope, schedule, and resources the team was able to reach agreement with their sponsor about what the team needed to do to be successful and what limitations they were under. Through negotiation they had been able to increase the percentage of time they could spend on the project during the analysis phase. They also understood that if the project started to grow, it was the schedule that had the greatest flexibility.

Step 7 Check

Check to make sure you have discussed scope, schedule, and resources with your sponsor. You should have

- ❏ A complete scope, schedule, and resources grid

- ❏ Agreement on where flexibility lies

- ❏ Agreement to renegotiate scope, schedule, and resources as necessary

ORGANIZE

The Big Picture

5. Estimate Project Requirements
6. Meet With Sponsors
7. Negotiate Scope, Schedule, and Resources
8. **Schedule Interviews**

Prework

- Create customer profile matrix
- Negotiate project scope, schedule, and resources

Time and Logistics

The time needed to schedule interviews varies from project to project. If you know everyone you want to interview, this work can be completed in a few hours. If, on the other hand, you need to identify companies or groups who meet your interviewee profile criteria, and find a contact there, scheduling interviews can take days.

Although one or two people may identify interviewees, it is best for the interview teams to arrange the final schedules.

Supplies and Equipment

- Calendar
- Copy of customer profile matrix

Outcomes

- Names, addresses, and phone numbers of interviewees
- Assigned interview teams
- A schedule for each interview

ORGANIZE

Step 8:

Schedule Interviews

Description

In this step you will choose customers using the criteria from the customer profile matrix. If you do not already have a contact in each organization, you will need to find a point of entry—someone who can direct you to the right people. Next, you will have to make contact with those people, and finally, you must mesh the busy schedules of your interviewees with your interview team.

Benefits

You will know precisely whom you will interview and how they fit your customer profile matrix. Interviewees and interviewers will have the necessary time allocated on their calendars.

Getting Your Bearings

The project team and sponsors have agreed on the scope, schedule, and resources. Now you are ready to identify specific customers who fit the profile of those you want to interview and then arrange those interviews. Time spent in preparation will pay off when you go on your customer interviews.

ORGANIZE

How to Schedule Interviews

A. Identify appropriate groups or organizations

It is important to start by reviewing the customer profile matrix created in Step 3. In this matrix you identified particular cells of customers that you wanted to interview. Now you must identify customers who fit in those cells. Below is the customer profile matrix that appeared in Part 2 of the New Photographic Film case study on page 60.

			Nontraditional Segments			
			Lead Users	Dissatisfied Customers	Cust. Had but Lost	Customers Never Had
Traditional Segments — Asia	Northern: South Korea	Shop Owners		1		1
		Shopkeepers	2		2	
	Southern: Malaysia	Shop Owners	1			2
		Shopkeepers			1	
Traditional Segments — Europe	Northern: Germany	Shop Owners			1	
		Shopkeepers	1	2		1
	Southern: Spain	Shop Owners	2		2	
		Shopkeepers				1

The team must now locate two shopkeepers in South Korea who are lead users and two who are former customers. They must also find one South Korean shop owner who is a dissatisfied customer and another who has never been a customer. Then they will move on to identify specific interviewees in Malaysia, Germany, and Spain.

On certain projects it may be easy to identify individuals who meet the profile criteria. More often, however, you will need to start your search by identifying appropriate groups, departments, or organizations, and then finding specific people within those entities. How you do this work depends on your project.

- If you intend to visit external customers, ask for assistance from your sales, marketing, or customer service departments. Department personnel should have data on customers and can help identify appropriate organizations. Even if someone from the department is working on this project with you and has identified customers to contact, it is always important to speak with the person responsible for maintaining a customer relationship prior to actually contacting customers.

- If you are exploring an internal issue, work with your sponsor or other managers, as appropriate, to identify which employees meet your profile characteristics.

- If you are targeting a customer group that is new for your company, you may need to employ an external research firm to recruit interviewees based on your criteria.

> *If any team members have personal relationships with appropriate customers, you can also draw on them to set up the interviews. However, those team members should not go on these interviews because their presence might influence what the interviewee says.*

ORGANIZE

The following examples describe ways companies found people to interview.

Examples of identifying interviewees

Initial Contact

When an imaging company team wanted to learn the needs of health care professionals, they were told they would never find plastic surgeons willing to give up their time for an interview. A team member found one plastic surgeon who was interested and got permission to use his name. This reference helped team members make initial contact with other plastic surgeons, who, in fact, were eager to have someone listen to them.

Sales Records

A company that sold training materials wanted to learn more about customer needs before updating one of its products. It was easy for the team to find both satisfied and demanding customers, and sales records also identified customers they had lost. But how could the team identify customers they never had? One team member suggested they look at people who had ordered preview copies, but never made an order, as well as people who had returned orders.

Lead Thinkers

A company wanted to know more about current and future developments in digital imaging for medical application. It was interested in exploring technology, funding, regulatory issues, and customer perceptions. Because the team was trying to look into the future, they wanted to find lead thinkers. Team members attended seminars and read publications to identify a few lead thinkers. Their initial interviews facilitated referrals to others prominent in the field.

External Recruiters

A car manufacturer wanted to learn more about the future needs of customers before developing a new line of vehicles. Once the project team had developed their profile matrix, they hired an outside organization to recruit the types of people they wanted to interview. Knowing clearly what kinds of people they needed to interview helped the recruiters do their job well.

B. Determine interviewee time commitment

Before contacting a customer, you need to know what kind of commitment you are asking of them. Most interviews take approximately one hour. If interviews are shorter, you may not have time to probe for details; if longer, you may have a hard time finding people who can devote the time.

Decide if observation will add value to your project. It is especially valuable when considering the potential for a new product or service, improving an old one, improving or redesigning a process or procedure, or when trying to understand a specific dynamic or situation. In any project in which watching the relevant environment will help you gain insight, plan to include observation. This ranges from watching a single person perform a task for fifteen minutes to watching several people use your product or service through a complete cycle. Note that if you are doing multiple interviews at a single site, you do not necessarily have to observe every individual.

A general rule of thumb is to schedule one hour to one-and-one-half hours for the interview and observation, and one hour between interviews to process your experience.

Observation may not be as important when

- You are working on an internal project and everyone on the team is familiar with the environment.

- Your objectives for learning focus on understanding ideas, learning about policies and regulations, or gathering opinions.

 Although it may be tempting to interview two or more people at the same time, try not to. Remember that you want to let the interviewee take the lead; if you have two or more people in an interview, they are unlikely to want to go in the same direction. You are also more likely to get rich, detailed information if you interview only one person at a time because the interviewee is more likely to be relaxed and candid.

The following table summarizes guidelines for scheduling observations.

Guidelines for scheduling observations

No Formal Observation	Observing Before the Interview	Observing After the Interview
When you are familiar with the environment (such as internal projects) When the environment is abstract or intellectual (as when collecting opinions or policies)	When you are at least somewhat familiar with the environment and the observations can help shape the interview questions (most common situation)	When you are unfamiliar with the environment and the interviews are necessary to help you understand what you see during the observations (such as highly technical projects)

Occasionally, you will conduct your interviews in the workplace. Although this can present problems in terms of getting verbatim notes and following a train of thought without interruption, it provides a fuller, more robust experience of the customers' world.

The examples on the next page illustrate how decisions about scheduling observations should be tailored to the situation.

Examples of when to observe

No Formal Observation

A team was exploring the pace of change in a field to determine how long a current product might last before becoming outdated. They planned to interview researchers, lead thinkers, and policy makers. Because the team was working mostly with ideas, they decided formal observations were unnecessary.

Observing Before the Interviews

A team was exploring potential improvements in documentation film. They decided that, before interviewing photographers, they would watch the entire process of taking passport photos from the time a customer requested a photo to the time the customer walked out of the shop with a photo in hand. In various locations around the country, they noticed that many photographers were using hair dryers to speed up the process. Having observed this procedure, the interviewers were able to follow up during the interviews and learn more about what photographers were trying to accomplish with the hair dryers.

Observing After the Interviews

A knowledgeable technical team wanted to understand the problems in their current test software before designing the architecture for its next generation. They decided to schedule a demonstration of the test equipment after their interviews; this way the on-site technicians could demonstrate any problems identified during the interviews.

ORGANIZE

A sample schedule for a full-day customer visit is shown below.

Sample schedule for customer visit

Time	Activity
8:30 – 9:00	Meeting with contact to review schedule
9:00 – 10:00	Facility tour or operational view
10:00 – 11:00	Interview #1
11:00 – 12:30	Debriefing #1 and lunch
12:30 – 1:30	Interview #2
1:30 – 2:30	Debriefing #2
2:30 –	More interviews (if scheduled)

 The scheduling guidelines given here represent what is ideal for you. However, that may not be possible in your customer's workplace. Be flexible to accommodate your customer's schedule and needs.

C. Find point of entry

In some projects, you can contact potential interviewees directly. In other projects, you may need to find a point of entry. The sales, marketing, or customer service department is often a good source of potential contacts within an organization. Alternatively, you may choose to hire an outside research firm to find potential interviewees.

With either method, making the right contact can be a delicate procedure. Most organizations understand the importance of maintaining good relationships with key customers. Those relationships are carefully managed, and nothing should happen that is not cleared through the person responsible for the relationship. If you find yourself stymied in finding the appropriate contacts, your sponsors may be able to help you gain access to customers.

D. Make contact with group or individuals

After you have identified appropriate people to contact and know what you need to ask them, you are ready to start making phone calls. Begin this work as soon as possible because you may need to make several calls before speaking directly with the appropriate people. The following checklist shows what topics to cover in the call.

 If this is an internal project, be careful not to discount the value of your fellow employees' time. Before making contact, you may want to check with your sponsor to see if approval is necessary before going into different parts of the organization.

ORGANIZE

Phone Call Checklist

Use this checklist as a reminder of the topics you need to cover when calling a contact or interview candidate.

❑ Introduce yourself.

❑ Indicate you are asking permission to visit and ask if this is a convenient time to talk.

❑ Briefly describe the reason for your project. Emphasize it is not a troubleshooting call or a sales visit, but rather an exploration.

❑ State how much time is needed, the number of interviews you would like to do, and what type of people you are visiting.

❑ Answer any questions the person has.

 Keep a list of interviewees' names, addresses, phone numbers, and fax numbers. You will need to send the interviewees a list of interview topics and confirm the arrangements right before your visit.

The following case study provides an example of an initial phone call.

Case Study: Product Redesign (Part 1 of 2)

"My name is Juanita Barker, and I'm the marketing vice president at Value Container Corporation. We're initiating a product redesign effort and would like to know if several people from my company could visit your organization. Is this a convenient time for you to speak with me?...

"Let me give you a little background first if I may. We're about to develop a new generation of containers and want to first understand how our customers use our plastic containers and what their needs for the future might be.

"We plan to visit only 16 companies across the country. Ship-a-Lot is one of our most valued customers, and we think it would be a great place for us to better understand our customers' requirements. We'd like to come for a day sometime in the next few weeks to conduct three separate interviews with someone from your customer service, shipping, and purchasing departments. Would that be possible?..."

E. Assign interview teams

When assigning interview teams the most important guideline is to pair people with different backgrounds or perspectives. People bring their own preconceptions and biases to an interview, no matter how open-minded they try to be. By including two people with different frames of reference, you are more likely to create a broad, balanced perspective. For example, if you are working on a product development project, do not send two engineers or two marketing specialists. Mix them up: engineering with marketing, marketing with manufacturing, and so on. In other projects you may want to mix people from different employment levels, such as manager and staff, executive and manager, executive and staff. Each person will naturally attune to comments that enlighten their perspectives. The marketing person may be focused on more general needs while the engineer may be listening for more detailed technical issues. Both of their perspectives are important and together they are able to get more out of the interview than either could alone.

The following case study illustrates how team members can help expand one another's perspectives.

Case Study: Product Redesign (Part 2 of 2)

Sylvia and Steve were paired for interviews they hoped would lead to a new design concept. Sylvia was from marketing and Steve was from engineering. When they went into the first interview they were each certain they knew what the product should be, but their individual solutions were not at all the same. During the interview they both listened for responses that supported their own perspectives. During the debriefing after their first interview they found their preconceptions being challenged. They both realized they had been wrong. When they went into their second interview they were both more open-minded.

ORGANIZE

Matching the schedules of three or more busy people—the interview team and the interviewee—can be challenging. You may be tempted to settle for one person conducting the interview alone. Teams that have tried this have regretted it. Not only did they lose the second perspective, but the quality of both the interview and the notes suffered significantly. It is difficult for one person to conduct the interview and take detailed notes to the degree that is necessary for this process to be successful.

Each person on the team should participate in at least four interviews. People who only participate in one or two interviews tend to give undue weight to the points of view they hear. Therefore it is best if everyone can hear several different viewpoints. If you have a large team, you may want to add an observer to the interview team to give everyone more exposure.

Interview teams are often assigned during other preparation work. Make sure the team is available to interview the customer before confirming the time. In order to accommodate everyone's schedule, you may occasionally have to compromise on the diversity of a team, but do so with caution.

 Encourage team members to remain as flexible as possible when scheduling their interviews.

F. Create interview schedule

The team should decide who will call to arrange for interviews and prepare follow-up correspondence. It is important to know the schedules of project team members when arranging interviews, especially if the interviews require overnight travel. As you assign teams and confirm interviews, create a schedule showing where the interviews will happen and who will be involved. Share the schedule with the interview teams.

When on a site visit, you may be tempted to pack in back-to-back interviews with as many people as you can possibly see. The time in between interviews is extremely valuable though: it gives the interview team a chance to reflect on what they heard and allows flexibility should the interview run longer than scheduled.

The following case study describes how a project team worked through the process of scheduling interviews.

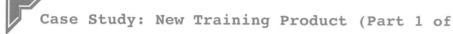

Case Study: New Training Product (Part 1 of 4)

A training company wanted to learn more about its customers' needs regarding a new product it was considering developing. How were people currently training in this area? What had early adopters learned? Where did people tend to have trouble?

To identify people who fit their profile matrix, the project team went first to their customer data base to find customers who had requested information in this area. They also used professional publications to identify organizations involved in training and implementing programs in the content area. As they followed leads, they were able to identify a mix of service and manufacturing organizations, large and small firms, and early and late adopters.

Next, they asked their contacts in each organization to help them identify executives, managers, trainers, and end users they might be able to interview. When they had completed this work, they prepared their customer profile matrix with four traditional segments and five nontraditional segments.

	Nontraditional Segments				
	Lead Users	Happy Customers	Demanding Customers	Customers We Lost	Customers We Never Had
Key Influencers (Executives)	J. Morariu			M. Tear	C. Lee
Decision Makers (Managers)	D. Harris		G. Diaz R. Gitlin	A. Perry	K. Hansen (D. Harris)
Trainers	M. Nguyen	J. Couden	L. Ng (M. Nguyen)	P. Hajduk	F. France D. Wilson
End Users		F. DiVesta		M. Stone P. Schultz	L. Soto

(Names that appear in parentheses are lead users who also fit in a second category.)

Continued...

They decided to interview two satisfied customers to make sure they understood what made them happy, but they were more interested in customers they had lost or never had. Over half their interviews ended up in the "customers we lost" and "customers we never had" columns. They also focused more heavily on two of the four traditional segments: decision makers (managers) and trainers. Although all four segments were important, these two had the most influence over buying decisions. To fill in the names on their matrix, they identified thirteen organizations of different types and sizes. Then they found individuals in the companies who would be willing to participate.

They decided to split their project team of six people into three interviewing teams of two people each. Each pair would visit six people to observe their work (when appropriate), and conduct the interviews. Each team would also be responsible for setting up the final interview schedule. However, as they started setting up schedules Cathy and Aaron could not find a time when they could both visit Best Book Printing, so Brian and Cathy traded places for two interviews.

	Quality Health Care	Best Book Printing	Superior Mfg.	1st Continental Bank	MadCon, Inc.	Silicon Solutions	H. L. Lee and Sons	Condon Engineering Corp.	Jackson Electronics	BioCo International	General Financial Corp.	MidCity Hospital	PMG, Inc.
Aaron	X							X				X	
Cathy	X							X					
Brian			X				X				X		
Elise			X				X						
Dana		X				X		X		X			X
Felipe									X				
Aaron		X											
Brian													
Cathy					X								
Elise													

(The number of Xs in a cell indicates the number of interviews to be conducted at that site.)

Continued...

Aaron and Cathy set up their interview schedule with Quality Health Care. They had two people to interview: Marjorie Tear and Philip Schultz. So each could experience the roles of interviewing and notetaking, they decided Aaron would interview Marjorie and Cathy would interview Philip. Quality Health Care was located within driving distance of the training company, but it was a long drive; they decided to leave the evening before and stay overnight.

Interview Schedule for Quality Health Care

8:00 – 8:30	Meeting with M. Tear to review schedule
8:30 – 9:00	Facility tour
9:00 – 11:00	Observation of people working/training
11:00 – 12:00	Interview with M. Tear (Aaron)
12:00 – 2:00	Lunch and interview debriefing
2:00 – 3:00	Interview with P. Schultz (Cathy)
3:00 – 4:00	Interview debriefing
4:00 – 4:30	Meeting with M. Tear to express thanks

ORGANIZE

Step 8 Check

Check to make sure you have scheduled all customer interviews. You should have

- ❏ Interviewee names, addresses, and phone numbers
- ❏ Assigned interview teams
- ❏ A schedule for each interview

ORGANIZE

Section Summary

You have now worked through the second phase of the FOCUS process, Organize Resources. You should have completed the following:

❏ Estimated project requirements to identify resources needed

❏ Met with sponsors and come to mutual agreement on project scope, schedule, and available resources, and established future checkpoints

❏ Identified interviewees

❏ Scheduled interviews

❏ Created interview schedule

Looking ahead...

Now it is time to move on to the third phase of the FOCUS process, Collect Data, where you will prepare for and conduct the customer interviews.

ORGANIZE

Out of FOCUS

A project team was ready to interview customers about a new product they were considering developing. They created an interview guide and customer profile matrix, and set up interviews.

The four member team divided into pairs for the interviews: one pair would interview local customers; the other, out-of-town customers. To minimize expenses, the traveling pair was able to set up ten interviews in a single metropolitan area over a two and one-half day period. On each interview team, one person was selected to conduct the interviews while the other took notes. However, once they started on the interviews, they realized that switching roles occasionally would be helpful, if only to give the notetaker a rest.

The pair on the road returned to their hotel every night too exhausted to debrief. Only later did they realize they each had a different approach to notetaking. One person had almost verbatim notes; the other had only short synopses. The team working locally took time to debrief every day. And based on the debriefing they would try different approaches. If one person asked leading questions in an interview and got the answers the team was hoping to hear, the other team member tried the same approach. When taking verbatim notes seemed difficult, they decided to try other methods. There were no standards and each interview was approached somewhat differently.

When the full team met to begin analyzing their data, they had a mess. Verbatim notes were easier to analyze, but it was tempting to focus on interviews where leading questions had elicited hoped-for responses. In the end, they decided to select the interviewing methods that had provided the richest data, practice those techniques, and conduct additional interviews using a standard approach.

COLLECT Data

COLLECT

F

FRAME THE PROJECT
1. Determine Purpose
2. Review Existing Data
3. Create Customer Profile Matrix
4. Create Interview Guide

O

ORGANIZE RESOURCES
5. Estimate Project Requirements
6. Meet With Sponsors
7. Negotiate Scope, Schedule, and Resources
8. Schedule Interviews

C

COLLECT DATA
9. Prepare for Visits
10. Polish Your Skills
11. Finalize Preparations
12. Conduct Interviews
13. Follow Up

U

UNDERSTAND THE VOICES
14. Check Your Direction
15. Focus Your Data Analysis
16. Structure the Data
17. Determine Key Areas to Address

S

SELECT ACTION
18. Generate Ideas
19. Evaluate Ideas and Create a Complete Solution
20. Develop an Action Plan

COLLECT

Overview

Interviewing customers is the pivot point of the FOCUS process. All that comes before is designed to make the interviews go well so that you will have good data on which to base your analysis and decisions. All that comes after is dependent on the data collected during the interviews.

Up to this point your team has done much planning work for the upcoming interviews. In this section you will make sure that both you and the interviewees are prepared for the visit. To prepare yourself, you should review any existing information about the customer, assign roles to the interview teams, finalize logistics, and practice your interview skills. To prepare the interviewees, you should confirm the arrangements and send them a list of the topics you hope to cover.

The better prepared you are, the more likely the interviews will be worthwhile. Even if things do not go exactly as planned, you will be in a good position to take advantage of unforeseen opportunities.

COLLECT

What You Gain by Collecting Data

- Smooth interview process due to thorough preparation
- Skilled interview team members
- Rich customer data for comprehensive analysis

Questions You Will Be Answering

- What will each team member be doing during the interviews?
- What do we need to do to prepare for the visits?
- What do we need to do after the visits?

Logistics

Much of the work in Collect Data will be done by the individual interview teams. The interview schedule will determine how much time this phase of the FOCUS process takes.

In Step 9, Prepare for Visits, the team as a whole should decide how to capture notes and set interview ground rules.

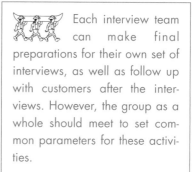 Each interview team can make final preparations for their own set of interviews, as well as follow up with customers after the interviews. However, the group as a whole should meet to set common parameters for these activities.

The remaining work of Collect Data will be completed by individual interview teams.

In Step 13, Follow Up, the team should come back together to reflect on this phase of work.

The following table shows how long this work typically takes.

Step	Estimated Time
Step 9: Prepare for Visits	Approximately 2 hours
Step 10: Polish Your Skills	Approximately 4 hours
Step 11: Finalize Preparations	Approximately 1 hour
Step 12: Conduct Interviews	Approximately 2 – 3 hours per interview, plus travel and observation
Step 13: Follow Up	15 – 20 minutes per interview to send thank-you notes and approximately 30 minutes to reflect on the interviews as part of a team meeting

COLLECT

The Big Picture

9. Prepare for Visits
10. Polish Your Skills
11. Finalize Preparations
12. Conduct Interviews
13. Follow Up

Prework
- Schedule customer interviews
- Assign interview teams

Time and Logistics

There are two types of work in Prepare for Visits. The team will need to meet together for approximately 1 hour to decide how to capture notes and set interview ground rules.

Individual interview teams will need another hour to complete arrangements and confirm schedules.

Supplies and Equipment
- Copy of customer interview schedule
- Calendar

Outcomes
- Interview team roles
- Method for notetaking
- Common understanding of ground rules for customer visits
- Confirmed schedule
- Confirmed travels plans, if needed

COLLECT

Step 9:

Prepare for Visits

Description

You know whom you are going to interview, and who from your organization will conduct the interviews. Now you need to decide what roles people will play and what the associated responsibilities are. You will also confirm the interview schedule and make travel plans, if necessary.

Benefits

Having an interview team that understands what each member should do during the interview prevents confusion, presents a positive image to the customer, and helps the interview process run smoothly. Good preparation should translate into efficient interviews that optimize getting appropriate data.

Getting Your Bearings

Everything up to this point has been in preparation for the interviews, and now decisions will be made on the roles and responsibilities of the interview team members. Ideally, each individual on the project team should participate in at least four interviews. Doing several interviews allows a person to experience and hear different points of view so during analysis each teammate's input is based on an adequate sample of customer voices.

COLLECT

How to Prepare for Visits

A. Decide on interview team roles

When conducting the customer interviews, each team member assumes a role: interviewer, notetaker, or observer. It is extremely difficult for one person to ask good questions, track the responses, observe the interviewee's behavior, and take verbatim notes. Separating these tasks improves the quality of both the interview and the notes.

At a minimum, the interview teams should consist of two people: an interviewer and a notetaker. Having two people hear and experience the same discussion provides a good reality check for both people and helps build the common frame of reference needed when analyzing the data. Sometimes the interview team includes a third person: an observer. This person's responsibilities are to observe the interview process, as well as relevant aspects of the interview environment, and provide feedback on these observations during the debriefing. If the project team is large, you can use the role of observer to get everyone involved in more interviews. The following table outlines the responsibilities associated with each role.

Interview role responsibilities

Interviewer's Responsibilities	Notetaker's Responsibilities	Interview Observer's Responsibilities (Optional Role)
• Build rapport • Conduct the interview • Manage the discussion • Take a few notes • Capture observations • Debrief with the notetaker (and observer)	• Take verbatim notes • Keep up with capturing the discussion as much as possible • Act as a backup for the interviewer • Ask clarifying questions (at the end) • Debrief with the interviewer	• Soak up impressions • Listen between the lines • Note the interviewer's skills • Take notes about the environment • Debrief with the interviewer and notetaker

The interview teams should decide which person will fulfill which role. If at all possible, participants should perform each role at least once during different interviews to develop some experience and comfort with the role. You should not switch roles during an interview because this may confuse the interviewee. You can prevent confusion if you create a schedule like the one in the following example:

	Mon	Tues	Wed	Thurs	Fri

Week 1		**Quality HC**
		M. Tear-
		    Interviewer: Aaron
		    Notetaker: Cathy
		P. Schultz-
		    Interviewer: Cathy
		    Notetaker: Aaron
			Best Book
			J. Couden-
			    Interviewer: Brian
			    Notetaker: Aaron
			
			Superior Mfg.
			R. Gitlin-
			    Interviewer: Dana
			    Notetaker: Felipe
				MadCon, Inc.
				F. DiVesta-
				    Interviewer: Cathy
				    Notetaker: Elise
					Condon Eng. Corp.
					K. Hansen-
					    Interviewer: Cathy
					    Notetaker: Aaron
					L. Soto-
					    Interviewer: Aaron
					    Notetaker: Cathy

Week 2	**1st Cont. Bank**
	L. Ng-
	    Interviewer: Elise
	    Notetaker: Brian
	G. Diaz-
	    Interviewer: Brian
	    Notetaker: Elise
			Silicon Solutions
			D. Harris-
			    Interviewer: Felipe
			    Notetaker: Dana
			
			Mid-City Hosp.
			J. Morariu-
			    Interviewer: Cathy
			    Notetaker: Aaron
				H. L. Lee & Sons
				C. Lee-
				    Interviewer: Brian
				    Notetaker: Elise
				F. France-
				    Interviewer: Elise
				    Notetaker: Brian	

COLLECT

B. Decide how to capture notes

When analyzing the results of your interviews, it is important to have verbatim notes—these are your customers' voices. You want to capture what the interviewees say as closely as possible, using their words, not yours. When you change their language, write a synopsis, or summarize, you risk losing critical information or adding filters to it. The FOCUS process uses specific language data, not general idea data, so it is important to have the interviewees' actual language. Rewording what customers have said is risky because the words you use may change the intended meaning. Also, using the interviewees' own words in your notes is a sign of respect. You have decided these visits are valuable, and the interviewees are giving you their time and information.

Each interview team, or the entire project team (if appropriate), should discuss how to capture these notes. The method you choose will be influenced by where the interview takes place. Using devices such as computers, video recorders, or audio recorders is not always practical (you may be on a shop floor or construction site, for instance). Keep in mind, also, the notetaker's comfort with the various methods. Some people can type faster than they can write. (See Options for Capturing Notes on the next page for a discussion of the methods.) If you choose a method other than handwritten notes, be sure to check with the interviewees before your visit to make sure they are comfortable with the method you have chosen. If you are using a method with which they are unfamiliar, such as typing into a portable computer, you may also want to check after the first five or ten minutes to make sure they are still comfortable.

Options for Capturing Notes

There are several ways in which you can capture verbatim interview notes. You will need to select the method or combination of methods that works best for you and your customers.

Handwriting: Taking verbatim notes by hand is a reliable method that most people find challenging but rewarding. The rule of thumb when taking notes during an interview is to allow the words to flow directly from the ear to the pen, bypassing the brain. Even if you capture notes by technical means, it is advisable to take verbatim notes longhand as a backup. Testing the speed of various pens, pencils, and paper surfaces ahead of time will help optimize this approach.

Tape Recorder: Tape recorders provide a faithful record, but the notes must be transcribed afterward (an often expensive and/or time-consuming effort), and some people are sensitive to having their conversations taped. In some countries, for instance, using a tape recorder would be unthinkable, and people would never speak openly if they knew their words were being taped. But other people may not have any problem at all with being taped. If you use a tape recorder, take handwritten notes as a backup for reference during your debriefing.

Computer: The sounds of someone typing into a computer can be distracting, but some people type more quickly than they write. If you choose to use a computer, make sure you have either a place to plug it in or a long-lasting battery.

Videotape: Videotaping has not been used in any known projects using the FOCUS process, although one team leader wished she had videotapes of customers in action to show to people who joined the team during the implementation phase. Videotaping not only provides an exact reproduction of the inter-viewee's words, but also captures tone of voice, facial expressions, and body language. It can therefore be a rich source of information. However, like tape recording, it requires transcription afterward. To be as rich as the original tape, the transcription should include all nonverbal elements.

One advantage of videotaping is that the tapes can be used later to help new teams get a feel for the interview process and to provide others in the company with a better understanding of their customers. However, as with tape recorders or computers, many people or organizations will be uncomfortable with video recorders, so check with them before your visit if you want to use this technology.

COLLECT

C. Discuss interview ground rules

As part of a customer interview team, you will be seen as a representative of your organization. Everyone on the team needs to understand what this means and review any pertinent organizational guidelines or policies. At a minimum, the team should have an authentic attitude of respect. When interviewees see you are genuinely interested in what they say and appreciate their contributions, they will work harder to make your effort worthwhile. Remember the four Ps of successful interviews: be Prepared, Punctual, Positive, and Professional.

The checklist on page 143 illustrates some of the basic ground rules many companies have found valuable. You may want to include additional ground rules that are appropriate for your own situation.

COLLECT

Suggested Ground Rules Checklist

❑ Be professional and courteous. Remember that you are representing your company, organization, or department.

❑ When speaking of your company, organization, or team, say "we," not "they" or "I."

❑ Be careful not to reveal confidential information about your organization. Remember that you are vulnerable to being quoted: "A source at X Corporation revealed today…"

❑ Make sure the interviewee knows how the interview notes will be used and how confidential they will be.

❑ Defer requests for help until after the interview; then assist if you can or make a referral to an appropriate person. You are there to listen, not troubleshoot.

❑ Resist the temptation to sell, or in general talk too much. You are there to listen.

❑ If there is a valid reason to mention competitors, speak only positively about them.

❑ Dress appropriately for the situation in a manner that balances representing your organization and putting the interviewee at ease.

COLLECT

D. Make final arrangements and confirm schedule

Making the final arrangements for the interviews includes the following tasks:

- Determine logistical needs. If possible, arrange to interview people in their own work spaces to get a better sense of their daily work. If this would disrupt coworkers, you may need a separate room for the interview. In any case, if you are conducting multiple interviews at one organization, you will need a room where you can conduct the interview debriefings.

- Confirm times, places, and participants. When you think you have everything arranged—the interview team is assigned, a location for the interview designated, a debriefing room arranged, and a time has been chosen—confirm these arrangements with all involved parties.

- Make travel arrangements if needed. If you are traveling offsite—whether across town or around the world—you need to make travel arrangements. If traveling to unknown locations, allow enough time to arrive at the customer site with time to spare. If you are traveling by plane or train, plan your departures at least two to three hours after the end of your scheduled interviews, or even the next day. Interviewees are often enthusiastic about sharing their experience. You do not want to cut an interview short, miss an opportunity for a spontaneous interview, or forego an opportunity to observe their operations because you need to catch a plane.

Step 9 Check

Check to make sure interview teams are prepared for their visits. They should have

- ❑ Agreement on interview roles
- ❑ Agreement on how to take interview notes
- ❑ Common understanding of customer visit ground rules
- ❑ A finalized schedule
- ❑ Confirmed travel plans, if necessary

COLLECT

The Big Picture

9. Prepare for Visits
10. Polish Your Skills
11. Finalize Preparations
12. Conduct Interviews
13. Follow Up

Prework
- Create interview guide
- Create observation guide, if necessary
- Assign interview teams
- Assign interview roles
- Decide how to capture notes

Time and Logistics
If you have little or no experience conducting interviews, allow approximately 4 hours to practice your skills. If you have prior experience, allow 1 – 2 hours for practicing with your current team. To set up mock interviews, interview teams will need to work together.

Supplies and Equipment
- Copy of interview guide
- Copy of observation guide
- Paper
- Pens or pencils
- Tape recorder/video recorder/computer, if necessary
- Videotape/VCR/monitor (for observation practice exercise)

Outcomes
- Listening skills
- Probing skills
- Notetaking skills
- Observation skills
- Debriefing skills

Step 10:

Polish Your Skills

Description

This step provides a chance to have a dress rehearsal of sorts. Team members will practice the different interview roles and test the interview guide. Interview skills are best developed through practice and reflection: try out the skills, think about what did and did not work, and continually improve what you do. Try to arrange sufficient time to do several rounds of practice interviews so you get a chance to practice all of the necessary skills: listening, probing, notetaking, observing, and debriefing.

Benefits

Practicing the interview roles gives everyone a chance to develop comfort with each role. Testing the interview guide allows you to make adjustments if something does not work or seems awkward. Practicing your interviewing skills and receiving feedback increases the likelihood of having successful interviews with no unwanted surprises. You will avoid confusion among team members and make a better impression on the customer. Practicing your observation skills and testing the observation guide will help you know what to look for in an unfamiliar environment.

Getting Your Bearings

At this point you know who is interviewing whom and have completed your arrangements. It probably feels like it is time to get started. Before you do, though, you should take the opportunity to practice. Even if you have previously interviewed customers, you are probably teamed up with new people this time. Also, a practice session will help you recall learnings from previous interviews.

How to Polish Your Skills

Before practicing your interview skills, read the following important points on listening, probing, notetaking, and observing. Keeping this information in mind will increase the effectiveness of your mock interviews.

What Every Interviewer Should Know About Listening

Every interviewer needs listening skills. Although this may seem obvious, listening is not always as easy as it sounds. We tend to want to fill in pauses or offer explanations when we should be listening.

Passive Listening

Passive listening includes a wide range of subtle but powerful behaviors that communicate you are paying attention to the speaker. Most people are familiar with simple behaviors that indicate genuine interest in what someone else is saying. When doing interviews, the key is to remain comfortable enough to do what comes naturally. Here are some tips:

- Sit around a corner from the interviewee. Sitting at an angle is less formal than sitting across a table. Sitting next to the person puts you in an awkward position for watching their expressions. Use good posture; do not slouch or slump.

- Use simple verbal or nonverbal cues as encouragement. Showing you are still engaged with the conversation by leaning forward slightly, nodding, or murmuring "uh-huhs" encourages people to keep talking.

- Do not fill every silence. Although some people seem to have little trouble putting their thoughts into words, others take longer to formulate what they want to say. If the person is speaking at length on a relevant topic, do not interrupt. If you sense the interviewee is formulating an answer, do not jump to fill the silence.

Continued...

COLLECT

Active Listening

Whereas a passive listener unobtrusively encourages a person to keep talking, without signaling any reaction or assessment, an active listener enters the conversation by reflecting his or her understanding of what has just been communicated. Most often, this reflection is done in the form of a paraphrase: "You sound frustrated by the speed of the service."

Some people believe active listening helps them get more out of an interview. Those who prefer only passive listening believe it best to elicit and capture the interviewee's view of the world without the potential of introducing bias.

The following table lists some of the pros and cons of using active listening during interviews.*

Active Listening

Pros	Cons
• Makes speakers feel heard and acknowledged, and therefore more likely to share their thoughts	• Can interrupt a speaker's train of thought or their mounting enthusiasm
• Clarifies a speaker's meaning (if the interviewer has misunderstood, the speaker can clarify and continue)	• Can interject the interviewer's own interpretation of the issue through paraphrasing
• Summarizes key themes from a wide-ranging discourse and helps create an effective transition to a new topic	• Can mislead the interviewee into thinking topics that are paraphrased are more significant than those not paraphrased
• Provides another tool, along with probing, to surface a speaker's underlying needs	• If not done well, can move the focus from the interviewee to the interviewer
• Allows time for the notetaker to complete a recent passage	

COLLECT

*See Appendix B, *The Team® Memory Jogger™*, for more information on active listening.

What Every Interviewer Should Know About Probing

Collecting language data is challenging because the kinds of information you need to shape your decisions—specific, concrete facts and experiences—are generally not what people give you at first. Instead, human conversation is typically a mix of opinions, emotion, abstract statements, and conclusions. Consider this example:

> An organization trying to adopt a new management philosophy interviewed employees to discover what the problems were. One employee spoke his mind freely: "It's obvious management doesn't believe in this change." The interviewer asked for more detail. "They didn't even begin training until six months after they announced the change."

Now suppose you were working on a team that was formulating recommendations for how to make a smooth transition to new methods. This employee's first statement does little to help you understand what the current barriers are and what could be done. The second statement provides more useful information: that a perceived delay in implementation was interpreted as lack of commitment.

As an interviewer, you will hear many abstract or emotionally charged words such as "obvious," "great," "lousy," "hard," and "easy," as well as lots of conclusions, like "management doesn't believe in the change." The key is to move speakers beyond their initial words to a more specific, concrete level.

Build your skill at moving down the ladder of abstraction by learning to probe for details, when appropriate.

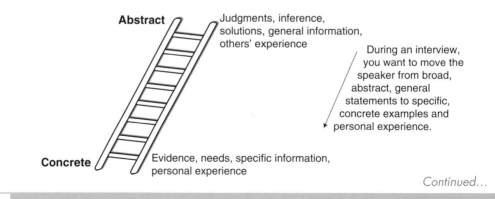

Abstract — Judgments, inference, solutions, general information, others' experience

During an interview, you want to move the speaker from broad, abstract, general statements to specific, concrete examples and personal experience.

Concrete — Evidence, needs, specific information, personal experience

Continued...

The following table provides guidelines for probing.

When you hear this . . .	Probe for . . .
A proposed solution: *"We should do . . ."*	Why the interviewee thinks the solution is a good idea: *"What would that do for you?"*
Loaded or emotionally charged words: *"This so-called solution . . ."*	What drives the emotion: *"Could you give me an example of how it affected your job?"*
Speaking in third person: *"They think that . . ."*	Personal experience: *"Could you describe an instance when this happened to you?"*
An inference or judgment: *"This gadget here is great!"*	Evidence that led to the judgment: *"What does it do for you that you couldn't do before?"*

COLLECT

What Every Notetaker Should Know

Most people, when they first begin to take notes, are not sure how much to write down or how to keep track of who is speaking. It helps to keep in mind that it does not matter if you understand what is said; this is the interviewer's responsibility. Your goal is to produce a verbatim transcript that sounds like the interviewee speaking—this is the customer's voice. To do that, you have to direct your energy into writing down the speaker's words without interpreting or translating them in any way. For example:

- Keep the original pronouns. Do not say "he said" or "she said." If the person says, "I use the widget press," that is what the notes should say, not "he uses the widget press" or "uses widget press." If you change or omit the pronouns, you can get confused later about who is doing what.

- Do not interpret what you hear; let the words flow directly from your ear to your hand. Any change you make in the words takes time—even just to convert "I use the widget press" to "uses widget press." Processing the words also puts you into the interview—your knowledge and attitudes will color the way you take notes. For example, if

someone says something you believe to be wrong, you may want to leave it out or correct it.

The following tips will help you become proficient at notetaking without becoming a court stenographer.

- Develop your own shorthand. You can expand the words later.

- Distinguish questions from answers; concentrate more on capturing the answers verbatim than the questions. Jot down only a key word or two from the question and use the time when the interviewer is asking a question to finish writing what the interviewee said.

- Do not interpret or react; simply write or type. Do not react to what you hear, even if you disagree or think it does not make sense.

- Do not summarize.

- Leave blanks if you are falling behind, but try to capture key words. You can fill the blanks in during the debriefing.

- Do not edit the interviewee's language. Every time you decide to leave out something the interviewee says you are making a judgment, which is not the role of the interview team.

COLLECT

What Every Team Member Should Know About Observing the Environment

"I just couldn't believe what I saw," said Karl. "I thought our customers would study all the information we sent them about how to use our product. But this guy had literally hundreds of product brochures in his office. There's no way he'd have time to read all the detailed specs we had in our instructions!"

The purpose of observing people in the workplace is to develop the kind of visceral appreciation for what their jobs are like that can never come from just listening to them talk.

You can also use the opportunity to identify constraints or needs that might never arise in conversation. One part of the observation experience is to simply note the physical factors that shape the person's work environment; the other part is to develop a sense of what it feels like to be that person.

When developing your interview questions, you may have also developed an observation guide of specific behaviors or uses you want to note. For instance:

- What do you want to know about the physical environment? Possibilities include lighting, temperature, humidity, cleanliness, types of equipment, amount of floor space, and amount of clutter and noise.

- What do you want to observe in the use of your product, service, or process? Possibilities include ease of use, points of frustration, unintended uses, work-arounds, and posting of instructions. Is the person sitting at a desk? standing in one place? moving from location to location?

- What do you want to notice about the emotional environment? Are people friendly? curious? hurried? relaxed? nervous? Are there rhythms to the day or a pace of work that might influence your project?

When you are in the other person's environment, it is all right to ask questions as long as you do not disrupt the work. (Remember to ask open-ended questions as in the interview!) For example:

- "What exactly are you doing when you do that?"

- "What makes this a typical work day? What's different about it?"

- "How often does ____ occur? What happens then?"

COLLECT

With these tips in mind, you are ready to begin polishing your interview skills.

A. Practice your interview skills

Set up mock interviews with your interview team members. If you need additional help, ask others on the FOCUS project team. This way you can test your skills in the safety of a familiar, supportive environment.

Try to involve two interview teams, rotating the roles of interviewee, interviewer, notetaker, and observer. The Interview Practice Exercise on page 155 describes one way to construct the practice sessions. For each practice session:

- Use the interview guide you intend to use in the real interview. Use it for at least two or three interviews before deciding whether any modifications are needed.

- Conduct a debriefing after each rotation, discussing what went well and what could be improved.

Once you have developed your interview skills with others on your team, interview other people in your organization—people who are familiar with your issue so they can give you as true an interview as possible.

If observation will be included as part of your customer visits, be sure to practice this also. The mock interviews will not give you the sense of observing the workplace or a process. Take time to practice this skill using the Observation Practice Exercise on page 158.

B. Review and revise your interview guide

After practicing with your interview guide, decide whether any adjustments are necessary. Take a few minutes as a group to reflect on people's experiences using the interview guide. While no two interviews will be alike because the flow will be influenced by the customer's responses, identify any areas where the questions seemed awkward or didn't evoke what was intended and make adjustments as necessary.

Interview Practice Exercise

Work in groups of four so you can each take a turn with the different roles.

1. Assign the roles of interviewee, interviewer, notetaker, and interview observer. During this practice, the observer will take notes on the interview process to provide feedback in the debriefing session.

2. Conduct an interview for approximately 15 minutes using the interview guide (if you want to go longer, stop halfway through and provide feedback so the person interviewing has an opportunity to improve). The interview observer should note specifically how well the interviewer listens, probes for more detail, and asks open-ended questions.

3. Conduct a debriefing session:

   - The interviewee gives feedback to the interviewer on what behaviors made it easy for the interviewee to contribute and what behaviors impeded participation.

   - The interview observer, who can provide a more objective view of the interview process, reflects on how well the interviewer elicited useful information.

   - The interviewer comments on what he or she would like to improve during the next practice or for the real interview.

   - The notetaker remarks on what it was like taking notes and what he or she would like to improve the next time.

4. The interviewer and notetaker continue the debriefing by finding and discussing at least one gap in the notes that they fill in from memory with the interviewee's words (in a real interview you fill in all of the gaps), and discuss insights and learnings, without consulting with the interviewee.

5. Switch roles and repeat steps two through four. Continue until everyone has had a chance to practice all four roles.

COLLECT

The following case study illustrates the new training product team's experience with their interview practice and debriefing.

Case Study: New Training Product (Part 2 of 4)

Aaron and Cathy, who were conducting the first interviews, were the first to practice their skills as interviewer and notetaker. Felipe and Elise helped out in the roles of interviewee and interview observer. Because none of the team members had been involved in this sort of interviewing before, they thought it would help to have an observer during their practice sessions.

At the end of the first interview, they went back through the notes together to try to fill in the gaps. In the places where Cathy had fallen behind in her notetaking, she and Aaron tried to reconstruct what had been said. Filling in the gaps was most difficult when Cathy had only left a space to indicate something was missing. When she had been able to capture the basic theme with a few key words, completing the notes was easier.

After the team had reviewed the notes, they discussed what they had observed about the interview. Aaron mentioned how hard it had been to ask open-ended questions.

Elise observed that he had done well with the main questions, but often asked leading questions to probe for more information. Felipe had noticed this as well. Several times he felt Aaron was pushing for a particular "right" answer. Aaron thought he was simply trying to get the information he needed, but everyone agreed it was more important to let the interviewee determine the path the interview would follow. They realized that other people in other interviews would provide some of the additional information.

Continued...

Felipe also noticed that Aaron did not always give him enough time to respond. "Sometimes I would be trying to frame a more complete answer, and you would jump in with the next question," he commented. Aaron, on the other hand, had been concerned that if he hesitated the interview would lose momentum.

When they went over the notes, they discovered the meaning was ambiguous in places. Cathy had kept up fairly well with the notetaking, but she had translated Felipe's "I's" into "he's." When Felipe referred to someone else, the meaning was unclear. Did "he does most of the training" mean Felipe did the training or another person did the training? Fortunately, Felipe was on hand to sort out the meaning, but they knew that in real interviews that would not be the case. Although they could go back to the interviewee to clarify meaning or ask follow-up questions, they did not want to do that too often because they did not want to look incompetent.

All in all, the team members felt they had learned a lot from their first practice. They had a much better idea of the level of skill they needed and the amount of practice they would need to feel comfortable.

C. Practice your visit observation skills

If you will be observing your customer's workplace, practicing observation skills is as important as practicing the other interview skills. As you observe your interviewee's environment, you will note how they use a product, how a process works for them, and so forth. Now is the time to review and test your observation guide using the following pointers:

- If there are people in your organization who perform work similar to that of your interviewees, get permission to spend some time watching how they do their jobs.

- If you will be observing consumers, try to simulate the situation as closely as you can. Go to a store that sells your product or similar products, or ask relatives or friends if you can observe them using the product or service.

COLLECT

- When you are observing, take notes on what you see, hear, and experience. Draw sketches of the workplace, if relevant. Some of the things you might want to notice are:
  - the physical environment
  - the emotional environment
  - how people work
  - how people use your product or service

The following exercise provides detailed directions for practicing your observation skills.

Observation Practice Exercise

Work as a whole team, if possible.

1. Choose a clip from a videotape that has a lot of environmental detail, such as a busy street, factory, or office. If possible, select a passage with an environment similar to those you are likely to encounter on your visits.

2. Show the clip for five minutes or so.

3. Stop the tape and have the team members individually jot down from memory everything they observed.

4. Discuss the differences in what individuals recall and why these differences might occur. Note any patterns of difference.

For instance, people who are more familiar with the environment might notice different aspects than people who are less familiar; people with engineering backgrounds might notice different aspects than people with marketing backgrounds.

5. As a group, identify aspects of the environment that particularly merit observation.

6. Rewind the tape and show the clip again. This time have everyone jot down observations as they watch the tape.

7. Discuss how much more people saw when they focused on specific aspects of the environment.

D. Review and revise your observation guide

After practicing observation, review your guide to decide whether any adjustments are necessary. Take a few minutes to reflect on your practice observations. Did you forget to pay attention to any elements of the environment listed on the observation guide? If so, what additional prompts should you include in your guide as reminders? Were any elements of the environment omitted from the observation guide? Make revisions as necessary.

Step 10 Check

Check to make sure the interview teams have the skills they need for customer visits. They should have

- ❏ Practiced conducting interviews
- ❏ Practiced taking verbatim notes
- ❏ Practiced interview debriefing
- ❏ Practiced observing the environment

The Big Picture

9. Prepare for Visits
10. Polish Your Skills
11. **Finalize Preparations**
12. Conduct Interviews
13. Follow Up

 ## Prework

- Schedule customer interviews
- Make final interview arrangements
- Assign interview teams
- Make travel plans, if necessary

 ## Time and Logistics

This work can be done by an individual or the interview teams. It should take approximately 1 hour to contact interviewees and convey the general topics of discussion.

 ## Supplies and Equipment

- Copy of customer interview schedule
- Interviewee names, addresses, and phone or fax numbers

 ## Outcomes

- Review of customer background information
- Receipt of agenda and topics by interviewees
- Complete set of interview supplies and equipment

COLLECT

Step 11:

Finalize Preparations

Description

Think of this as your last chance to make sure that both you and your interviewees are prepared for your visit.

Benefits

By performing a final check before departure, the interview teams will have all the supplies they need, will know the interview schedule, and will feel relaxed and confident going into the interviews.

Getting Your Bearings

You have now had the opportunity to practice the interview roles and test the interview and observation guides. All final preparations should ensure that you encounter no unwanted surprises. To this end, take time to quickly review the company's history with the customer, make final contact with your interviewees, and organize any supplies and equipment needed for the visit.

COLLECT

How to Finalize Preparations

A. Review customer background information

In Frame the Project you reviewed data relevant to the project. Before conducting the interview, the team should review data relevant to the particular customer you will be visiting. Being as knowledgeable as possible about the customer will give you a better understanding of what factors might influence the customer's attitude or responses. This preparation will also prove valuable in asking appropriate follow-up or probing questions. For external customers, check trade journals or other publications for articles that describe their business, their competition, and their industry in general. Check your own organization's records to review their sales history and/or service history. For internal projects, look for employee surveys or suggestion systems, project reports, meeting notes, or other documents containing relevant information to the issue being studied.

B. Send topics to interviewees

To help prepare the interviewees, use your objectives for learning and interview guide to create a list of general topics that will be covered in the interview. Make sure you phrase the items as general topics and not specific questions. Sending this list ahead of time will allow people to marshal their thoughts. You should be clear that they do not need to make detailed notes in preparation.

Send the interviewees a copy of the day's schedule and the list of general topics. If you are working through a contact person, ask that he or she share copies with all interviewees.

The following case study shows the letter sent by the new training product team to prepare their interviewees.

Case Study: New Training Product (Part 3 of 4)

As part of their final preparations, the team composed a letter to send to each of their targeted interviewees. Then each interview pair tailored the letter to their own situation. Aaron and Cathy sent the following letter to Dr. Marjorie Tear at Quality Health Care.

Dear Dr. Tear:

Leading Edge Training Corporation is planning a new product in the area of organizational change. Because Quality Health Care has been a long-time customer of ours, and because you are currently involved with organizational change and the training that goes with it, we are pleased you have agreed to talk with us from 11:00 to 12:00 P.M., on Wednesday, October 4.

Although the discussion will be open-ended, we expect to cover the following topics:

- The biggest problems you are facing with regard to organizational change
- Materials you are currently using to help solve these problems
- The major strengths you have found with these materials
- The major weaknesses you have found with these materials
- Characteristics you would like to see in future products

We appreciate the time you are taking to help us with this project. If you have any questions prior to the interview, please contact Aaron Weiss at (608) 555-1234.

Sincerely,

Aaron Weiss   Cathy Dmitri

COLLECT

C. Pack supplies and equipment

Create a checklist of the supplies and equipment you will need and get them ready. Make sure all interview teams have a complete set of everything they will need.

Supply Checklist

Supplies needed

- ❏ Interview schedule
- ❏ Interview guide
- ❏ Observation guide
- ❏ Notetaking pads
- ❏ Pens or pencils
- ❏ Quick reference guides for interviewing, notetaking, and debriefing (see Step 12)

Optional Items

- ❏ Thank-you tokens
- ❏ Tape recorder, tapes, batteries
- ❏ Laptop computer, floppy disks for backup, batteries, printer
- ❏ Camera, film, batteries

Step 11 Check

Check to make sure your interview preparations are complete. You should have

- ❏ Reviewed customer background information
- ❏ Sent discussion topics to interviewees
- ❏ Packed necessary supplies and equipment

COLLECT

The Big Picture

9. Prepare for Visits
10. Polish Your Skills
11. Finalize Preparations
12. Conduct Interviews
13. Follow Up

Prework

- Create interview guide
- Create observation guide
- Make final interview arrangements
- Make travel plans, if necessary
- Practice interview skills and roles
- Test interview guide
- Send copies of topics to interviewees

Time and Logistics

Completing and debriefing the interviews will take 2 – 3 hours per interview plus travel time. If you are observing the environment, the customer visits may take longer.

Supplies and Equipment

- Copy of interview schedule
- Copy of interview guide
- Copy of observation guide, if necessary
- Notetaking equipment
- Copy of quick reference guides (included in this step)
- Thank-you tokens
- Camera/film/batteries, if necessary

Outcomes

- Set of verbatim notes for all interviews
- Observation notes for all interviews

Step 12:

Conduct Interviews

Description

In this step you will be conducting your interviews. This will include observing the environment, setting the tone of the interviews, covering the questions in the interview guide, closing the interviews, and debriefing. There are three quick reference guides included here for interviewing, notetaking, and debriefing.

Benefits

Conducting in-person, face-to-face interviews will give you invaluable information. Having the opportunity to experience the customer's environment firsthand cannot be equaled.

Getting Your Bearings

This is the moment for which you have been preparing. You have written the questions and practiced your interview skills. Now it is time to conduct the customer interviews.

For the novices in the group, it is time to take a deep breath and confidently walk through the customer's door. For those who have conducted customer interviews before, encourage your less experienced colleagues. Wherever you fall in the range of experience, remember to open your eyes and ears to the customer's world, and be conscious of collecting a 360° perspective. Doing a thorough job now assures that you will collect the customer voices that you need in the next phases of the FOCUS process.

COLLECT

How to Conduct Interviews

A. Get a good start

Part of getting the interview off to a good start is arriving with time to spare. Allow extra time for unknowns, such as distance from the parking lot to the door, security measures, and procedures for getting to the person you will be meeting. After your greetings and introductions, check to see if any adjustments are needed in the schedule.

Going As an Explorer

When using the FOCUS process, you are embarking on a journey to explore the needs, views, and attitudes of people central to a decision you are facing. Approach each interview as an explorer—someone who wishes to understand the world from another person's viewpoint. Explorers spend time in an environment, seeing what it is like to live there day by day.

You also want to remain open to surprise. Surprise is one of the best ways to come up with ideas that shake up traditional solutions. Explorers may have theories about what they are going to see and experience, but they have to remain open to the unexpected. Absorb everything you see and hear. Suspend your judgment as much as possible and set aside your own views and filters. This also allows you to remain open to seeing and hearing things you may not have paid attention to before.

Look for inconsistencies and incongruities between the way you think about the world and what is really happening. And lastly, use your interview guide as a jumping-off point or checklist of reminders, not a rigid survey that you march through point by point. Let the interviewee lead you, rather than vice versa.

B. Observe the environment

Taking a tour of a facility or observing people at work is not always necessary, but in all situations observation is advantageous. If you will be given a tour, remember to review your observation guide prior to arrival. During the interview you will be trying to develop a 360° view of this customer's world through words. Your observations will help you develop a complete picture, as well as provide you with vivid images that should be easy to recall when you analyze the data you collect. In situations where you are familiar with the environment (such as internal projects) or where the environment you are exploring is abstract or intellectual (as when collecting opinions or policies), conducting formal observations may not be important. However, you should still pay attention to the environment because you may discover something relevant.

Understanding Context

Each of us understands intuitively that words can be properly interpreted only if we understand the context in which they are used. Even young children can understand the difference between a "Come here" spoken in loving tones when being invited onto a parent's lap and a "Come here!" yelled impatiently across the room as the same parent points to evidence of a mishap.

Children learn almost as early that the same behavior may be experienced differently in different locales; behavior that is acceptable at a kitchen table may not be at a dining room table, or at a restaurant or at someone else's home. The context, the physical or emotional surroundings, may vary the meaning of what is experienced.

One of the key strengths of the FOCUS process is interviewing customers in their own environment. This allows you to establish contextual awareness that later enables you to understand the meaning behind statements you hear during interviews. Such awareness can be anchored by capturing an image, story, or metaphor that conveys the feeling of place or event. These contextual anchors often illuminate other words or phrases, helping teams understand more of the subtlety of what they have heard.

COLLECT

What to Do in Foreign Countries

Different cultures have different sensitivities to various aspects of an interview, including the questions you ask, how you phrase the questions, the behaviors you exhibit, and whether you use equipment like a tape recorder to capture notes. For instance, in some cultures, looking people straight in the eye or leaning forward is considered poor manners. In others, recording a conversation on a tape recorder is unthinkable. When traveling abroad, be sure to check with your host to learn about respectful behavior in that culture.

If possible, practice your interview skills with natives of the countries to which you will be going. This preparation will help you calibrate verbal language and body language so you do not inadvertently confuse or offend people. Even though your company's in-country personnel will most likely be involved in setting up or participating, use professional translators to simultaneously translate the interviews. You may be tempted to use bilingual company employees to save money, but they are not trained as translators and often have their own biases, which might be reflected in the translation.

The new photographic film team used their own service representatives as interpreters in Korea. In one interview, a Korean shopkeeper talked at length in response to a question about problems with the current film. When he finished, the translator said, "They want quicker drying time." The richness of the customer's answer was lost. For the notetaker to capture the customer's answer verbatim, the translator must provide the customer's voice.

C. Set the tone

Before asking your interview questions, take a few moments to set the stage.

- Introduce the members of the interview team, emphasizing the diversity of professional backgrounds

- Provide a brief background about the project, including its purpose and boundaries

- Emphasize that only a limited number of people are being interviewed

- Clarify why notes are being taken (if you are using a method like tape recording or typing into a computer, check to make sure it is okay with the interviewee)

- Comment on the degree of confidentiality of the notes (most teams agree on keeping them confidential within the project team)

D. Cover the interview guide questions and take verbatim notes

As you begin working through the questions in the interview guide, keep in mind that you are trying to stand in your interviewee's shoes and develop a 360° view of the issue.

- Use the interview guide as a springboard; do not feel compelled to follow it strictly

- If you think the interviewee's comments about a topic not on your guide are relevant, explore them

- Be led by what is important to the interviewee

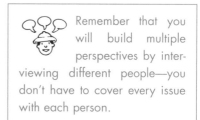 Remember that you will build multiple perspectives by interviewing different people—you don't have to cover every issue with each person.

Remember that during the interview, the notetaker is a backup for the interviewer. For the most part, notetakers should be silent, concentrating on taking notes. They can occasionally interrupt if they miss points where they think it might be important to clarify language, but they should not confuse the interviewee by asking interview questions. Some teams agree ahead of time that the notetaker can ask questions of clarification at the end of the interview.

COLLECT

Using Images to Build Understanding

Images can help a team build a deep and shared understanding of their customers' world by going one step further into that world, beyond the words people use. These images may be things you see during your observations, or descriptions you hear during the interviews. In either case, images help you ground yourself in the personal experiences of your customers in order to better understand their unstated needs.

For example, when manufacturers of window air conditioners talk with their customers, they learn that people want quiet air conditioners. But what does that really mean? If a company actually observed an air conditioner in use, or asked customers to describe their experiences with air conditioners, they might get at some unstated requirements.

For instance, one user told a company representative that he had a window air conditioner in his bedroom at his summer home. But in the evening when the air conditioner came on, he had to get up from his bed to turn up the volume on his television set in order to hear the audio. From this image of the man watching TV in his bedroom with the volume turned up, the company learned not only that their customer wanted a "quiet air conditioner," but also that the unit had to be quiet enough to hear a television over it. In addition, the air conditioner manufacturer might be able to infer that, for this customer, the value (and therefore the price) of a quieter air conditioner would have to be comparable to the cost of the customer's alternative solution, a television remote control.

Be on the alert for images you can gather during your visits with customers. Through these images you can understand limitations that customers simply accept. Here is where you often gain your greatest insights. It is much like a children's puzzle where a picture of a landscape has images of animals or household items hidden in it. You will find valuable treasures hidden away in the images you collect during interviews that will help you move from a solution that will meet your customers' basic, and more obvious, needs to a solution that will provide delight.

A more sophisticated use of images to discover latent customer requirements can be found in Concept Engineering™, a methodology developed by the Center for Quality of Management for use when a more rigorous development process is necessary.*

*See Appendix B for more information on Concept Engineering™.

Quick Reference for Interviewing

❏ Sit around a corner of the table, not across the table.

❏ Use good posture. Do not slump or slouch. If anything, sit slightly forward.

❏ Make eye contact (if appropriate to the culture).

❏ Encourage the speaker with gestures like head-nodding and phrases like "uh-huh."

❏ Even when you think the interviewee is done speaking, wait a moment longer before asking your next question.

❏ Accept what you hear. If the interviewee says something with which you do not agree, do not physically react (frown, furrow eyebrows, shift in chair, divert eyes).

❏ Refrain from offering information or explanations when the interviewee describes problems or failures with your product or service. Table the issue until the end of the interview, and then arrange for someone to follow up on the problem.

❏ Probe when you want to hear more about something the interviewee is saying. Also use follow-up questions when the person is speaking in abstract terms or using highly emotional or judgmental language.

❏ Ask open-ended questions to elicit more concrete statements. For example:

- Could you give me an example of what you mean by...?
- What specifically...?
- Anything else...?
- Could you describe a personal experience you had with this?
- How would that help you?
- What would that solution do for you?

COLLECT

Quick Reference for Notetaking

❏ Develop your own shorthand.

❏ Distinguish questions from answers.

❏ It is more important to capture the answers verbatim than the questions. If you get behind, use the time when an interviewer is asking a question to finish writing or typing what the interviewee has just said. Jot down only a key word or two from the question.

❏ Do not interpret; simply write or type. Do not react to what you hear, even if you disagree or think it does not make sense.

❏ Do not summarize.

❏ Use the speaker's words. Do not translate "I did X" to "she did X."

❏ Leave blanks if you miss something. You can fill them in during the debriefing.

❏ Ask the speaker to repeat something only if it is absolutely necessary because this can interrupt the flow of the interview.

❏ Ask any questions of clarification at the end of the interview.

COLLECT

The following case study shows an excerpt from an interview transcript.

Case Study: Home Heating Products (Part 1 of 2)

A company was interested in learning more about how people used their home heating products, so they interviewed builders, installers, merchants, end users, and others in the customer chain. The following interview excerpts show how the interviewer used follow-up questions to probe for more information in an interview with a merchant who sold the company's products.

Interviewer:	Could you give me some background on your business, how it evolved as a business?
Merchant:	Yes, well, our company was started in 1975. Its purpose originally was to supply domestic heating controls to the trade, but over the years the emphasis of the business has been more toward the replacement market rather than the new installation.... So we're more or less there for, these days, for replacement of parts in existing central heating systems.
Interviewer:	Typically who is the guy who walks through the door to your counter? What kind of guy is he?
Merchant:	Most of the people who approach us are installers. A lot of the time from small independent businesses. There are lots of them around and they buy on a "one-of" basis; they don't carry their own stock except perhaps on some certain items....
Interviewer:	What sort of mix do you have between selling to installers and to second line merchants, roughly?

In this first segment the interviewer uses follow-up questions to probe for more details about the customer's business. In the next excerpt the interviewer hears something he has not been expecting and follows up with an additional question, which leads to a continued discussion of a topic that had not been in the original discussion guide.

Continued...

Interviewer: Just casting your mind sideways a little bit in a slightly different direction, could you describe what a typical day for somebody working out here in your business is— one of the guys working out here actually on the counter—what sort of things would he see in a day?

Merchant: He'd be faced with quite a lot of telephone calls. We spend a lot of time trying to help people. We get requests from customers with incomplete information, and we spend a lot of time trying to help the customers. Sometimes we feel perhaps that we're the last chance to help sort the problem out.... Myself, I'm involved more in such things as the policy and procedures of the company; I'm also involved with credit control procedures.

Interviewer: Tell me more about your procedures.

E. Close the interview

Always structure an interview to end on time—this indicates to interviewees that you value their time. About ten minutes before the scheduled end, alert the interviewee that time is almost up. Often, they will give you a few more minutes if they have more to say. The choice to extend an interview should always be theirs, not yours.

About five minutes before the scheduled end

- Ask the interviewee if he or she has anything to add

- Ask if the notetaker has any questions to ask

- Thank the interviewee for his or her time

- Ask for permission to make a follow-up call if you have questions

F. Give tokens of appreciation (optional)

If you would like to recognize the contributions of the people you have interviewed, it may be appropriate to give them a thank-you gift as a token of appreciation. Depending on your type of business and the culture of the company you are visiting, some of your products may be appropriate gifts. The nature of the gift should be tailored toward the people you have interviewed. If you are conducting interviews in other countries, check to see that your gift is considered appropriate there. Business practices in many countries are more formal than those in the United States. If your company's product does not serve as an appropriate gift, consider giving:

- Something with your company logo

- Desk accessories

- Lunch or dinner gift certificates for a local restaurant

G. Conduct interview debriefing

Immediately after the interview, while the experience is still fresh, the interview team should spend sixty to ninety minutes discussing what happened. This is a time to reflect on new insights, write down observations about the environment, fill in any gaps in the notes, and check on ways to improve the next interview. Here are some tasks that will help you make the most of your debriefing session.

- Read the notes together, filling in gaps with the interviewee's actual words or reconstructing messages that may have become garbled.

- Discuss insights and general observations. What themes did you identify? What surprised you?

- Evaluate the interview guide. Discuss what did and did not work. What areas should be emphasized or de-emphasized in future interviews?

 The voices in the interview transcripts are key to your future work. If you have taken notes by hand, make a photocopy of the notes as soon as possible. If you have used a computer to take notes, quickly make a backup copy of the file.

COLLECT

- Assess the interviewer's technique and skills. Discuss posture, probing opportunities that were taken or skipped, unintended hints about the interviewer's bias, and so on. Pick one skill area to improve in the next interview.

- Plan follow-up actions. Did any questions or issues arise during the interview that require follow-up? If you tape-recorded the interview, decide who will be responsible for getting it transcribed. Decide who will write a letter of thanks to the interviewee. Assess whether other issues need to be addressed.

- Make copies of the interview notes. Your interview notes will form the basis for the rest of the FOCUS process, so protecting them is critical. It is nearly impossible to reconstruct the entire interview later in enough detail to analyze the data in the next stage of this process.

  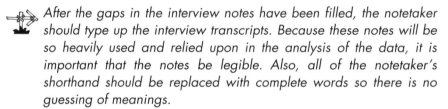 *After the gaps in the interview notes have been filled, the notetaker should type up the interview transcripts. Because these notes will be so heavily used and relied upon in the analysis of the data, it is important that the notes be legible. Also, all of the notetaker's shorthand should be replaced with complete words so there is no guessing of meanings.*

The following case study illustrates how the heating products team conducted their debriefing.

Case Study: Home Heating Products (Part 2 of 2)

When the interview with the merchant was over, the interviewer and notetaker had a debriefing meeting.

At one point in the interview the merchant had been talking rapidly about his problems with customers who do not have accurate parts numbers. The notetaker had fallen behind and left a blank: "Sometimes they don't have any information on parts numbers—they just describe it. There are a lot of occasions where we've had parts numbers quoted_____." The interviewer remembered that the merchant had described people who provide what they think is a parts number but is actually a date code. The notetaker added this information in brackets so the team would remember it was not a direct quotation.

This was the interview team's fourth interview together. The interviewer had improved at asking open-ended questions through the earlier interviews, but in going over the notes the team still noticed several places where he had asked closed questions which elicited only yes or no answers. On the other hand, he had done a good job of not biasing the discussion of competitors' products.

One of the themes that had surprised the interviewer was the emphasis on processes within a small business. The notetaker found it interesting that most of the merchant's business was with small independent installers who bought items one at a time, rather than carrying their own stock.

As with their previous interviews, the team decided that the person who had taken the notes would type them up and the person who had conducted the interview would send a letter of thanks.

COLLECT

Quick Reference for Debriefing

- ❏ Review the notes together
- ❏ Discuss insights and general observations
- ❏ Evaluate the interview guide
- ❏ Assess the interviewer's technique and skills
- ❏ Plan follow-up actions
- ❏ Make copies of the interview notes

Step 12 Check

Check to make sure your customer interview process is complete. You should have

- ❏ Complete notes for each interview
- ❏ Observation notes for each interview

COLLECT

The Big Picture

9. Prepare for Visits
10. Polish Your Skills
11. Finalize Preparations
12. Conduct Interviews
13. **Follow Up**

Prework

- Complete customer interviews

Time and Logistics

The first part of this step, sending out thank-you notes, will probably take approximately 20 minutes per interview. This work can be done by the individual interview teams. The second part of the step, which involves a quick check on the interview process, should be done by the entire team and will take approximately 30 minutes.

Supplies and Equipment

- Thank-you cards or stationery
- Interviewee names and addresses

Outcomes

- Acknowledgment of interviewees' contributions
- Confirmation that data meets project goals
- Reflection on the interview experience

Step 13:

Follow Up

Description

In this step the interview teams express appreciation for their interviewees' efforts and reflect on their interview experiences with the project team as a whole.

Benefits

The simple act of sending a formal thank-you card or letter is invaluable in maintaining relationships with your customers. Also invaluable is the opportunity for interview team members to reconvene and reflect on their recent experiences as a group. Talking about the customer visits and capturing the lessons learned will be helpful for the next project.

Getting Your Bearings

You have invested a lot in completing your interviews. Before you continue, it is good to pause briefly to acknowledge your customers' contributions of time and effort and to reflect as a team on the experience.

COLLECT

How to Follow Up

A. Send a thank-you letter

In most cases, sending a thank-you letter or card is the most appropriate way to let people know you appreciate the time they took on your behalf. However, if you know the interviewees well and interact with them regularly, you might feel awkward being that formal. Use your judgment.

If you have used contacts to arrange your interviews, do not forget to acknowledge and thank them for their contributions. Remember to also send a copy of the customer thank-you letter to the people within your organization who handle the customer account or to anyone who provided you with a contact name.

The following is an example of an effective letter of appreciation.

Case Study: New Training Product (Part 4 of 4)

Dear Dr. Tear:

On behalf of Leading Edge Training Corporation and our project team, we would like to thank you for giving us so much of your time on Wednesday, October 4. The information we learned will be invaluable to us in developing a useful training product in the area of organizational change.

We especially appreciated your perspective on both the changes occurring in health care today and those you forsee coming down the road.

We appreciate your interest and continued participation in our project. As discussed, we look forward to meeting with you in a few months to review our new training product.

Sincerely,

Aaron Weiss   Cathy Dmitri

B. Reflect on the experience

Before you begin a formal analysis of the interview and observation notes, it often helps for the entire project team to reflect on the experience of meeting and interviewing customers. Teams typically begin to process the information by talking about what happened and comparing people's general impressions about what they saw and heard.

One of the benefits of reflecting on the interview experience is to capture the lessons learned. Regardless of the size of the team, everyone involved should be part of the discussion. Suggested topics for discussion include the following:

- What worked well?

- What did not work well?

- What changes to the process would we make?

- Were there things we did not do that we wished we had done?

- What was the biggest insight we had when talking to customers?

Identify any necessary data that you have not obtained. Review your objectives for learning to determine whether the information in your interview transcripts covers all of the issues you planned to explore. You may have discovered along the way that some of your objectives turned out to be less important than you anticipated; it is not necessary to have extensive coverage on these. If you discover major gaps, decide as a group what to do about them. You may have to follow up with phone calls to interviewees or even plan another interview or two.

COLLECT

Step 13 Check

Check to make sure you have reached closure on the interview process. You should have

❑ Letters of thanks to all interviewees

❑ The data needed to meet your project goals

❑ Reflection by the team on the interview experience

Section Summary

You have now worked through the third phase of the FOCUS process, Collect Data. You should have completed the following:

❑ Determined interview team roles

❑ Decided how to capture interview notes

❑ Discussed interview ground rules

❑ Practiced your interview skills

❑ Tested and revised the interview guide if necessary

❑ Sent interviewees general topics of discussion

❑ Packed all of your necessary interview supplies and equipment

❑ Conducted your customer interviews

❑ Sent the interviewees a thank-you note

❑ Reflected with the team on the overall interview experience

❑ Obtained the data necessary to meet your project goals

Looking ahead...

Now it is time to prepare for the analysis of the interview data. In Understand the Voices you will begin to decipher the customers' words and determine what they mean in the context of your project's purpose and goals.

COLLECT

Out of FOCUS

A team was working on an internal improvement project. They had created an employee profile matrix that would give them a good representation of perspectives across the company. From their interviews they learned how people perceived the problems with the process they were trying to improve. Impatient to get a solution in place, they decided to skip the Understand the Voices phase of the FOCUS process. Because they were working on an internal project and they all had involvement in the process to be improved, they thought they already understood the situation well enough.

As a cross-functional team, each member had heard the interviews according to his or her own perspective. Jumping straight from conducting interviews to proposing solutions, the team members missed creating a common understanding of the problem. They recommended actions to solve only the parts of the problem with which they were concerned, not the overall problem. Team meetings became divisive, with the representatives of different company functions arguing for their own perspectives.

In the end, the most vocal and assertive team members "won." A solution was implemented that did indeed improve parts of the process, but at the expense of some other, critical components. Within a year people were clamoring to improve the process, but no one wanted to serve on an improvement team.

UNDERSTAND the Voices

SECTION CONTENTS

UNDERSTAND

F

FRAME THE PROJECT

1. Determine Purpose
2. Review Existing Data
3. Create Customer Profile Matrix
4. Create Interview Guide

O

ORGANIZE RESOURCES

5. Estimate Project Requirements
6. Meet With Sponsors
7. Negotiate Scope, Schedule, and Resources
8. Schedule Interviews

C

COLLECT DATA

9. Prepare for Visits
10. Polish Your Skills
11. Finalize Preparations
12. Conduct Interviews
13. Follow Up

U

UNDERSTAND THE VOICES

14. Check Your Direction
15. Focus Your Data Analysis
16. Structure the Data
17. Determine Key Areas to Address

S

SELECT ACTION

18. Generate Ideas
19. Evaluate Ideas and Create a Complete Solution
20. Develop an Action Plan

Overview

The Understand the Voices phase is the very heart of the FOCUS process. You have completed the rich and rewarding experience of conducting interviews with your customers, but what you gained from these explorations is just the first level of insight. Much more will be learned as you analyze the verbatim interview transcripts.

In other stages of the FOCUS process, the basic steps are the same regardless of the type of project. In Understand the Voices, the analysis differs, depending on what you want to accomplish and how much time you can commit to the analysis. The following is a brief description of the three paths covered in this section.

- The Targeted Path (p. 201) allows you to analyze interview statements related to one key question that is the target of your investigation. This path is ideal if you are working on a problem that is relatively straightforward or are looking for an overview of main themes.

- The Requirements Path (p. 241) helps you translate customer needs or concerns (extracted from the interview notes) into performance requirements. This path is useful if you are trying to design or improve a product, service, process, policy, and so forth.

- The Systems Path (p. 295) is a more complex version of the Targeted Path. Here, you analyze interview statements for different dimensions of the problem, looking for key factors that determine system performance. Then you identify the interactions between these factors to find the leverage points, places where your intervention will have the greatest impact. This path is designed for use on relatively complex issues, such as situations that have proven resistant to change or where many potential factors should be studied. It is also useful for identifying specifically where opportunities lie in a complex environment.

UNDERSTAND

What You Gain by Understanding the Voices

- Identify the most significant themes from the interviews

- Zero in on the areas where further action will have the biggest payback

- Identify specific performance requirements, where appropriate

Logistics

Regardless of the path you select, the steps in Understand the Voices involve two distinct types of work: preparation, which includes highlighting and extracting statements from the interview notes, and analysis, which includes working with the statements to identify patterns and generate insight. Much of this work will be done by the whole group, although some work can be done by individuals.

In Step 14, Check Your Direction, the team will select which path to follow. This step is common to all three paths. The work in Steps 15, 16, and 17 will vary depending on which path you take. Additional logistics information can be found at the start of each path.

The following table shows how long this work typically takes for each of the three different analytical paths.

Step	Targeted Path	Requirements Path	Systems Path
Step 14: Check Your Direction	1 hour or less	1 hour or less	1 hour or less
Step 15: Focus Your Data Analysis	30 minutes	1 hour per interview	1 – 3 hours
Step 16: Structure the Data*	1 hour per interview and 4 hours to create affinity diagram	Approximately 8 hours	1 – 1½ hours per interview and 4 hours per dimension
Step 17: Determine Key Areas to Address	1 hour or less	5 hours plus elapsed time for return of questionnaires	Approximately 8 hours

* If you have a team, divide the work of structuring the data among team members so it will go more quickly. Ideally, all team members would review transcripts of the interviews they were a part of. At a minimum, transcripts should be reviewed by the person who conducted the interview.

UNDERSTAND

The Big Picture

14. Check Your Direction
15. Focus Your Data Analysis
16. Structure the Data
17. Determine Key Areas to Address

Prework

- Determine project purpose
- Identify objectives for learning
- Negotiate scope, schedule, and resources
- Complete customer interviews

Time and Logistics

Reviewing your learnings and deciding on a path for analysis should take less than 1 hour to complete.

Supplies and Equipment

- Copy of project purpose statement
- Copy of objectives for learning
- Copy of scope, schedule, and resources grid

Outcomes

- Selection of an analytical pathway
- Understanding of scope, schedule, and resources

UNDERSTAND

Step 14:

Check Your Direction

Description

Due to the nature of an exploration, you may have been surprised by what you learned in your customer interviews. Now is the time to compare your original purpose and objectives for learning with what you actually discovered. Based on what you now know, you will choose the best path for analysis.

Benefits

This step gives you the opportunity to correct your course and to purposefully select the best path forward.

Getting Your Bearings

This step is about getting your bearings. The philosopher C. I. Lewis once said, "...knowing begins and ends in experience, but it does not end in the experience in which it began."[5] This statement is a perfect summary of what often happens with Voice of the Customer projects. You begin the project believing one thing based on your experience and come out of the customer interviews with new insights. Pausing now will help you chart the best course forward.

UNDERSTAND

---

[5]C.I. Lewis, "Experience and Meaning," *The Philosophical Review*, 1934, vol. xliii, p. 134.

How to Check Your Direction

A. Review and refine your purpose

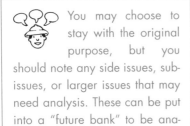 You may choose to stay with the original purpose, but you should note any side issues, sub-issues, or larger issues that may need analysis. These can be put into a "future bank" to be analyzed later.

As a team, reflect on and discuss what you saw and heard during the interviews. Review the purpose statement and objectives for learning you developed in Frame the Project.

- Are your original intentions still appropriate given the current knowledge you gained from the interviews?

- Is your purpose too narrow or too broad?

- Should it be shifted slightly in one direction or another?

The following case study shows how the employee benefits team refined their purpose statement.

 Case Study: Employee Benefits (Part 2 of 6)

A team working to understand what kinds of benefits their company's employees needed had originally selected this purpose statement:

> "To better understand employees' insurance needs in order to provide an optimal benefit package at reasonable company expense."

Now the team reviewed what they had learned in their interviews. Although various types of insurance had been discussed, employees were primarily concerned with health insurance issues. The team, therefore, refined their purpose statement to more accurately reflect employee needs:

> "To better understand employees' health insurance needs in order to meet maximum employee needs at reasonable company expense."

UNDERSTAND

B. Choose appropriate path for analysis

As outlined in the Overview to this section, three different analytical paths are commonly used in Voice of the Customer projects: Targeted, Requirements, and Systems.

Review the following table to gain insight on which path is most appropriate for your particular situation.

Choosing a path for analysis

	Choose this path if...	Purpose	Examples	Comments
Targeted Path	You are exploring a known or suspected weakness or problem OR you only need an overview of high level themes	Gain insight into one question	• Identifying employee concerns about changing health plans • Finding the obstructions in the order fulfillment process • Identifying the biggest barriers to producing reliable budgets • Determining the obstacles to implementing reorganization	This path is the best choice for many FOCUS users. It lets you quickly identify the main themes from the interviews. If you decide later you need to learn more, you can use the same set of interview notes for additional analysis.
Requirements Path	You need to define performance requirements for a product, service, process, or policy	Understand customer requirements for a product, service, process, or policy	• Understanding consumer needs for new electronic entertainment products • Defining needs of retail stores to help field service reps design incentive programs • Identifying shared concerns among constituent groups to draft new statewide policy	This pathway is ideal for people who need to design or redesign a product, service, process, or policy that impacts the operating environment. If you are looking at issues that affect very different groups of people, you can compare the requirements of each group to find shared concerns.
Systems Path	The issue you are exploring is part of a system with multiple dimensions OR your issue is impacted by diverse factors	Discover the interrelationships between multiple dynamics	• Analyzing program management processes in order to do the work better in less time and at lower costs • Discovering key influences changing the home heating market	This path is best for people who are studying a complex problem that involves several dimensions of an overall system. These systems problems often become evident when a change made to one process has unexpected, and frequently unwanted, consequences for another process. This occurs because both processes are part of an overarching and complex system. In order to implement sustainable change it is necessary to understand the interactions of many different factors.

UNDERSTAND

If after the interviews you find the issue is significantly different, a check with your sponsor might be prudent to calibrate the team's next steps. You may find it necessary to review and renegotiate your scope, schedule, or resource allocations before getting too deeply involved in analyzing the interview data.

Here is how the employee benefits team chose the path for analysis that best met their needs.

Case Study: Employee Benefits (Part 3 of 6)

The team was essentially looking at their employees' health insurance needs. Some team members, therefore, thought they should follow the Requirements Path. On the other hand, one team member saw the problem within the larger context of what the company could afford, what was happening with health care in general, and how the insurance industry was adapting to changes. She thought they might learn more if they followed the Systems Path.

Because the team lacked initial consensus, they went back to their revised purpose statement: "To better understand employees' health insurance needs in order to meet maximum employee needs at reasonable company expense." After discussing the issue, they agreed that they were exploring a weakness and that the Targeted Path would best provide them with the insight they needed to make recommendations.

If their analysis showed that they needed to frame specific requirements or that many of the issues involved larger systems perspectives, they could enlist the support of their sponsor in performing a more detailed analysis. At that point they would understand the issue more clearly and would be better able to justify spending more time on the problem.

Step 14 Check

Check to make sure you have a plan for the analysis of your interview data. You should have

- ❏ A refined purpose statement, if necessary

- ❏ An agreed upon path for analysis of your interview data

- ❏ Met with your sponsor to check your scope, schedule, and resources, if necessary

UNDERSTAND

Understand the Voices

Targeted Path

"The best salesman is a satisfied customer."

> Peter Vermeeran, Executive Vice President of Global Operations
> ADAC Laboratories

Overview

The Targeted Path is designed to focus on the customer's perspective of your key issue. Initially, you will develop a question that helps you zero in on the statements that specifically relate to your issue. You will then use these voices to identify the main themes where actions will have the greatest impact.

Step T15: Develop Key Question (details begin on p. 205)

Write a question that will help you extract those voices or statements from the interview transcripts that pertain to the issue you are trying to resolve.

Step T16: Structure the Data (details begin on p. 211)

Select the strongest voices from the interview transcripts and then organize them in a way that helps you identify a handful of key themes.

Step T17: Identify Key Themes (details begin on p. 235)

Select one to three themes that represent the greatest opportunities for taking effective action.

Questions You Will Be Answering

- What is our key question?

- What are the customers' key issues around this question?

- What are the larger themes represented by the customers' voices?

- Where will it be most advantageous for us to take action?

Logistics

The Targeted Path of Understand the Voices is relatively quick and straightforward. Crafting the key question and creating the affinity diagram are done as a group, whereas selecting statements from the interview transcripts is done by the individual team members.

The group will work together in Step T15, Develop Key Question.

In Step T16, Structure the Data, team members work individually to review interview transcripts and extract statements that help answer the key question. Then as a group they create an affinity diagram to identify common themes among the statements.

In Step T17, the group uses their affinity diagram to identify key themes on which to take action.

The following table shows how long this work typically takes.

Step	Estimated Time
Step T15: Develop Key Question	Approximately 30 minutes
Step T16: Structure the Data	1 hour per interview to identify voices (interviews can be reviewed concurrently by all team members)
	4 hours to create the affinity diagram
Step T17: Identify Key Themes	1 hour or less

The Big Picture

Targeted Path

T15. Develop Key Question

T16. Structure the Data

T17. Identify Key Themes

Prework

- Complete customer interviews
- Select path for analysis
- Meet with sponsor, if necessary

Time and Logistics

Allow approximately 30 minutes for the team to develop their key question.

Supplies and Equipment

- Copy of project purpose statement
- Flipchart paper
- Flipchart markers

Outcomes

- Key question used to focus the analysis

Step T15:

Develop Key Question

Description

To begin getting a deeper understanding of your interview data, draft a key question that will help you identify or select relevant statements in your interview transcripts and images from your observation notes.

Benefits

The key question helps you maintain a clear focus throughout this phase of work.

Getting Your Bearings

After conducting your customer interviews and transcribing the interview notes, you then paused to reflect on what you heard and compared it with your purpose statement. With this information, the team decided the Targeted Path was most appropriate for analyzing the interview data. The team will now focus thinking and analysis by developing a key question. Based on this question, team members will review the interview transcripts and identify key voices that relate to the question.

How to Develop a Key Question

A. Draft key question

A key question will provide focus for your thinking during the analysis phase. This question should help you understand what you most want to know about the subject of your exploration in order to accomplish your purpose. You will use this question to extract the relevant voices from your interview transcripts.

Typically, the question begins with the words "What are…" For example:

- What are the barriers to _____?
- What are the weaknesses of _____?
- What are the primary factors influencing _____?
- What are the customers' greatest concerns regarding _____?

Examples of key questions

Purpose Statement	Key Question
To better understand employees' health insurance needs in order to meet maximum employee needs at at reasonable company expense.	What are the key health insurance concerns of our employees?
To understand the key factors causing the problems of incompleteness in delivery in order to take preventive action.	What are the key breakdowns in our delivery process as perceived by our customers?
To learn what problems may be encountered in auditing and follow-up in order to develop a better auditing system.	What are the weaknesses in our current auditing and follow-up process?
To learn how to sell into high-end Information Technology environments in order to survive in the business of dealing with big customers directly.	What are the key factors that enable productive relationships with large customer IT decision makers?
To understand the internal criteria used in screening/selecting external resources for product development in order to optimize company-vendor relationships.	What are the key criteria our company uses to screen and select vendors for our product development process?

B. Check question for content

The question should be stated in the same terms as the issue or problem, not as a solution. In the first example, for instance, an incorrect way to phrase the question would be "What is the lowest cost health insurance plan we can offer?" "Offering low cost health insurance" is one possible solution to the problem.

If your project purpose is to clarify a fuzzy problem, use a weakness-oriented question that asks about problems, obstructions, and so forth. Looking for weaknesses helps you pick out statements that describe past and current reality rather than speculate about future solutions. Working with the data gathered from past problems and current experience will help you more fully understand the structure of the problem.

C. Check question for scope

The key question may be written at the same level of abstraction as your purpose statement or one rung down on the ladder of abstraction, that is, more concretely. If you get too specific, however, you might overlook important and relevant information in the interviews. See the examples in the following diagram.

Example of checking the scope of key questions

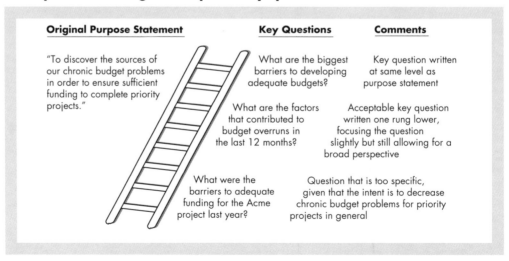

Original Purpose Statement	Key Questions	Comments
"To discover the sources of our chronic budget problems in order to ensure sufficient funding to complete priority projects."	What are the biggest barriers to developing adequate budgets?	Key question written at same level as purpose statement
	What are the factors that contributed to budget overruns in the last 12 months?	Acceptable key question written one rung lower, focusing the question slightly but still allowing for a broad perspective
	What were the barriers to adequate funding for the Acme project last year?	Question that is too specific, given that the intent is to decrease chronic budget problems for priority projects in general

The following case study shows how one company drafted its key question and checked it for content and scope.

Case Study: Medical Imaging Technology (Part 1 of 1)

A company that was considering creating a product for the medical field wanted to learn more about the future of digital imaging technology in that market. They had begun their project with this purpose statement:

> "To discover what factors are influencing the shift from analog to digital technology in the medical field so we can determine whether the time is right for investment in digital product development."

They crafted a key question:

> "What developments in digital imaging technology are influencing the shift from analog to digital in the medical field?"

When they checked this question for content, however, they realized it was likely a key part of the answer to their question, rather than a key question that would help them select appropriate voices more broadly. So they revised their key question:

> "What are the factors influencing the shift from analog to digital technology in the medical field?"

Next, they checked the question for scope. Because they had focused their interviews primarily in the field of mammography, they decided their question should reflect that narrow scope:

> "What are the most significant factors shaping the transition in the field of mammography from analog to digital?"

Step T15 Check

Check to make sure you will be able to identify relevant statements in your interview transcripts. You should have

- ❏ A clear, concise question at the appropriate level of abstraction

The Big Picture

Targeted Path

    T15. Develop Key Question

    T16. Structure the Data

    T17. Identify Key Themes

Prework

- Complete customer interviews
- Transcribe interview notes
- Develop key question

Time and Logistics

Individual team members will extract relevant statements from transcripts of the interviews they conducted. Allow about 1 hour per interview for this work. Using statements from all of the interviews, the team will create an affinity diagram which will take approximately 4 hours.

Supplies and Equipment

- Copies of verbatim interview transcripts
- 3" x 3" self-stick notes
- Black, red, and blue pens for each participant
- Flipchart paper
- Highlighting markers
- Black flipchart marker
- Tape or pushpins

Outcomes

- Affinity diagram showing relationships among statements

Step T16:

Structure the Data

Description

In this step you will go back to your interview and observation notes and identify the voices that represent important aspects of your key question. Then you will create an affinity diagram to discover connections among these statements that will provide important insights into your issue.

Benefits

This process will help you better relate your customers' concerns to your key question. Using this structured approach helps a team gain a common understanding of the issues and to see them in a broader context.

Getting Your Bearings

You now have a key question related to your issue. In this step you will review all of the interview transcripts and highlight voices or statements that help answer that question.

During this process you will alternate between divergent (broad) and convergent (focused) thinking. For instance, you will start out thinking broadly in order to extract diverse statements from the interview notes; then you narrow the field by selecting only the strongest of those statements. When looking for connections, you again start broadly, looking for as many connections as possible; then you narrow your focus to find the most insightful themes.

> The statements you highlight in your interview transcripts reflect the customer's voice. In this book the terms voices and statements are used interchangeably.

Two tools, described later in detail, will help you do the work in this step:

1. The Method for Priority Marking™ (MPM) is a useful technique for narrowing down the number of interview statements from potentially several hundred to about two dozen. Your final subset of statements should include the strongest statements that still provide a 360° view of the issue.

2. An affinity diagram is a tool for finding connections among statements. The affinity diagram technique described in this book is designed specifically to help you move slowly up the ladder of abstraction from detailed statements to increasingly broad themes.

How to Structure the Data

A. Identify relevant statements in interview notes

The first task in understanding the data is to identify the voices you heard in the interviews that relate to the key question. Read through the verbatim interview notes and highlight any statements that are relevant to this question. You should also check for any relevant images or insights from your observation notes.

Next, transcribe these statements onto 3" x 3" self-stick notes. This will make them easier to work with during the rest of this process.

 It is ideal for each interview team to work on their own transcripts. Although it is enriching for team members to read all the transcripts, it is not necessary to do so. Later, when creating the affinity diagram, learnings will be shared.

- Write the statements word for word, as much as possible, putting quotation marks around direct quotes. If the speaker is referring to a previous comment, you may need to add a few words for the statement to make sense. Show any added words with brackets [ ]. If you want to delete irrelevant information from a statement, use three dots (…) to indicate something is missing.

- Print the statements in black, block letters so that everyone will be able to read them. In later stages you will be using different ink colors to indicate more abstract themes, so it is best to use black to represent the lowest level of abstraction.

- Code each note so that you know from which interview it came and from which transcript page. This coding is important for tracking your thinking and decision making back to the Voice of the Customer. You may want to use numerical codes instead of initials for your notes so that you do not introduce bias into the selection process.

If your transcripts have been entered into a computer you can print your files in 3" columns instead of copying the statements onto self-stick notes. Then cut out the relevant statements and either sort them on a table or tape them to self-stick notes for use on a flipchart.

If you find that many statements from a single interview cover the same issue, you need not transcribe them all. Select the ones that are lower on the ladder of abstraction—phrased in the concrete, verifiable language of first-person experience. (In the next substep, you will compare statements across all of the interviews; here, focus on each interview separately.)

 If you find you are completely filling the note, you may have multiple statements that should be divided onto separate notes.

The next case study follows the employee benefits team as they extract relevant statements from their interviews.

 Case Study: Employee Benefits (Part 4 of 6)

The team had agreed on this key question: "What are the key health insurance concerns of our employees?" The team members then highlighted relevant statements in the interview transcripts.

Here is an interview excerpt with relevant statements highlighted:

The benefits package was one of the things that really sold me on this job. I have four kids and making sure I can afford to take care of all their health care needs, including dental and vision, is really important to me. In fact, I turned down a job with a higher salary and fewer benefits. If we start losing benefits now, I don't know how I'm going to manage. It scares me, too, if we change carriers because my husband has rheumatoid arthritis. That's a preexisting condition. What if it's not covered? And I already have one kid in braces.

The following notes were taken from this interview excerpt. Each team member transcribed the statements from the interviews he or she conducted, for a total of 250 notes from 16 interviews. The code in the upper right corner of each note indicates from which interview the statement was taken and the transcript page on which it can be found. This code is helpful if anyone needs to check on the context of the statement later in the process.

Continued...

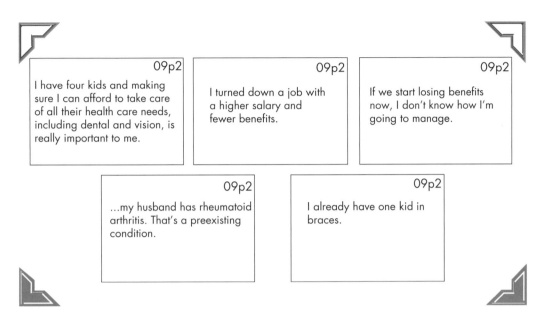

B. Select strongest statements

It is not unusual to identify between 50 and several hundred statements in the interview transcripts. Some interviewees will have made similar statements and many voices may represent the same issue. Now is the time to review the statements and eliminate duplication. To extract themes from all of this data, most people find they must reduce the number of statements to about two dozen. This selection is made by carefully considering which statements reflect both the depth and diversity of sentiments expressed in the interviews.

Gather together all of the statements from all of the interviews. If there are more than about two dozen, put all of the ones you think sound similar together and pick the strongest from each group. Continue the process of grouping and selecting until you have two dozen or fewer notes. (If you have a significant number of notes, see "Selecting the Strongest Statements" on page 217 for more details on narrowing your selection.)

 Be careful that in selecting the strongest statements you do not lose sight of the diverse viewpoints represented. To get a 360° view, sometimes you will need to include a weak statement that represents a different perspective. Think of the statements chosen as being symbolic of others.

Strong voices are clear, concise, and specific. They often reflect personal experience. Weak voices are vague and imprecise. People often begin talking at a high level of abstraction, but later in the passage or after a probe make stronger, more detailed statements.

Examples of weak and strong voices

Weak Voice	Stronger Voice
"Any procedure that is going faster and smoother is easier for the patient." (This voice is fairly high in abstraction; we don't know what faster and smoother mean.)	"Because a patient has to lie still during a procedure, a short procedure is easier on them." And, "The most uncomfortable position for older patients is lying on their faces." (These voices begin to detail "faster and smoother.")
"It's no good to be better if it's so much more expensive." (If this is the best voice, it would be better than nothing; but in reading further, other voices were found that gave more detail.)	"Nowadays, especially up here, more than down in the States, getting money for equipment, it really has to be better " And, "If a product is better it can be more expensive, but it has to be within reach, not so much more expensive." (Even more detail would be valuable—for example, what are the criteria for "a better product"—but these quotes begin to define "expensive" and are better choices than the voice that is more vague.)

Some team members may have difficulty letting go of so many customer statements. Having done the customer visits, all of the statements may seem important. To help with this, remember to do the following:

- Check back to the key question often

- Recognize that the process will help the team focus on the most important issues without getting lost in a sea of data

- Remember that issues chosen symbolize others that are similar

- Check for omissions to make sure a key issue has not been neglected

Selecting the Strongest Statements

One way to narrow down your statements to a manageable number and, at the same time, sort out the strongest notes is to use the Method for Priority Marking™. This method involves four steps: sorting, unrestrained pickup, focused pickup, and final check.*

Sorting

Start by posting all the notes on one or more sheets of flipchart paper. To find notes representing similar thoughts, you may find it helpful to sort the notes into general categories, using whatever categories come to mind.

Unrestrained Pickup

Next, focus on those notes that seem to best reflect your theme. Working simultaneously, team members should mark a red dot on the lower right corner of notes they think are worth keeping. Individually read through all the notes and look for those that are specific or clearly expressed. Look also for notes that represent or symbolize different perspectives, even though they may not be stated as well as some of the others. The objective is to eventually eliminate notes that are repetitious without losing a 360° view. It is best for everyone to work silently. There are no limits to how many notes may be marked, but each note should get only one dot. This is not voting; if someone likes a note that already has a dot on it, he or she should simply leave it and move on. When everyone is finished, remove the unmarked notes (but save them in case you need them later to answer any questions).

If you have more than 35 to 40 notes left, go through the marking process again, adding a second dot to the notes you want to keep. At the end of this round, remove all notes that have only one dot on them. Continue with additional rounds until you get down to about 35 to 40 notes.

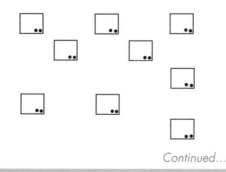

Continued...

---

*See Appendix B for more information on the the Method for Priority Marking™.

Focused Pickup

To narrow your choices to roughly 24 notes, divide 24 by the number of people on the team. This is the number of final selections each person gets. If the answer is not a whole number, round up. For instance, if you have a team of seven, each person gets four selections. Each person, in turn, selects one note that he or she thinks is important to keep, reads the note aloud, and explains why it is important. The note is then moved to one side and the next person selects a note, reads it aloud, and explains the selection. The rotations continue until all have completed their specified number of selections.

Final Check

Finally, check to make sure a 360° view has been preserved. Look over the notes that were not selected in the focused pickup and decide if any need to be added. Discuss the notes that have been selected to make sure everyone has a common understanding of their meaning. At this point you should have a workable number of voices that provide clear, strong, and diverse perspectives of your question.

In this illustration, six team members are selecting from notes chosen in unrestrained pickup and placing their selections to the right. Three team members have made three selections each, whereas the other three have made only two selections so far. In the end, each team member will get four selections in this round for a total of 24 notes.

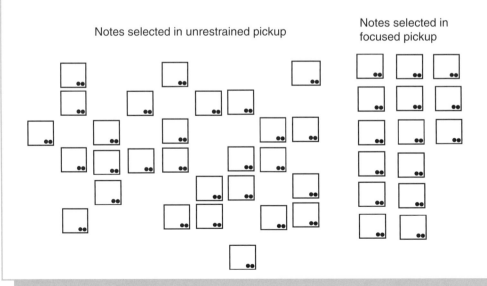

Notes selected in unrestrained pickup

Notes selected in focused pickup

Here is how the employee benefits team used the MPM™ method to select their strongest statements.

Case Study: Employee Benefits (Part 5 of 6)

The benefits team sorted the statement notes into broad categories. Those with a dot in the lower right corner were first-round selections.

- The first note in the Basic Medical grouping was left out because it covered multiple issues: dental, vision, and basic health.

- The second note in the Dental grouping was left out because it did not include as much detail as the other note.

- The third note in the Managed Care vs. Fee for Service grouping was left out because it did not identify the person's concern.

- Although not very strong, the left note in the Other grouping was included because it represented a different viewpoint.

The team continued with this process until they had reduced the number of statement notes from 250 to 25. The following illustration shows a small portion of the team's notes.

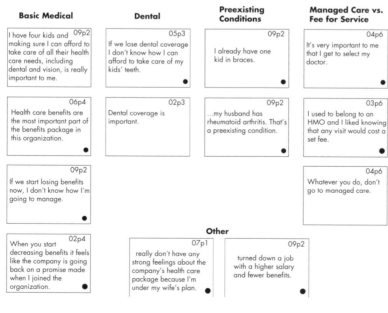

C. Create Level 1 groupings

The categories you used to organize your notes in the MPM™ process created logical groupings. Now you need to look for different types of connections in order to deepen your understanding of the common themes discussed. Considering many alternative groupings allows you to think about your customers' concerns in new ways. (For additional help in creating groups and titles, see "Affinity Diagrams" on page 222.)

- Spread the notes randomly on a flipchart.

- Group the statements into small clusters that reflect a common, yet fairly concrete, theme. Try to keep these themes at a low level of abstraction, only one rung up from the notes themselves. If you started with 24 diverse statements, it should be hard to find a common theme in more than three statements at a time.

- Avoid cause-and-effect groupings; these do not have an overlapping common element. Your intent in this part of the process is to gain insight by moving up the ladder of abstraction from the fairly concrete statements to a higher conceptual level. Cause-and-effect relationships will make it difficult to do this.

- Keep moving the notes around until you have approximately 8 to 12 groups.

Begin this work of creating groupings silently to avoid interrupting others' train of thought. Toward the end of this activity, however, people may have questions about why notes are being moved, and this discussion can provide new insights.

The first groupings will probably reflect connections you already are aware of or the similarity of words used. To reach new understandings, it is necessary to try new combinations based on different kinds of similarities.

The following illustration shows how the employee benefits team regrouped several of their statements.

Case Study: Employee Benefits (Part 6 of 6)

The original category titles are shown on the notes. What the notes have in common is shown at the top of each cluster. The following illustration shows notes taken from the broad categories, now clustered in Level 1 groupings.

What these two notes have in common: I like to choose medical sources based on my own criteria.

> 04p6
>
> It's very important to me that I get to select my doctor.
>
> **(Managed Care vs. Fee for Service)** ●

> 06p4
>
> I don't like having to drive across town to get my prescriptions filled.
>
> **(Not shown previously)** ●

What these three notes have in common: I worry that my family will be less well cared for.

> 09p2
>
> If we start losing benefits now, I don't know how I'm going to manage.
>
> **(Basic Medical)** ●

> 09p2
>
> I already have one kid in braces.
>
> **(Preexisting Conditions)** ●

> 05p3
>
> If we lose dental coverage I don't know how I can afford to take care of my kids' teeth.
>
> **(Dental)** ●

Affinity Diagrams

An affinity diagram helps you group items so you can see what they have in common.* In the FOCUS process, we recommend that you keep the number of notes in a group relatively small. This should be fairly easy because you have already reduced your number of notes.

Create Level 1 Groupings

Begin by writing the key question in the upper left corner of two flipchart pages taped side by side on a wall. Spread all the statement notes randomly on the paper. Then start grouping the statements, looking for common themes. It is natural to want to group statements into cause-and-effect relationships; that is, one statement is the cause of another. It is better in the long run not to do this. Instead, look for notes that share a common element.

If you start getting groupings larger than two or three notes, you are probably working at too high a level of abstraction. Break the groups apart, looking for the subtle distinctions among them. Sometimes single notes do not relate to any others and will continue to stand alone.

Keep moving the notes around, remembering they can always be moved back. This helps you see connections you might not have noticed at first. Making and breaking connections is how you will often gain new insights. You should end up with 8 to 12 clusters.

Create Level 1 Titles

Write a summary title sentence that captures the common theme in each group. These titles are critical because they will become the basis for whatever actions you decide are necessary.

Level 1 titles should be fairly specific and are easier to write if you have only 2 or 3 notes in the grouping. If the title is too abstract, it will be difficult to take action later in the process.

A good way to create titles is to start with key words or phrases that reflect what the statements have in common. Then write a sentence that relates the concept reflected in the notes to the key question. When possible, use action verbs in your titles. When the title is complete, print it in red on a self-stick note and place it at the top of the grouping.

Sometimes you may find that one of the notes actually works well as a title. In that case, simply draw a red box around the text to distinguish it from the other notes and move it into position as the title.

Continued...

*See Appendix B, Language Processing Method™, for information on a more rigorous method for grouping notes.

Once you have titles for all your groups, check to see if any single notes now fit into one of the groupings. Sometimes having clarified the groupings through titling helps you see how another note is related.

Create Level 2 Groupings

Repeat the clustering steps by looking for ways to group the Level 1 titles into common themes. Stack the groupings so that only the title can be seen on top. This focuses attention on the titles and not the underlying notes.

Again, aim for groupings of 2 or 3 titles. If you start getting larger groupings, you are probably working at too high a level of abstraction. A single note that remained ungrouped might now fit in a Level 2 group.

You will probably still move the groupings around. Sometimes you may find that several groupings can be made from the same set of titles. If you are not sure which is best, check to see which cluster best fits your key question. You should end up with 4 to 8 clusters.

Create Level 2 Titles

Again, write a summary title that captures the common theme in each grouping. These titles are at a higher level of abstraction and will help you capture overall themes that will help you see the big picture. Identifying

these themes helps people communicate with managers and others in the organization.

To create Level 2 titles, start with key words or phrases that reflect what the Level 1 titles have in common. Then write a sentence that relates the concept reflected in the titles to the key question. When the title is complete, print it in blue on a self-stick note and place it at the top of the group.

When you have all your Level 2 titles, check to see if any of the remaining single notes or Level 1 clusters now fit into one of the Level 2 groupings. Sometimes having clarified the groupings through titling helps you see how another note is related. If any Level 1 clusters or single notes do not fit into Level 2 groupings, they may remain alone.

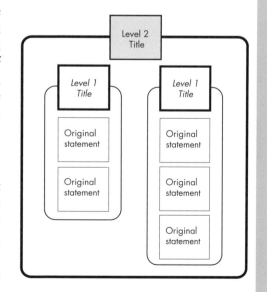

The following case study shows how one team created their Level 1 groupings.

Case Study: Compensation Process Improvement (Part 1 of 5)

A company wanted to understand their employees' problems with the compensation system in order to make improvements. The team started with this key question: "What are the major problems with our compensation system?" With this question in mind, they went through their interview notes and transcribed relevant statements onto self-stick notes.

Next they selected the most diverse statements. Because their project focused on identifying areas to improve, they primarily selected voices oriented towards problems or weaknesses. They put up all the notes on flipchart paper and everyone read through them silently. Then they started looking for notes that seemed to go together. One person found two she thought were related and moved them into a cluster. Other people found different groupings. As they worked, the groupings changed as people found new ways to think about the statements.

As the process continued, the team members moved fewer and fewer of the notes as they gradually became satisfied with the clusters. In one case, two people kept rearranging three clusters. Finally, one person explained the connections he saw, the other person explained her perspective, and together they reached agreement on the clustering. Eventually, everyone was satisfied and the clusters were complete. Two notes stood alone. They were important, but did not seem to fit with any others. All together, they had 11 Level 1 groupings, as shown in the following diagram.

Continued...

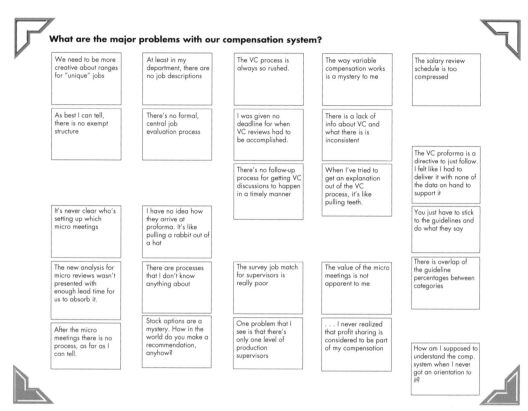

What are the major problems with our compensation system?

We need to be more creative about ranges for "unique" jobs	At least in my department, there are no job descriptions	The VC process is always so rushed.	The way variable compensation works is a mystery to me	The salary review schedule is too compressed
As best I can tell, there is no exempt structure	There's no formal, central job evaluation process	I was given no deadline for when VC reviews had to be accomplished.	There is a lack of info about VC and what there is is inconsistent	
		There's no follow-up process for getting VC discussions to happen in a timely manner	When I've tried to get an explanation out of the VC process, it's like pulling teeth.	The VC proforma is a directive to just follow. I felt like I had to deliver it with none of the data on hand to support it
It's never clear who's setting up which micro meetings	I have no idea how they arrive at proforma. It's like pulling a rabbit out of a hat			You just have to stick to the guidelines and do what they say
The new analysis for micro reviews wasn't presented with enough lead time for us to absorb it.	There are processes that I don't know anything about	The survey job match for supervisors is really poor	The value of the micro meetings is not apparent to me	There is overlap of the guideline percentages between categories
After the micro meetings there is no process, as far as I can tell.	Stock options are a mystery. How in the world do you make a recommendation, anyhow?	One problem that I see is that there's only one level of production supervisors	. . . I never realized that profit sharing is considered to be part of my compensation	How am I supposed to understand the comp. system when I never got an orientation to it?

D. Write Level 1 titles

Identify what is common in each Level 1 grouping and write a concise summary title. Remember that Level 1 titles should show the connections among the statement notes and will eventually be used to determine where to take action. The more concrete they are, the better.

The tendency at first is to write titles that simply repeat everything in the original notes. Instead, the title needs to represent the common link between the notes.

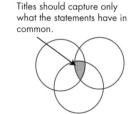

Titles should capture only what the statements have in common.

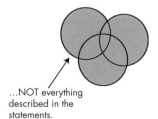

...NOT everything described in the statements.

You may find that it works best for the group to discuss the notes and come up with a single title, or you may prefer to have each person write his or her own title for each cluster. You can then select one that seems best or combine ideas into a single new title.

 Be wary of titles that are too long to fit on a self-stick note or that contain the word "and."

 Avoid cause-and-effect relationships; that is, do not pick a title that is the cause or the result of the statements in the grouping.

 It is easy to spend lots of time trying to perfect the title wording. Sometimes that effort pays off; other times, approximately right is good enough. Use your judgment.

Examples of Level 1 titles

Level 1 Grouping	Possible Level 1 Titles		
Functional mgrs. readily provide Prod. Mgrs. with the required deliver-ables in a timely manner	*Corporate decision makers, functional managers, product managers, program managers, and the marketing group are all aligned*	*Everyone aligns on roles in the organization*	*Roles and responsibilities are clear at all levels of new product development*
Marketing group aligns with other functions on its role in new product delivery	This title is really not a summary. It is the total of everything written on the notes.	This title is too high on the ladder of abstraction. It encompasses more than what is expressed in the three notes.	This title is better for this group of notes because it captures what they have in common at an appropriately specific level of abstraction.
Corporate decision makers and prod. mgrs. align on roles and responsibilities of Program Managers			

The next case study follows the compensation team as they write titles for their Level 1 groupings.

Case Study: Compensation Process Improvement (Part 2 of 5)

Once the team was satisfied with their Level 1 groupings, they looked at each cluster and tried to find a single statement that would encompass the key points in each of the individual statements. They discussed why they had grouped the statements together as they tried to find a summary statement.

Sometimes their first efforts were too high on the ladder of abstraction and had to be revised. Other times their titles were too long, covering everything in the cluster rather than just what was common to all the notes. Eventually, the team came up with titles with which they were all satisfied. The following diagram shows five of their clusters and the titles they selected.

What are the major problems with our compensation system?

Information about the VC process is not readily available.	The micro meeting process is confusing	There are compensation processes that are not understood	Some processes in the salary review are too directive	HR does not market compensation products and services
The way variable compensation works is a mystery to me	It's never clear who's setting up which micro meetings	I have no idea how they arrive at proforma. It's like pulling a rabbit out of a hat	The VC proforma is a directive to just follow. I felt like I had to deliver it with none of the data on hand to support it	The value of the micro meetings is not apparent to me
There is a lack of info about VC and what there is is inconsistent	The new analysis for micro reviews wasn't presented with enough lead time for us to absorb it.	There are processes that I don't know anything about	You just have to stick to the guidelines and do what they say	. . . I never realized that profit sharing is considered to be part of my compensation
When I've tried to get an explanation out of the VC process, it's like pulling teeth	After the micro meetings there is no process, as far as I can tell.	Stock options are a mystery. How in the world do you make a recommendation, anyhow?	There is overlap of the guideline percentages between categories	

E. Create Level 2 groupings

Repeat the clustering steps, but this time cluster the Level 1 titles rather than the individual notes. This second round of grouping helps identify larger themes that can provide a broader frame of reference for your thinking.

 Stack the groupings so that only the title can be seen on top. This focuses attention on the titles and not the underlying notes.

- Look for groups of two or three titles that have something in common. At this point you can also include single, ungrouped notes in these new clusters. You should end up with four to eight clusters.

- Once again, avoid cause-and-effect relationships within groupings.

- Begin by working silently. Each team member will probably see different ways to create groupings. Trying to see what others see will help everyone gain a deeper understanding of the issues.

- Sometimes you may find that several groupings can be made from the same set of Level 1 titles. If you are not sure which is best, check to see which cluster best fits your key question.

Here is how the compensation team created their Level 2 groupings.

Case Study: Compensation Process Improvement (Part 3 of 5)

The team stacked each cluster of statements so that the Level 1 title was on top. Then they looked for ways to group the titles. At a higher level of abstraction, did any of the clusters have anything in common? Occasionally, someone needed to pick up the stack and reread the individual notes to remember what was included.

As before, the clusters kept changing. Each team member would see different relationships and different ways to group. Eventually, the team reached a point where everyone was satisfied, if not quite in full agreement. The illustration on the next page shows four of the team's Level 2 groupings.

Continued...

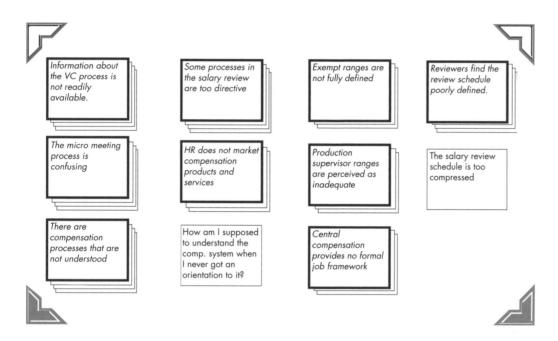

F. Write Level 2 titles

Repeat the titling steps to find a concise summary title for each Level 2 grouping. These titles should answer your key question. Team members may resist working at this level of abstraction. It may seem that the summaries lose all the power of the customer statements. The affinity diagram will preserve all levels of abstraction—the customer voices and the summaries.

- Identify what is common in each Level 2 grouping.

- Write a title that is only one rung higher on the ladder of abstraction than the Level 1 titles.

- Avoid cause-and-effect relationships.

Write a title as a team or have each person write his or her own title; then either select the best one or combine ideas into a single new title.

The compensation team was now ready to write their Level 2 titles.

Case Study: Compensation Process Improvement
(Part 4 of 5)

When they had created the new groupings, the team needed to find new titles that would identify what these clusters had in common. Once again, they needed to move up one level on the ladder of abstraction.

For the cluster of titles concerning compensation processes that were not understood, the team started with a Level 2 title that included each process mentioned. This title, however, was too long and specific. The team decided "some compensation processes" would be a better summary. They also felt the real problem was not that the processes were necessarily confusing, but that they were not communicated well. In the end, they chose this Level 2 title: "Some compensation processes are not well communicated."

They wrote the new titles in blue on self-stick notes and placed them above their groupings.

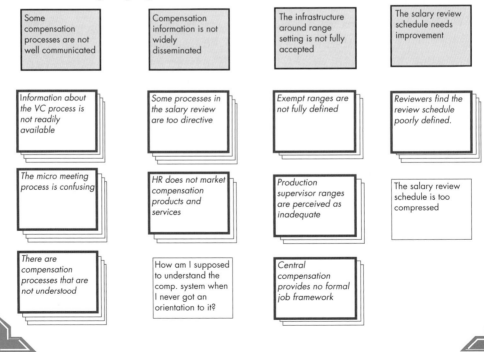

G. Lay out the affinity diagram

If you placed the self-stick notes on top of each other while you were sorting, spread them out again into the appropriate clusters so that you can see each individual note. If you need more space, add another sheet of flipchart paper.

- Draw black lines around each Level 1 grouping.

- Draw heavy black lines around each Level 2 grouping.

- Tape the notes to the paper to make this a more permanent document.

- Write the date on the final diagram. You may also want to add the name of the team and each team member. Some teams sign their names as a way of acknowledging their consensus.

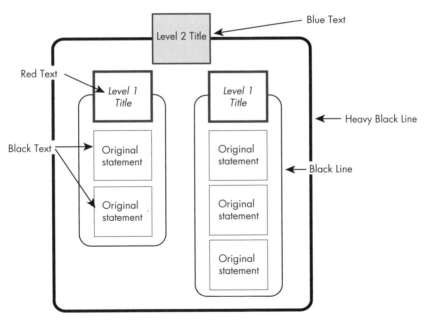

This next case study shows how the compensation team finished structuring their data.

Case Study: Compensation Process Improvement (Part 5 of 5)

The compensation team completed their affinity diagram. When they start the next step, they will be able to clearly see the big picture provided by the Level 2 titles, as well as the details provided by the individual statement notes. A portion of their final affinity diagram follows.

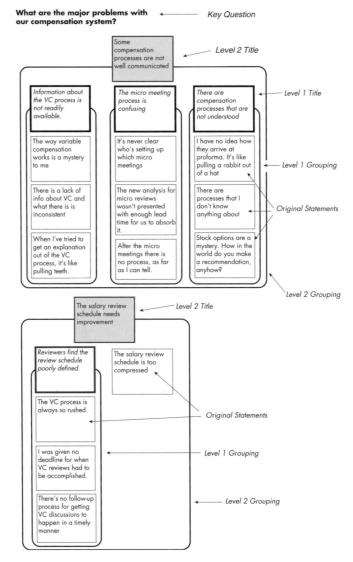

Step T16 Check

Check to make sure you understand the relationships in your data. You should have

❏ About 24 of the strongest statements that provide a 360° view of the key question

❏ Groupings that show how the statements relate to one another

The Big Picture

Targeted Path

T15. Develop Key Question

T16. Structure the Data

T17. Identify Key Themes

Prework

- Create affinity diagram

Time and Logistics

Deciding on the key themes should take approximately 1 hour or less and is usually done at the end of the working session in which the affinity diagram is created.

Supplies and Equipment

- Black and red pens
- Copy of affinity diagram
- 3" x 3" self-stick notes
- Tape or pushpins

Outcomes

- 3 or fewer key themes on which to take action

Step T17:

Identify Key Themes

Description

After reviewing the affinity diagram to make sure nothing important is missing, you will analyze it to identify the key themes on which to take action. The process will help you determine what points will have the greatest impact on your issue.

Benefits

The process used to identify key themes will ensure that everyone in the group has an equal voice in selecting the areas in which to move forward.

Getting Your Bearings

The work done in the previous two steps has helped everyone focus on what is most significant to the issue you began exploring. You started the process of Understand the Voices with a tremendous amount of knowledge gained through your customer interviews, and then used that knowledge to determine the primary focus for your data analysis. Maintaining that focus is especially important as you prepare to select what actions to take based on your findings. In this step you will determine the top three themes—the areas that will have the most significant impact on your issue.

How to Identify Key Themes

A. Reflect on and revise affinity diagram

The process of creating an affinity diagram helps you analyze the messages buried in the mass of interview notes, but it cannot replace the human brain's ability to synthesize information. Although you could simply accept the affinity diagram titles as the potential key themes from the analysis, you would run the risk of overlooking an important point not captured in the diagram.

Take a few minutes to study your affinity diagram. Review your purpose statement and think back to everything you have seen and heard throughout the project.

- Based on everything you have learned to date, is there anything your intuition tells you is missing? If so, write down these statements and add them to the diagram at the appropriate level.

- Does the wording of the Level 1 and Level 2 titles make sense? Check to make sure the titles capture the common elements in the clustered notes and are only one rung up on the ladder of abstraction.

B. Select Level 1 titles to target for action

Level 1 titles are generally where your actions will have the most impact and be most effective. At this point you have approximately 8 to 12 titles and may find it beneficial to choose no more than three titles that you will try to address in your action plans.

Revisit the affinity diagram and have each team member vote for the top three Level 1 titles. Put yourself in your customers' shoes: how would they vote? An easy way to vote that ensures equal participation is to use a 3-2-1 voting method, described below.

- Each person gets three votes. An individual's top choice gets a score of 3, the second choice a score of 2, and the least favorite a score of 1.

- Working simultaneously, team members write the scores for their top three selections directly on the notes. Single notes that are not part of a cluster should also be included in the voting.

- Add up the numbers on each note. Some notes may have several votes, whereas others have none.

- Select the top vote-getters.

Step T17 Check

Check to make sure you understand the major themes in your data. You should have

❏ No more than three Level 1 titles to target for action

Section Summary

You have now worked through the Targeted Path of Understand the Voices. You should have completed the following:

❑ Developed a key question to focus your analysis of the interview data

❑ Identified relevant statements in the interview notes

❑ Created an affinity diagram showing what your strongest customer statements had in common

❑ Identified key themes in your data to target for action

Looking ahead...

The final phase of the FOCUS process, Select Action, provides steps on how to translate your learnings into a complete solution, as well as some background on the creation of an action plan. Many teams at this point have gained so much insight into their issue that their next steps are clear. Other teams have only to make a report of their learnings to their sponsor or management. Review Select Action to see how these steps can best be used to meet your team's requirements.

Understand the Voices

Requirements Path

"At L.L. Bean we believe in listening to our customers; it is part of our heritage. If they have something to say about a product or service we pay close attention. What we in Product Development have not done previously is listen to our customers before we develop products. Collecting the Voice of the Customer saves time, keeps us focused on what the customer values and directs us to catalog copy that has real power."

Harry McPherson, Product Manager Outerwear
L.L. Bean

Overview

The purpose of this path is to understand customer requirements—usually for a new or redesigned product, service, process, or policy.

The first step in this path exposes unmet needs among your customers. However, simply hearing these needs seldom points the way toward specific actions. Further steps help you translate the customers' stated problems and needs into performance requirements.

Step R15: Identify Key Customer Concerns (details begin on p. 245)

Review the interview transcripts to identify the customers' key issues, needs, concerns, problems, and solutions. These voices will lead you to requirements on which action can be taken.

Step R16: Construct Requirement Statements (details begin on p. 255)

Convert the customers' language into specific performance requirements for whatever you are designing or redesigning.

Step R17: Assess Requirement Priorities (details begin on p. 273)

In order to assess which requirements are most important, get input from the people who will ultimately use what you design.

Questions You Will Be Answering

- What are our customers' key concerns?
- What requirements underlie these key concerns?
- What are the larger themes represented by the customer requirements?
- Which of the key requirements have the highest priority for customers?

Logistics

The Requirements Path involves several different types of work: individual work, small group work, and work with the entire team.

In Step R15, Identify Key Customer Concerns, team members work individually to review interview transcripts and extract statements that identify customer concerns.

In Step R16, Construct Requirement Statements, the team translates customer voices into requirement statements. If you use the complete set of customer voices, this work can be completed by small groups working independently. If you use a subset of the voices, the entire team should work together.

In Step R17, Assess Requirement Priorities, the group creates an affinity diagram to identify relationships among the requirement statements. Then you need to create a questionnaire to help you identify which requirements are most important to your customers.

Step	Estimated Time
Step R15: Identify Key Customer Concerns	1 hour per interview to identify voices (interviews can be reviewed concurrently by all team members) Optional: 1 2 hours to select strongest statements
Step R16: Construct Requirement Statements	If using the full set of voices, at least 8 hours with small groups working concurrently If using a reduced set of strongest voices, approximately 4 hours with entire team working together
Step R17: Assess Requirement Priorities	Approximately 5 hours plus elapsed time for return of customer surveys

The Big Picture

Requirements Path

R15. Identify Key Customer Concerns

R16. Construct Requirement Statements

R17. Assess Requirement Priorities

Prework

- Complete customer interviews
- Select path for analysis
- Meet with sponsor, if necessary

Time and Logistics

Individual team members will extract relevant statements from transcripts of the interviews they conducted. Allow about 1 hour per interview for this work. An optional exercise involves selecting only the strongest statements to work with. This work takes an additional 1 – 2 hours and should be done in a team meeting.

Supplies and Equipment

- Copies of verbatim interview transcripts
- Highlighting markers
- 3" x 3" self-stick notes
- Black and red pens for each participant
- Flipchart paper
- Tape or pushpins

Outcomes

- Identification of customer voices representing key ideas, needs, problems, concerns, and solutions from all the interviews.

Step R15:

Identify Key Customer Concerns

Description

The goal of the Requirements Path is to translate your customers' needs into specific requirements that you can use to design a product, service, process, or policy. You begin this translation by identifying statements from the interviews that reflect your customers' needs. These statements may be phrased as explicit needs, but they may also be stated as problems, concerns, or proposed solutions.

Benefits

Identifying the ways customers express their underlying needs will help you arrive at the requirements that can be acted on to meet those needs.

Getting Your Bearings

The interview process helped you build a tacit understanding of your customers' world—their key issues, problems, needs, concerns, and proposed solutions. Now it is time to analyze all the language data you collected. Developing a common understanding of your customers' voices and translating them into requirements that you can act on is what gives the FOCUS process its power.

> The statements you highlight in your interview transcripts reflect the customer's voice. In this book the terms voices and statements are used interchangeably.

The Method for Priority Marking™ (MPM) is a useful technique you may later use to narrow down the number of interview statements from potentially several hundred to about two dozen.

How to Identify Key Customer Concerns

A. Identify need statements in interview notes

Use the following question to help you recognize need statements in your interview notes: "What voices identify key issues, needs, problems, concerns, images, or solutions that will help us understand customer requirements?"

Read through the verbatim interview notes and highlight statements that help answer this question. Remember, at this point you are not looking for requirements but for clues that will lead to requirements. You should also check for any relevant images or insights from your observation notes.

Some statements may reflect needs or offer solutions; others may express problems or concerns. Some thoughts may be stated explicitly, whereas others may be implied. Using divergent thinking, highlight anything you think may lead to understanding customer requirements. The interview statements represent the Voice of the Customers. A voice may be a phrase, a sentence, or several sentences—whatever is needed to capture a distinct thought or issue.

Next, transcribe these statements onto 3" x 3" self-stick notes. This will make them easier to work with during the rest of this process.

It is ideal for each interview team to work on their own transcripts. Although it is enriching for team members to read all the transcripts, it is not necessary to do so. Later, when creating the affinity diagram, learnings will be shared.

- Write the statements word for word, as much as possible, putting quotation marks around direct quotes. If the speaker is referring to a previous comment, you may need to add a few words for the statement to make sense. Show any added words with brackets [ ]. If you want to delete irrelevant information from a statement, use three dots (…) to indicate something is missing.

- Print the statements in black, block letters so that everyone will be able to read them. In later stages you will be using different ink colors to indicate more abstract themes, so it is best to use black to represent the lowest level of abstraction.

- Code each note so that you know from which interview it came and from which transcript page. This coding is important for tracking your thinking and decision making back to the Voice of the Customer. You may want to use numerical codes instead of initials for your notes so that you do not introduce bias into the selection process.

> If your transcripts have been entered into a computer you can print your files in 3" columns instead of copying the statements onto self-stick notes. Then cut out the relevant statements and either sort them on a table or tape them to self-stick notes for use on a flipchart.

If you find that many statements from a single interview cover the same issue, you need not transcribe them all. Select the ones that are lower on the ladder of abstraction—phrased in the concrete, verifiable language of first-person experience. (In the next substep, you will compare statements across all of the interviews; here, focus on each interview separately.)

> *If you find you are completely filling the note, you may have multiple statements that should be divided onto separate notes.*

The following case study illustrates how the document management team, discussed earlier in Frame the Project and Organize Resources, went through their interview transcripts to identify need statements.

Case Study: Document Management (Part 8 of 9)

The document management team had conducted interviews to learn how employees used the company's document management system. Now they went back through the interviews looking for need statements. They found some in descriptions of people's current work, while they identified others in passages where people talked about what they would like to be able to do in the future.

The team recognized that the excerpts they highlighted were not all requirement statements. However, these voices, which expressed what people thought they needed to get their work done, would lead to requirement statements. Here are some need statements the team identified:

- "I need to have both a PC and a Mac at my workstation."

- "Tom and I are working together off-site with a client. But since we both save our work on our own laptops, it's difficult to share work while we're in the create mode."

- "One of the things that would be helpful is the state-of-the-art laptops that are using the telephone. Say I'm in a hotel room and I plug in to send you something. It would be helpful if we could talk while we're looking at the same document on-line."

- "I need to be able to use a lot of different software: Word, Claris, Quark, Illustrator, PowerPoint."

- "We need a way for people working off-site to know what everyone else is doing. Otherwise we can't learn from each other—leverage off each other's work."

- "Ellie wanted to use three pages out of a seminar that had been done a couple years ago. First I had to find a printed binder for that seminar, then I went through to find the right pages, and I faxed them to her to make sure I was looking for the right thing. After I found the paper copies, I had to get the codes off the bottom and then find them in the electronic files."

B. Select strongest statements (optional)

It is not unusual to identify between 50 and several hundred statements in the interview transcripts. Some interviewees will have made similar statements and many voices may represent the same issue. Depending on the project and its associated level of risk, the team may choose to translate all of the customer voices into requirements, or to reduce the number of statements to about two dozen.

If you choose to translate all of the customer voices, you can now proceed directly to Step R16, Construct Requirement Statements. If you choose to reduce the number of statements before translating them into requirements, this selection is made by carefully considering which statements reflect both the depth and diversity of sentiments expressed in the interviews.

 When developing new products and services it is often worth the additional time to translate all the voices into requirements. Working with the complete set of customer voices will often provide greater insight than working with only the strongest statements. Putting in the extra day or two now will assure that you have been thorough in identifying all the requirements which will bring you closer to providing a product or service that will truly delight your customers.

Gather together all of the statements from all of the interviews. If there are more than about two dozen, put all of the ones you think sound similar together and pick the strongest from each group. Continue the process of grouping and selecting until you have two dozen or fewer notes. (If you have a significant number of notes, see "Selecting the Strongest Statements" on page 251 for more details on narrowing your selection. For an example of how to use this process, see the Employee Benefits case study on page 219 of the Targeted Path.)

Strong voices are clear, concise, and specific. They often reflect personal experience. Weak voices are vague and imprecise. People often begin talking at a high level of abstraction, but later in the passage or after a probe make stronger, more detailed statements.

Examples of weak and strong voices

Weak Voice	Stronger Voice
"A briefcase to suit my needs must be made of vinyl."	"I travel weekly, so my bag gets banged and scratched by airport baggage handlers—plus, when I get to the construction site for the assessment, who knows where it will get put—on rough cement, an iron beam, gravel..."
"My briefcase is useless in bad weather."	"When my briefcase is full, the flap on the top doesn't fasten and the contents get wet in the rain."

Some team members may have difficulty letting go of so many customer statements. Having done the customer visits, all of the statements may seem important. To help with this, remember to do the following:

- Check back to the key question often

- Recognize that the process will help the team focus on the most important issues without getting lost in a sea of data

- Remember that issues chosen symbolize others that are similar

- Check for omissions to make sure a key issue has not been neglected

Be careful that in selecting the strongest statements you do not lose sight of the diverse viewpoints represented. To get a 360° view, sometimes you will need to include a weak statement that represents a different perspective. Think of the statements chosen as being symbolic of others.

Selecting the Strongest Statements

One way to narrow down your statements to a manageable number and, at the same time, sort out the strongest notes is to use the Method for Priority Marking™. This method involves four steps: sorting, unrestrained pickup, focused pickup, and final check.*

Sorting

Start by posting all the notes on one or more sheets of flipchart paper. To find notes representing similar thoughts, you may find it helpful to sort the notes into general categories, using whatever categories come to mind.

Unrestrained Pickup

Next, focus on those notes that seem to best reflect your theme. Working simultaneously, team members should mark a red dot on the lower right corner of notes they think are worth keeping. Individually read through all the notes and look for those that are specific or clearly expressed. Look also for notes that represent or symbolize different perspectives, even though they may not be stated as well as some of the others. The objective is to eventually eliminate notes that are repetitious without losing a 360° view. It is best for everyone to work silently. There are no limits to how many notes may

be marked, but each note should get only one dot. This is not voting; if someone likes a note that already has a dot on it, he or she should simply leave it and move on. When everyone is finished, remove the unmarked notes (but save them in case you need them later to answer any questions).

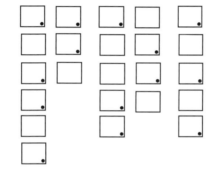

If you have more than 35 to 40 notes left, go through the marking process again, adding a second dot to the notes you want to keep. At the end of this round, remove all notes that have only one dot on them. Continue with additional rounds until you get down to about 35 to 40 notes.

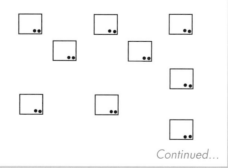

Continued...

* See Appendix B for more information on the Method for Priority Marking™.

Focused Pickup

To narrow your choices to roughly 24 notes, divide 24 by the number of people on the team. This is the number of final selections each person gets. If the answer is not a whole number, round up. For instance, if you have a team of seven, each person gets four selections. Each person, in turn, selects one note that he or she thinks is important to keep, reads the note aloud, and explains why it is important. The note is then moved to one side and the next person selects a note, reads it aloud, and explains the selection. The rotations continue until all have completed their specified number of selections.

Final Check

Finally, check to make sure a 360° view has been preserved. Look over the notes that were not selected in the focused pickup and decide if any need to be added. Discuss the notes that have been selected to make sure everyone has a common understanding of their meaning. At this point you should have a workable number of voices that provide clear, strong, and diverse perspectives of your question.

In this illustration, six team members are selecting from notes chosen in unrestrained pickup and placing their selections to the right. Three team members have made three selections each, whereas the other three have made only two selections so far. In the end, each team member will get four selections in this round for a total of 24 notes.

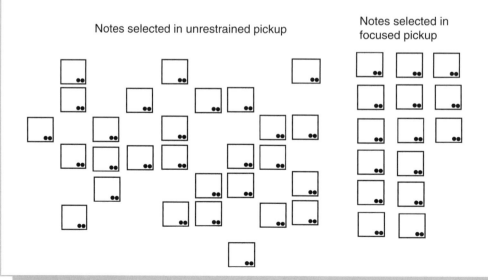

Notes selected in unrestrained pickup

Notes selected in focused pickup

Step R15 Check

Check to make sure the statements you have selected represent key customer concerns. You should have

❏ Customer need statements representing relevant voices from your interviews

❏ An emerging sense of your customers' concerns and requirements

The Big Picture

Requirements Path

R15.   Identify Key Customer Concerns

R16.   Construct Requirement Statements

R17.   Assess Requirement Priorities

Prework

- Identify relevant customer voices
- Identify strongest customer statements, if necessary

Time and Logistics

If you are using the complete set of customer voices, the team should begin this step by translating requirements as a group. Once people become comfortable with the work, the team can split into small groups of two or three to work independently on different voices. This step can take at least 8 hours and ideally should be completed in two or three half-day sessions.

If you have selected only the strongest customer voices, this step will take approximately 4 hours and should be completed by the entire team working together.

Supplies and Equipment

- Copies of relevant customer voices on 3" x 3" self-stick notes
- Flipchart or overhead projector
- Flipchart markers or overhead pens
- Overhead transparencies, if necessary

Outcomes

- A set of requirement statements

Step R16:

Construct Requirement Statements

Description

The purpose of this step is to develop a set of key requirements that describe as accurately as possible what customers need. You will translate each customer voice into language that describes specific, unambiguous performance requirements for the product, service, process, or policy you are designing or redesigning.

Benefits

People often run into difficulty when they try to act on the Voice of the Customer because their customers have described their needs either in vague language or in terms of specific solutions. This step will help you identify the requirements necessary to develop a solution in the next phase of the FOCUS process, Select Action.

Getting Your Bearings

The key customer concerns you identified in the previous step were not all worded as requirements. Some were needs, some were images, others were proposed solutions, and some just expressed general concerns. To take meaningful action, you need to understand these concerns in terms of requirements. This step helps you translate concerns into requirements upon which action can be taken. You will repeat the substeps listed here for each of your customer voices.

This work can be tedious and requires patience and clear thinking. Do this work when the team is fresh. Most teams report that the efforts here to understand their customers' stated and unstated requirements paid off immensely in developing the best solutions for their customers.

Once you have identified all of your customer requirements, you will prioritize them in the next step. The most important requirements will be the focus of your work in Select Action, the final phase of the FOCUS process.

How to Construct Requirement Statements

A. Write customer voice on a translation worksheet

In this substep you will use a translation worksheet, similar to the one on page 258, to translate customer concerns into requirements. To start the process, choose one voice and write it on a translation worksheet. You will eventually complete a worksheet for all of the voices, working through them one at a time.

Sometimes a customer voice can be dry, without much contextual information. However, during your customer visits you may have seen or heard something that would help to enrich the voice. Whether it is an image you saw during your observations or an image that was conjured up by a story you heard, you can add these to your customer voice on the translation worksheet.

If you are translating all of the customer requirements, it is best to work in interview teams to do the translation work. It would take a significant amount of time for the entire group to translate all of the requirements. Due to the volume of requirements, team members will still be exposed to a broad perspective in the voices they translate.

Example of a customer voice

Customer Voice

"I need a really tough briefcase."

(Image: "I travel weekly, so my bag gets banged and scratched by airport baggage handlers—plus, when I get to the construction site for the assessment, who knows where it will get put—on rough cement, an iron beam, gravel...")

Key Items

Customer Requirements/Needs

R

A translation worksheet consists of three key elements as described below.

Translation worksheet

Customer Voice

This is a verbatim phrase, sentence, or group of sentences taken from the interview notes. Include only one voice per worksheet.

(You can also add images that you saw or heard during your customer visits to help provide context for the voice. Images may or may not be verbatim statements).

Key Items

Key items can be almost any issues or considerations that come to mind when you think about the voice in the context of any images you may have included. They serve as a bridge between the customer voice and the requirement statement.

Customer Requirements/Needs

A concise one-sentence statement that describes the functionality or performance requirement you will need to address in order to fulfill your customers' needs. It is possible you will identify more than one requirement from a single voice.

 Use a flipchart or an overhead projector to complete the worksheets.

Using Images to Understand Requirements*

As you move from customer voices to requirements, you will recall images of your customers' environment. It can be difficult to understand what the customer really needs, and an understanding of their environment often helps get at the real issues.

Anecdotes will provide you with vivid images and rich detail. Storytelling often moves individuals to a more emotional level of experience, and it is from this basis that much of their behavior is motivated. The following story shows how an anecdote helped a team better understand customers' pharmaceutical needs.

A pharmacy merger team heard in some of their interviews about the impact of polypharmacy. What made the issue vivid was the rich detail in a nurse's anecdote of an elderly woman coming to a clinic with a brown grocery bag filled with medications. She was taking fifteen different medications prescribed by several physicians. This story conveyed a concern about the potential adverse effects when patients unwittingly combine drugs prescribed by multiple doctors who are unaware of the other prescriptions. The team framed some of their requirement statements around this concern.

Seeing customers in their own environment is also a powerful experience that can add insight into how customers might use a product or service, or what latent needs they may have. The following story shows what one team learned by observing their customers' environment.

A team was designing a piece of equipment for shops in Europe. As part of their interviews, they visited some shops to be sure their designs would work. They discovered that available floor space and surfaces were so limited that few retailers could use the equipment they had designed because there would be no place to put it. This image helped them understand the retailers' requirement for a compact piece of equipment in a more concrete way than interviews alone could have done.

In both these cases, images provided the team with contextual anchors that helped them frame their requirements. Because each interview team gathers different images on their visits, it is valuable at this point for the entire group to share their images. One method for sharing is to catalog the images into a single list to which you can refer as you complete your translation worksheets.

*See Appendix B for more information on images and their use in Concept Engineering™.

B. Identify key items related to the customer voice

No hard-and-fast rules exist about what is or is not a key item. Use this space on the translation worksheet to free-associate, jotting down words or sentences that capture issues you identify with the customer voice. These could be things you heard in the interviews, observations you made in the workplace, or related images that come to mind. If you have an image of the customer's environment that you have included with the Customer Voice, use it to help you generate more accurate or vivid key ideas.

As you complete a worksheet for each voice, you may identify key items already listed on other worksheets and translated into requirements. Take a moment to ask if there is anything new about this voice that you may have missed. Sometimes linking the voice with a different image can create new key ideas and requirements. If not, lay the worksheet aside and proceed to the next one. You can always come back to it later.

 If you have trouble thinking of key items, identify the significant words in the voice and use them to spark key ideas.

The following example illustrates some key items for the previous customer voice and related image.

Examples of key items

Customer Voice

"I need a really tough briefcase."

(Image: "I travel weekly, so my bag gets banged and scratched by airport baggage handlers—plus, when get to the construction site for the assessment, who knows where it will get put—on rough cement, an iron beam, gravel...")

Key Items

- Durable exterior
- Rugged construction
- Must stand up to daily rough wear and tear

Customer Requirements/Needs

C. Write a requirement statement

Writing a good requirement statement is often an iterative process. Rather than trying to write a perfect requirement statement the first time, it often helps to get down some words and then refine them to meet the criteria in the following table. The examples on the right page illustrate the difference between statements that do not meet the criteria below and statements that do.

Requirement statement criteria and examples

1. **Identify a functional need, not a solution.**
   A functional need tells what the solution should do; a solution tells how it should be accomplished.

2. **Be as concrete and specific as possible.**
   Abstract or vague terms allow for multiple interpretations.

3. **Use multivalued language.**
   Multivalued language lets you measure a requirement along a scale. If a requirement is either present or absent, it is not multivalued. You may have to make some trade-offs in requirements when you develop a solution. Having multivalued requirements will allow you more flexibility in your final design. Words such as "easily," "slowly," "freely," "thoroughly," and "completely" convey a multivalued degree of desired performance.

4. **Phrase the statement in positive language.**
   The word "not" indicates a weakness-oriented requirement statement.

The language you use in your requirement statements will also help make them clear and unambiguous.

- Use a simple sentence structure: subject—verb—modifier.

- Use action verbs; avoid "is" and "are."

- Avoid "must" or "should." These words usually indicate a lack of multivalued language.

- Use of "and" usually indicates more than one requirement.

Solution	Functional Need
The bag should be made of vinyl	The bag is durable
Mail statements 2nd day after closing	User accesses information

Vague	Specific
The bag is durable	Exterior of the bag resists abrasion
User accesses information	User accesses monthly charges at the close of the month

Yes/No Value	Multivalued
Bag fits under airplane seat	Bag fits easily under airplane seat
User accesses monthly charges at the close of the month	User accesses monthly charges promptly after the close of the month

Negative Language	Positive Language
User does not have to use a hand to carry the bag	User optionally carries bag hands-free
Computer-based training program does not require purchase of new equipment	Computer-based training program runs effectively on existing equipment

The following example illustrates a customer requirement for the previous customer voice and key items shown earlier on page 261.

Example of a customer requirement

Customer Voice

"I need a really tough briefcase."

(Image: "I travel weekly, so my bag gets banged and scratched by airport baggage handlers—plus, when I get to the construction site for the assessment, who knows where it will get put—on rough cement, an iron beam, gravel…")

Key Items

- Durable exterior
- Rugged construction
- Must stand up to daily rough wear and tear

Customer Requirements/Needs

Exterior of bag resists abrasion from wear and tear of daily handling.

The table on the next page shows how teams translated customer voices into requirements for several different projects.

Examples of translated customer voices

Customer Voice	Key Items	Customer Requirements
"I want to be reassured on paper that you have the parts there to support us."	reassurance, insurance high risk, not in control	Merchant checks status of the service easily, at any time
"We lose money by the minute when we can't get replacement parts." (Image: The conveyor belt did not move the entire time we were in the factory)	downtime, waiting for parts, buyers, expensive	Out-of-stock situations affect installers minimally
"Sending spreadsheets back and forth between site buyers and suppliers is a nightmare."	data, back and forth, spreadsheets, difficult	The supplier and customer share timely data easily
"Sometimes it is pretty hot. When having a bath you've got to put a lot of cold water in as well."	warm water, temperatures, temperature control	User adjusts warm water temperature easily
"If there's a fault in that particular item, we know it's going to get dealt with promptly and efficiently." (Image: "Can you believe it? I was transferred three times and *still* didn't have an answer.")	merchants operating effective businesses	Merchants access prompt help from manufacturers when a problem arises Merchants access efficient help from manufacturers when a problem arises

 If you are having trouble coming up with a requirement statement for a voice, put it aside and come back to it later. Do not try to force requirements.

Team members may not always agree on customer requirements because they interpret customer voices and key items differently. This is to be expected, given that individuals have different backgrounds and heard different interviews. Exploring these differences can help lead to new understandings and creative opportunities. It may be that a difference in understanding implies two requirements. If so, include both.

You may also identify potential solutions during this work. Do not try to disguise these solutions as requirements, but do not discard them either. Write them down and put them aside. You can come back to them in the next phase of work, Select Action.

When you are satisfied with your requirement statement, go back to the original customer voice and, keeping in mind your list of images, see if any other requirement statements can be derived from it. It is not uncommon to get multiple requirements from a single voice.

When you are satisfied that you have identified all of the requirements behind a single voice, select the next voice and repeat the process.

Requirement Statement Checklist

- ❏ The statement identifies a functional need rather than a solution

- ❏ It is concrete and as specific as possible

- ❏ It uses multivalued language, which allows the requirement to be measured on a scale

- ❏ The requirement is stated in the active voice with an action verb

- ❏ The statement is worded positively, without the word "not"

- ❏ The statement clearly expresses what is intended

- ❏ The statement is consistent with the voice from which it was derived

The following case study illustrates how the document management team translated a customer voice into requirements.

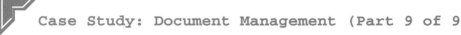

Case Study: Document Management (Part 9 of 9)

The team selected their first customer voice and wrote it at the top of a translation worksheet.

Customer Voice

"I need to have both a PC and a Mac at my workstation."

Key Items

They recognized that although the voice was stated as a need, it was really a solution to an unstated problem. So they discussed what they thought was key to this issue. They thought back to things they had heard and seen in their interviews. As they talked, they realized that this voice could be interpreted in different ways. They decided to start with graphics concerns, which were a problem for many customers they interviewed. When they completed the requirements related to graphics, they could look at the issue from other perspectives.

The team came up with three key items related to the need for a PC and a Mac when working with graphics, as shown below.

Customer Voice

"I need to have both a PC and a Mac at my workstation."

Key Items

- Creating graphics once and accessing from PC & Mac
- Accessing old docs created in MacDraw via a PC
- Macs & PCs handle graphics differently so there are changes in translation

Customer Requirements/Needs

Continued...

Next, the team was ready to identify a functional need behind this voice.

Their first attempt at writing a requirement statement was "User creates graphics anywhere in the system to be accessed anywhere in the system." This statement was too broad and covered two separate issues, creating graphics and accessing graphics. Therefore they separated the two issues and focused first on creating graphics: "Any user creates graphics anywhere in the system."

This statement was still not specific enough. What did "anywhere in the system" really mean? Also, the language was not multivalued: either people could or could not do it. To remedy these faults, they created two separate requirements and added the word "easily."

Customer Voice

"I need to have both a PC and a Mac at my workstation."

Key Items
- Creating graphics once and accessing from PC & Mac
- Accessing old docs created in MacDraw via a PC
- Macs & PCs handle graphics differently so there are changes in translation

Customer Requirements/Needs

~~User creates graphics anywhere in the system to be accessed anywhere in the system~~

~~Any user creates graphics anywhere in the system~~

Any user creates graphics easily from any platform in the system

Any user creates graphics easily from any geographic location

---

Continued...

Because the team had started with the need to both create and access graphics and then narrowed the focus to creating graphics, they now went back and developed parallel requirements for accessing graphics. From this first round of translation on the first voice, they developed four separate requirements.

Customer Voice

"I need to have both a PC and a Mac at my workstation."

Key Items

- Creating graphics once and accessing from PC & Mac
- Accessing old docs created in MacDraw via a PC
- Macs & PCs handle graphics differently so there are changes in translation

Customer Requirements/Needs

1. Any user creates graphics easily from any platform in the system
2. Any user creates graphics easily from any geographic location
3. Any user accesses graphics easily from any platform in the system
4. Any user accesses graphics easily from any geographic location

---

Continued...

Now it was time for the team to go back to the same customer voice and repeat the process from other perspectives. This time they added an image that one team member had observed of someone sitting in a coworker's area to do her work. This image led to related key ideas and eventually to another requirement statement.

Customer Voice

"I need to have both a PC and a Mac at my workstation."

(Image: Jan sitting at Sue's desk to create overheads to accompany a presentation because her computer didn't support the right software)

Key Items

- Creating diverse kinds of documents in the same system
- Presentations done on one platform; handouts done on another

Customer Requirements/Needs

User creates related documents efficiently on any platform

After the team had completed requirement statements for four different voices, they felt confident enough in the process to divide into pairs to work through the rest of the voices. When they were done, they would compile their completed worksheets and begin work on the next step.

R

Step R16 Check

Check to make sure you have translated customer needs into action-oriented requirements. You should have

❏ A set of requirement statements

The Big Picture

Requirements Path

R15. Identify Key Customer Concerns

R16. Construct Requirement Statements

R17. Assess Requirement Priorities

Prework

- Complete requirement translation worksheets for each customer voice

Time and Logistics

This step involves two distinct types of activities. First, the whole team creates an affinity diagram of the requirement statements. This work takes approximately 4 hours. Next, allow 1 hour to prepare a survey to find out what customers consider to be priorities. The time needed to send out the survey will vary depending on the nature of your project. Finally, it is important to remember that it can take from several days to a month or more to get the surveys back.

Supplies and Equipment

- Copy of customer requirement statements
- 3" x 3" self-stick notes
- Black, red, and blue pens for each participant
- Flipchart paper
- Black flipchart marker
- Tape or pushpins

Outcomes

- 24 or fewer key requirements
- Affinity diagram showing relationships among requirements
- Priority ranking of key requirements based on customer feedback

Step R17:

Assess Requirement Priorities

Description

In this step you will identify the strongest requirement statements and create an affinity diagram. Then you will prioritize these requirements with feedback from your customers.

Benefits

Even if you have translated only the strongest customer voices in the interviews, you are still likely to have a large number of requirement statements. Trying to address all of these requirements simultaneously is not only impossible but unnecessary, because not all of them will be equally important to your customers. This step helps you identify which requirements are most critical.

Getting Your Bearings

In the last step you used divergent thinking to create as many different requirements as possible. Now you will switch to convergent thinking to select the strongest requirements. By thinking broadly before becoming more focused, you are maximizing your possibilities and helping ensure that your final selection will include the strongest of all possible requirements.

In the final phase of the FOCUS process, you will use these requirements to design an appropriate solution.

How to Assess Requirement Priorities

A. Select the strongest requirements

If you selected two dozen voices and translated them you may have 35 to 40 requirements. If you translated all of the voices you may have hundreds of requirement statements. In either case, before you start looking at solutions, you need to identify those requirements that will have the greatest potential for delighting your customers.

- Transcribe all of the requirement statements onto self-stick notes.

- A key question that will help frame your thinking as you select the strongest statements is "What are the key customer requirements for _____?"

- Use the Method for Priority Marking™* (see "Selecting the Strongest Statements" on page 251) to identify about two dozen of the most important requirements.

B. Create Level 1 groupings

The next step is to discover the overlap between your requirements. This will help you focus your thinking when you start generating solutions in the final phase of the FOCUS process. The affinity diagram technique described here is designed to help you move slowly up the ladder of abstraction from specific requirements to broad themes. (For additional help in creating groups and titles, see "Affinity Diagrams" on page 277.)

Begin this work of creating groupings silently to avoid interrupting others' train of thought. Toward the end of this activity, however, people may have questions about why notes are being moved, and this discussion can provide new insights.

- Spread the notes randomly on a flipchart.

- Group the requirements into small clusters that reflect a common, yet fairly concrete, theme. Try to keep these themes at a low level of abstraction,

*See Appendix B for more information on the Method for Priority Marking™.

only one rung up from the requirements themselves. You should have no more than two or three notes in each group because what is common to a larger group will be too high on the ladder of abstraction.

- Avoid cause-and-effect groupings; these do not have an overlapping common element. Your intent in this part of the process is to gain insight by moving up the ladder of abstraction from the fairly concrete statements to a higher conceptual level. Cause-and-effect relationships will make it difficult to do this.

- Keep moving the requirements around until you have approximately 8 to 12 groups.

The first groupings will probably reflect connections you already are aware of or the similarity of words used. To reach new understandings, it is necessary to try new combinations based on different kinds of similarities.

The example on the next page illustrates how the clusters for an affinity diagram for the redesign of a pharmacy system differed from the broad categories that had been used in the Method for Priority Marking™.

Example of MPM categories vs. affinity diagram clusters

Sample of notes from the MPM process

Pharmacy Systems	**Drug Therapy**	**Collaboration**
Delivery system reduces the opportunity for human error significantly	Physician relies on pharmacist for collaboration re: drug therapy decisions	Pharmacist & physician participate "face to face" in the care of the patient
Redesigned pharmacy system accommodates increasing # of ambulatory patients' need for meds	Pharmacists participate on patient care teams influencing drug therapy outcomes	Pharmacists' involvement in pathway design improves outcomes
Pharmacy information systems integrate inpatient and outpatient data	Patients readily access drug therapy regardless of the ability to pay	Pharmacists participate in educating residents, med. students, and faculty re: clinical pathways, algorithm, & care guidelines
Pharmacy systems reduce potential harm resulting from the clinical effects of polypharmacy	Patients trust pharmacist to assess appropriateness of medical order	

Sample of how notes were reclustered into Level 1 groupings

What these three notes have in common:
Delivery system reduces the potential for error

Delivery system reduces the opportunity for human error significantly

(Pharmacy Sys.)

Incidences of error reliably prompt corrective action (including education)
(Not shown previously)

Pharmacy systems reduce potential harm resulting from the clinical effects of polypharmacy
(Pharmacy Sys.)

What these two notes have in common:
Pharmacists collaborate with physicians to optimize drug therapy

Physician relies on pharmacist for collaboration re: drug therapy decisions

(Drug Therapy)

Pharmacist & physician participate "face to face" in the care of the patient

(Collaboration)

Affinity Diagrams

An affinity diagram helps you group items so you can see what they have in common.* In the FOCUS process, we recommend that you keep the number of notes in a group relatively small. This should be fairly easy because you have already reduced your number of notes.

Create Level 1 Groupings

Begin by writing "What are the key customer requirements for _____?" in the upper left corner of two flipchart pages taped side by side on a wall. Spread all the requirement notes randomly on the paper. Then start grouping the requirements, looking for common themes. It is natural to want to group requirements into cause-and-effect relationships; that is, one requirement is the cause of another. It is better in the long run not to do this. Instead, look for notes that share a common element.

If you start getting groupings larger than two or three notes, you are probably working at too high a level of abstraction. Break the groups apart, looking for the subtle distinctions among them. Sometimes single notes do not relate to any others and will continue to stand alone.

Keep moving the notes around, remembering they can always be moved back. This helps you see con-nections you might not have noticed at first. Making and breaking connections is how you will often gain new insights. You should end up with 8 to 12 clusters.

Create Level 1 Titles

Write a title requirement that cap-tures the common theme in each group. These titles are critical because they will become the basis for what-ever solutions you decide are neces-sary.

Level 1 titles should be fairly specific and are easier to write if you have only 2 or 3 notes in the grouping. If the title is too abstract, it will be dif-ficult to use later in the process.

A good way to create titles is to start with key words or phrases that reflect what the requirements have in com-mon. Then write a new requirement that relates the concept reflected in the notes to the key question. When possible, use action verbs in your titles. When the title is complete, print it in red on a self-stick note and place it at the top of the grouping.

Sometimes you may find that one of the notes actually works well as a title. In that case, simply draw a red box around the text to distinguish it from the other notes and move it into position as the title.

Continued...

*See Appendix B, Language Processing Method™, for information on a more rigorous method for grouping notes.

Once you have titles for all your groups, check to see if any single notes now fit into one of the groupings. Sometimes having clarified the groupings through titling helps you see how another note is related.

Create Level 2 Groupings

Repeat the clustering steps by looking for ways to group the Level 1 titles into common themes. Stack the groupings so that only the title can be seen on top. This focuses attention on the titles and not the underlying notes.

Again, aim for groupings of 2 or 3 titles. If you start getting larger groupings, you are probably working at too high a level of abstraction. A single note that remained ungrouped might now fit in a Level 2 group.

You will probably still move the groupings around. Sometimes you may find that several groupings can be made from the same set of titles. If you are not sure which is best, check to see which cluster best fits your key question. You should end up with 4 to 8 clusters.

Create Level 2 Titles

Again, write a title requirement that captures the common theme in each grouping. These titles are at a higher level of abstraction and will help you capture overall issues that will help you see the big picture. Identifying these larger issues helps people communicate with managers and others in the organization.

To create Level 2 titles, start with key words or phrases that reflect what the Level 1 titles have in common. Then write a sentence that relates the concept reflected in the titles to the key question. When the title is complete, print it in blue on a self-stick note and place it at the top of the group.

When you have all your Level 2 titles, check to see if any of the remaining single notes or Level 1 clusters now fit into one of the Level 2 groupings. Sometimes having clarified the groupings through titling helps you see how another note is related. If any Level 1 clusters or single notes do not fit into Level 2 groupings, they may remain alone.

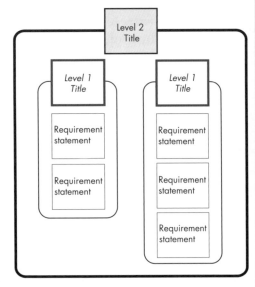

The following case study shows how one team created their Level 1 groupings.

Case Study: Product Development Process (Part 1 of 5)

A company wanted to learn more about what was needed to ensure success in developing new products. The project team started by asking: "What voices identify key issues, needs, problems, concerns, images, and solutions that will help us understand the requirements for a process to develop successful new products?" With this question in mind, they went through their interview transcripts and identified relevant concerns. Then they translated the concerns into requirement statements.

Next, they wrote a question to help them structure their data: "What are the key customer requirements for success in developing new products?" In this case, the word "customer" referred to people who were customers of the product development process, rather than the people who would ultimately purchase the products.

They placed all of the requirement notes up on flipchart paper and everyone read through them silently. Then they started looking for requirements that seemed to go together. One person found two she thought were related and moved them into a cluster. Other people found other groupings. As they worked, the groupings occasionally changed as people found new ways to think about the requirements.

As the process continued, fewer and fewer notes were moved. Team members gradually started stepping back to watch, satisfied with the clusters. Eventually, everyone was satisfied and the clusters were complete. One note stood alone. It was important, but it didn't seem to fit with any others. So it became a "cluster of one." The following illustration shows some of their Level 1 clusters.

Continued...

What are the key customer requirements for success in developing new products?

Reviewers on New Product Dev. teams confidently recommend stopping a program	Our culture, climate, structure & behavior systematically facilitate NPD	Marketing group aligns with other functions on its role in new product delivery	New Prod. Dev. teams document customer req'ts. early in the Product Delivery Process
NPD decision makers objectively evaluate all new product programs based on business criteria	Each business integrates a product development process	Corporate decision makers and prod. mgrs. align on roles and responsibilities of Program Mgrs.	NPD teams factor regional customer requirements into product requirements
Bus. Leaders make NPD commitments based on rigorous, quantifiable assessment of risk	Corporate Officers champion the Product Dev. Process	Functional mgrs. readily provide Prod. Mgrs. with the required deliverables in a timely manner	New Product Dev. teams readily access customer feedback during all phases of the PD Process

New Product Dev. team members commit the % of time necessary to feel ownership for a given program	Review participants reliably follow through on promised actions
Key functional team members predictably stay with a program from concept through commercialization	

C. Write Level 1 titles

Identify what is common in each Level 1 grouping and write a concise title. These titles should be written in the same requirements language as the original requirement statements, but they should be at a slightly higher level of abstraction. In addition to showing the connections among the requirement notes, the Level 1 titles must be concrete and operable. These titles will serve as the foundation for the solution you decide on in Select Action. If they are not written as clear requirements it will be difficult to complete the FOCUS process. Take the time now to phrase the Level 1 titles so that they meet the criteria for good requirement statements. (See page 262)

The tendency at first is to write titles that simply repeat everything in the original notes. Instead, the title needs to represent the common link between the notes.

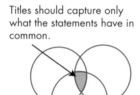

Titles should capture only what the statements have in common.

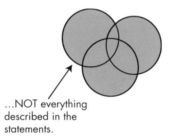

...NOT everything described in the statements.

You may find it works best for the group to discuss the notes and come up with a single title, or you may prefer to have each person write his or her own title for each cluster. You can then select the one that seems best or combine ideas into a single new title.

 Be wary of titles that are too long to fit on a self-stick note, or that contain the word "and."

 Avoid cause-and-effect relationships; that is, do not pick a title that is the cause or the result of the statements in the grouping.

Examples of Level 1 titles

Level 1 Grouping	Possible Level 1 Titles		
Delivery system reduces the opportunity for human error significantly Incidences of error reliably prompt corrective action (including education) Pharmacy systems reduce potential harm resulting from the clinical effect of polypharmacy	*Delivery system reduces error, prompting corrective action when errors do occur, especially with regard to polypharmacy* This title is really not a summary. It is the total of everything written on the notes.	*Redesigned pharmacy system delivers the "right" drug to the right patient at the right time* This title is too high on the ladder of abstraction. It encompasses more than what is expressed in the three notes.	*Redesigned pharmacy system continually reduces the potential for error* This title is better for this group of notes because it captures what they have in common at an appropriately specific level of abstraction.

The next case study follows the product development team as they write titles for their Level 1 groupings.

R

Case Study: Product Development Process (Part 2 of 5)

Once the team was satisfied with their Level 1 clusters, they tried to write a single requirement statement higher on the ladder of abstraction that would capture the similarities among all of the requirements in the cluster. Writing the Level 1 titles in the form of new requirement statements was not always easy. The following diagram shows four of their clusters and the titles they selected for three of the clusters. The requirement note that was ungrouped was placed on the same level as the Level 1 titles.

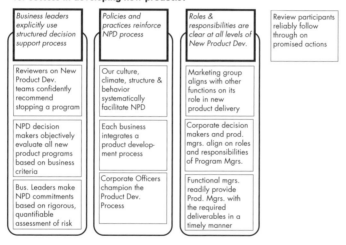

What are the key customer requirements for success in developing new products?

Business leaders explicitly use structured decision support process	Policies and practices reinforce NPD process	Roles & responsibilities are clear at all levels of New Product Dev.	Review participants reliably follow through on promised actions
Reviewers on New Product Dev. teams confidently recommend stopping a program	Our culture, climate, structure & behavior systematically facilitate NPD	Marketing group aligns with other functions on its role in new product delivery	
NPD decision makers objectively evaluate all new product programs based on business criteria	Each business integrates a product development process	Corporate decision makers and prod. mgrs. align on roles and responsibilities of Program Mgrs.	
Bus. Leaders make NPD commitments based on rigorous, quantifiable assessment of risk	Corporate Officers champion the Product Dev. Process	Functional mgrs. readily provide Prod. Mgrs. with the required deliverables in a timely manner	

For the grouping on the far left, the team discussed how these requirements were all things that needed to be done by people who make or control decisions in order to have a clearly defined decision process. But that was too long.

"People who make and/or control decisions" became "business leaders" because it was more succinct.

"Clearly defined decision process" became "structured decision support process" because it more accurately reflected what was important in the notes.

Their final Level 1 title for this cluster became: "Business leaders explicitly use structured decision support process."

D. Create Level 2 groupings

> Stack the groupings so that only the title can be seen on top. This focuses attention on the titles and not the underlying notes.

Repeat the clustering steps, but this time cluster the Level 1 titles rather than the individual notes. This second round of grouping helps identify larger themes that can provide a broader frame of reference for your thinking.

- Look for groups of two to three titles that have something in common. At this point you can also include single, ungrouped notes in these new clusters. You should end up with four to eight clusters.

- Once again, avoid cause-and-effect relationships within groupings.

- Begin by working silently. Each team member will probably see different ways to create groupings. Trying to see what others see will help everyone gain a deeper understanding of the issues.

- Sometimes you may find that several groupings can be made from the same set of Level 1 titles. If you are not sure which is best, check to see which cluster best fits your key question.

Here is how the product development process team created their Level 2 groupings.

Case Study: Product Development Process (Part 3 of 5)

The team stacked each cluster of requirements so that the Level 1 title was on top. Then they looked for ways to create new clusters with the titles.

As before, the clusters kept changing. Each team member would see different relationships and different ways of grouping the notes. The following diagram shows some of their Level 2 clusters. The single note became part of a cluster, but now there was one Level 1 cluster that stood alone.

Continued...

The illustration below shows three of the team's Level 2 groupings.

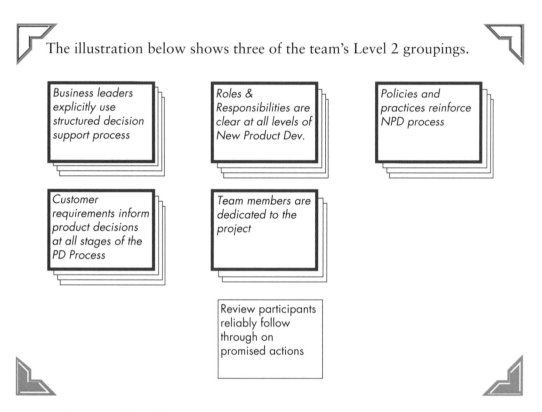

E. Write Level 2 titles

Repeat the titling steps to find a concise summary title for each Level 2 grouping. These titles should answer your key question. Team members may resist working at this level of abstraction. It may seem that the summaries lose all the power of the customer statements. The affinity diagram will preserve all levels of abstraction—the customer voices and the summaries.

- Identify what is common in each Level 2 grouping.

- Write a title that is only one rung higher on the ladder of abstraction than the Level 1 titles.

- Avoid cause-and-effect relationships.

Write a title as a team or have each person write his or her own title; then either select the best one or combine ideas into a single new title.

The product development process team was now ready to write their Level 2 titles.

Case Study: Product Development Process (Part 4 of 5)

When they had created the new groupings, the team needed to find new titles that would identify what these clusters had in common. Once again, they needed to move up the ladder of abstraction.

For the cluster on the far left, they decided that the two Level 1 titles were about the importance of making good decisions both as a member of the team and in support of the team. But that just seemed to sum up the two titles, rather than moving up the ladder of abstraction. In the end, they selected: "Business leaders base new Product Development decisions on thorough analysis" because that was what the two titles had in common.

For the Level 1 cluster that was not part of a larger Level 2 grouping, they did not need to write a new summary title.

The new titles were written in blue on self-stick notes and placed above their respective groupings. Even at this level the team still tried to word their titles in the form of requirements.

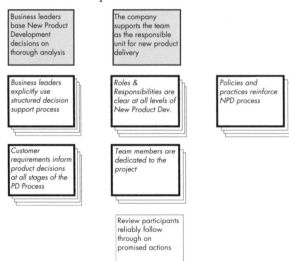

F. Lay out the affinity diagram

If you placed the self-stick notes on top of each other while you were sorting, spread them out again into the appropriate clusters so that you can see each individual note. If you need more space, add another sheet of flipchart paper.

- Draw black lines around each Level 1 grouping.

- Draw heavy black lines around each Level 2 grouping.

- Tape the notes to the paper to make this a more permanent document.

- Write the date on the final diagram. You may also want to add the name of the team and each team member. Some teams sign their names as a way of acknowledging their consensus.

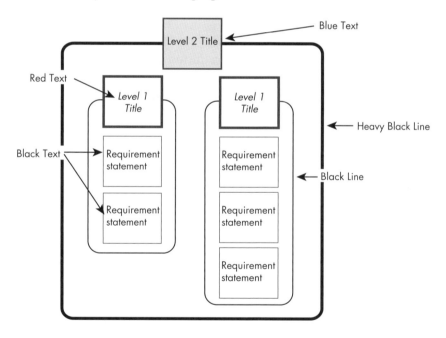

The next case study shows how the product development process team finished structuring their data.

Case Study: Product Development Process (Part 5 of 5)

To complete their affinity diagram, the team spread out the notes on the flipchart paper so they could all be read and then drew black lines around each of the Level 1 groupings with the red Level 1 title at the top.

Next, they drew heavy black lines around the new Level 2 groupings, to distinguish them from the Level 1 groupings, and put the blue Level 2 titles at the top.

When the team begins brainstorming possible solutions, they will be working with the Level 1 titles. But they need to be able to see clearly both the "big picture" provided by the Level 2 titles and all of the details provided by the individual requirements.

A portion of their final affinity diagram is on the following page.

Continued…

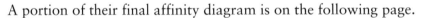

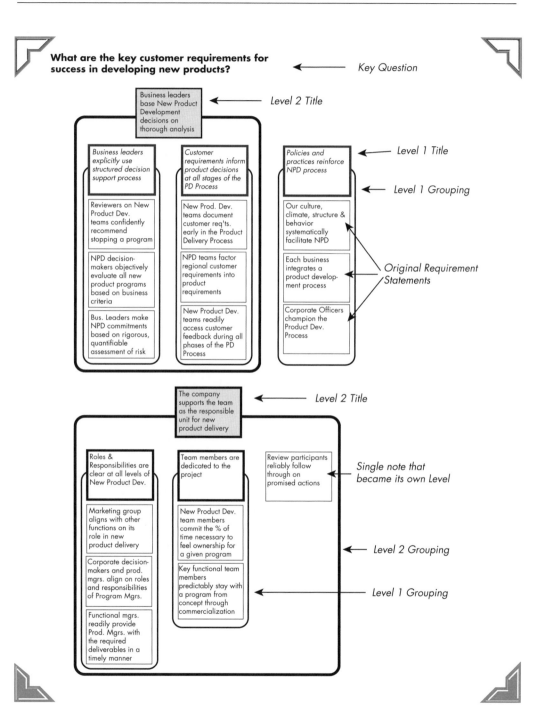

What are the key customer requirements for success in developing new products? ← Key Question

Business leaders base New Product Development decisions on thorough analysis ← Level 2 Title

Business leaders explicitly use structured decision support process ← Level 1 Title

Customer requirements inform product decisions at all stages of the PD Process

Policies and practices reinforce NPD process

← Level 1 Grouping

Reviewers on New Product Dev. teams confidently recommend stopping a program

New Prod. Dev. teams document customer req'ts. early in the Product Delivery Process

Our culture, climate, structure & behavior systematically facilitate NPD

NPD decision-makers objectively evaluate all new product programs based on business criteria

NPD teams factor regional customer requirements into product requirements

Each business integrates a product development process

← Original Requirement Statements

Bus. Leaders make NPD commitments based on rigorous, quantifiable assessment of risk

New Product Dev. teams readily access customer feedback during all phases of the PD Process

Corporate Officers champion the Product Dev. Process

The company supports the team as the responsible unit for new product delivery ← Level 2 Title

Roles & Responsibilities are clear at all levels of New Product Dev.

Team members are dedicated to the project

Review participants reliably follow through on promised actions

← Single note that became its own Level

Marketing group aligns with other functions on its role in new product delivery

New Product Dev. team members commit the % of time necessary to feel ownership for a given program

Corporate decision-makers and prod. mgrs. align on roles and responsibilities of Program Mgrs.

Key functional team members predictably stay with a program from concept through commercialization

← Level 2 Grouping

← Level 1 Grouping

Functional mgrs. readily provide Prod. Mgrs. with the required deliverables in a timely manner

R

G. Identify priorities

You have identified what you think are the most important requirements by interviewing a representative sample of your customers. A broader sample of customers should now prioritize the requirements on your affinity diagram. The questionnaire on page 291 is one common tool that will help you do this. Your organization may have other standard or preferred tools for this step.

- If you are developing a commercial product or service, get your marketing department involved in gathering customer input regarding your selected requirements. Telephone or mail surveys are often used to sample the opinions of your customers. There should be a direct correlation between the sample size and the level of risk associated with the development of your product or service.

- If you are working on an internal project or do not have a marketing department to provide support, you should still develop an Importance Questionnaire or a similar feedback device to get input from your customers.

- A rule of thumb is to survey approximately 100 – 150 customers for each market segment. If you created more than one customer profile matrix, each matrix represents one market segment. Sometimes, you will start with a single customer profile matrix, but as a result of your interviews you will find that one group of interviewees is very different than the rest. In this case, you should consider this different group as possibly representing a second market segment and should survey approximately 100 – 150 customers in *each* group. If you have a small customer base, or are doing an internal survey, and you do not have 100 people to survey, try to reach everyone possible.

- It is important to get a significant return rate for surveys to be meaningful. Experience shows that it is not unusual to get a 50% to 60% return rate for this type of survey. However, there are three steps you can take to help make sure you get enough surveys back: 1) Provide an incentive that has some value. This can be as simple as a report on the survey results. 2) Contact customers before sending out the survey to let them know you value their participation. 3) Follow-up with participants if you do not get a response.

Importance Questionnaire

The Importance Questionnaire is one method for gathering customer feedback to prioritize your requirements. Distribute the questionnaire to everyone you interviewed, as well as other customers if at all possible, and have them rate the importance of each requirement on a scale of 1 to 9. (You can also use a scale of 1 to 5 if you prefer.)

For each requirement statement, ask "How important is it or would it be if...?" Then have the customers rate the requirement on a scale from "Not at all important" to "Extremely important."

When the questionnaires are returned, add up the ratings for each requirement, and then divide by the number of responses to get the average rating. You will usually see a small cluster of requirements with top scores. These will be your most important requirements. A second small cluster often occurs within the top ten requirements. These would become your secondary requirements.

Numerous books and articles can provide you with additional information on conducting market surveys.[5,6]

How important is it or would it be if:	Not at all important		Somewhat important		Important		Very important		Extremely important
Our culture, climate, structure and behavior systematically facilitate new product development	1	2	3	4	5	6	7	8	9
Each business integrates a product development process	1	2	3	4	5	6	7	8	9
Corporate officers champion the product development process	1	2	3	4	5	6	7	8	9

[5] Abbie Griffin and John R. Hauser, "The Voice of the Customer," *Marketing Science*, 12, No. 1 (Winter 1993): 1-27.

[6] Glen L. Urban and John R. Hauser, *Design and Marketing of New Products*, [Rev. ed.] (Englewood Cliffs: NJ: Prentice Hall, 1993).

Step R17 Check

Check to make sure you understand which requirements are most important to your customers. You should have

❏ About 24 of the strongest requirements

❏ An affinity diagram showing the relationships among the requirements

❏ Feedback from your customers about which requirements are most important

Section Summary

You have now worked through the Requirements Path of Understand the Voices. You should have completed the following:

❏ Identified relevant statements in the interview notes

❏ Translated customer voices into customer requirements

❏ Created an affinity diagram showing what your customer requirements had in common

❏ Tested customer requirements with a broader sample of customers to prioritize the requirements and identify the most important

Looking ahead...

The final phase of the FOCUS process, Select Action, provides steps on how to translate your learnings into a complete solution, as well as some background on the creation of an action plan. Review Select Action to see how these steps can best be used to help you meet your customers' requirements.

Understand the Voices

Systems Path

"Using the Systems Path was a powerful tool for us in our strategy development. It helps you to approach strategy with the open mind necessary for real long-term thinking. But at the same time, you are forced to look closely at the most effective next steps to get there— looking for the maximum leverage."

Dr. Fiona Riddoch, Business Unit Manager
Honeywell Corporation

Overview

Sometimes your exploration will reveal that the problem you are studying is complex and involves the interactions of several dimensions. The Systems Path is designed specifically to identify how the multiple dimensions of a situation are related and where your actions can have the greatest impact.

Because trying to understand a complex system is difficult, this path provides a structured framework for thinking about the multiple dimensions and their interactions. The mechanics of working within this framework can seem very prescriptive. It is important to realize, though, that this is only a framework for your own thinking. The processes described in this path will not tell you what to do; they will only help you understand the system in a way that will help you decide what actions are most appropriate.

Step S15: Identify System Dimensions (details begin on p. 299)

Identify what dimensions of the issue are most appropriate for your project. The dimensions you choose will vary, depending on the nature of your exploration and whether you are looking at internal or external issues.

Step S16: Structure the Data for Each Dimension
(details begin on p. 307)

For each dimension select the strongest statements from the interview transcripts and create an affinity diagram.

Step S17: Identify High Leverage Points (details begin on p. 331)

Identify major factors that shape the system as a whole, and map out the interactions among these factors. Identify those factors that will have the greatest impact on your issue.

Questions You Will Be Answering

- What are the key dimensions of our system that we need to understand?

- What key question do we need to answer for each dimension?

- What are the customers' key issues in each dimension?

- What are the larger themes represented by the customers' voices?

- Which key factors will have the greater influence on the system as a whole?

Logistics

The Systems Path can be time-consuming, and most of the work needs to be done by the entire team.

The group will work together in Step S15, Identify System Dimensions. These dimensions provide a focus for the rest of your work in Understand the Voices.

In Step S16, Structure the Data for Each Dimension, team members work individually to review interview transcripts and extract statements that help answer the key question for each dimension. Then, as a group, they create an affinity diagram for each dimension to identify common themes.

In Step S17, Identify High Leverage Points, the team will identify key factors, learn how these factors influence one another, and discover which factors can provide the greatest leverage for action. This step is best done in a single day or two consecutive days. If too much time elapses during the course of this work, the group may require considerable time to become reoriented.

Step	Estimated Time
Step S15: Identify System Dimensions	1 – 3 hours
Step S16: Structure the Data for Each Dimension	1 – 1½ hours per interview to identify voices (interviews can be reviewed concurrently by all team members)
	4 hours per dimension to identify strongest voices and create affinity diagrams
Step S17: Identify High Leverage Points	Approximately 8 hours

The Big Picture

Systems Path

S15. **Identify System Dimensions**

S16. Structure the Data for Each Dimension

S17. Identify High Leverage Points

Prework

- Complete customer interviews
- Select path for analysis
- Meet with sponsor, if necessary

Time and Logistics

Allow approximately 1 – 3 hours for the team to identify system dimensions and determine a key question for each.

Supplies and Equipment

- Copy of project purpose statement
- Copy of objectives for learning
- Flipchart paper
- Flipchart markers

Outcomes

- System dimensions for analysis
- Key question for each dimension to focus the analysis

Step S15:

Identify System Dimensions

Description

In this step you will identify key dimensions of a complex system. Each dimension will illuminate the system from a particular perspective to provide you with a better sense of the whole.

Benefits

It is extremely difficult, if not impossible, to thoroughly grasp a complex system all at once. This step will allow you to focus on different dimensions individually and then build these perspectives into an integrated whole.

Getting Your Bearings

The dimensions you select as key for this process will depend on your problem statement and objectives for learning. Which dimensions of the system you are studying have the greatest impact on what you are trying to achieve?

The dimensions you select will form the basis for the rest of the work in this phase of the FOCUS process. For each dimension, you will identify related statements in your interview transcripts and then organize these statements into broader themes. These themes will then provide you with the key factors on which you can take action. Although identifying system dimensions may at first seem like a minor step, it is critical to take the time to make certain you have selected the dimensions that will shed the most light on your issue.

How to Identify System Dimensions

A. Select appropriate dimensions for analysis

The dimensions you select to study will depend on your project purpose and your objectives for learning. Some teams will need to look solely at internal issues, others solely at external issues, and some, a combination of both.

As a group, make a list of potential dimensions that seem to impact your issue. For instance, if you want to understand how changes in the market will affect your business, you should identify three to five elements impacting that market. These could include such things as government regulations, technology, behavior of potential customers, behavior of potential suppliers, or competitive forces. If you want to understand an internal problem, look for the factors that impact that issue.

- Review your objectives for learning. You may find that the objectives cluster around several themes or dimensions.

- In many internal projects, the three major dimensions relate to processes, policies, and people. A good way to begin is to see whether any or all of these dimensions fit your project.

- In external projects, one common way to look at dimensions is in terms of potential entrants, suppliers, buyers, substitutes, and industry competitors.[7]

---

[7]Michael E. Porter. *Competitive Strategy: Techniques for Analyzing Industries and Competitors* (New York: The Free Press, 1980).

The following table lists some relevant dimensions of sample projects.

Examples of possible dimensions

Sample Project	Possible Dimensions
Identify key competitive threats over the next five years	Mostly external... • Technology • Marketplace/consumer behavior • Value chain
Identify key barriers to implementation of new initiatives	Mostly internal... • Processes • Policies • People
Restructure delivery of services to the marketplace	Both internal and external... • Processes on receiver's end • Company policies • Processes on deliverer's end

Use divergent (broad) thinking to create an initial list of candidates. It is not unusual at this point to have more dimensions than you can work with. Discuss these as a group and use convergent (focused) thinking to narrow down your list to three to five key dimensions. Intuition grounded in what you learned in your interviews will likely play a role in your decision. This discussion of key dimensions will help team members articulate how they think about the problem and build a common knowledge base about the structure of the issue. If you cannot reach consensus as a group, have people vote for the dimensions they think will be most useful.

 Having only two dimensions is seldom sufficient. You need at least three dimensions for the breadth of perspective that provides you with the insights and understandings that make the Systems Path valuable.

Try to identify key dimensions one or two steps higher on the ladder of abstraction than where you think your problem lies. If you are too low on the ladder, you may limit your perspective. By working at a higher level, you may discover an important connection that lies outside the boundaries you would ordinarily consider.

Example of system dimensions

A company wanted to know how it could best compete in a market undergoing rapid change. Although numerous aspects of the field affected these changes, the team selected the following three dimensions as key to their business:

- Regulations
- Technologies
- Market forces

B. Write a key question for each dimension

A key question will provide focus for your thinking during the analysis phase. The question should help you understand what you want to know about each dimension of your exploration in order to accomplish your purpose. You will use these questions to extract the relevant voices from your interview transcripts. Typically, the question begins with the words "What are...." For example:

- What are the barriers to _____?

- What are the weaknesses of _____?

- What are the primary factors influencing _____?

- What are the customer's greatest concerns regarding _____?

The following table provides three possible key questions for the dimensions shown in the previous example.

Examples of key questions

Dimensions	Key Questions
• Regulations	• What are the regulations shaping the future of the field?
• Technologies	• What are the technologies shaping the future of the field?
• Market forces	• What are the market forces shaping the future of the field?

C. Check question for content and scope

The key questions should be stated in the same terms as the issue or problem, not as a solution. In the example of a key question for the Regulations dimension (shown above), an incorrect way to phrase the question would be, "How can we influence regulations shaping the future of the field?" "Influencing regulations" is one possible solution to the problem.

It is also important to check the scope of your key questions. They should either be written at the same level of abstraction as your purpose statement or one rung down on the ladder of abstraction, that is, more concretely. If you get too specific, however, you might overlook important and relevant information in the interviews.

The following case study illustrates how one team developed key questions for each of their dimensions.

Case Study: Program Management (Part 1 of 13)

A senior executive in charge of the inventory and supply operations for a large, geographically dispersed organization knew that massive internal changes were under way. With budgets tightening, his department would soon have to find new ways to operate so they could deliver the right kinds of goods and services in a fraction of the time at much lower cost.

To figure out what kinds of changes would promote this efficiency and be sustainable, the executive and several of his managers decided to use the FOCUS process. Their purpose statement was, "To explore the obstructions to program management in order to streamline operations." To gain relevant information, they interviewed other senior managers, program managers, specialists, and suppliers.

When discussing how to analyze the data, the team started with the basic dimensions of processes, policies, and people. They reviewed their objectives for learning and agreed that these dimensions would be appropriate because they had the greatest impact on their system.

Next, they developed three key questions, one for each dimension. Because they were concerned with obstructions to program management, they phrased their questions as follows:

- What are the process-related obstructions to program management?

- What are the policy-related obstructions to program management?

- What are the people-related obstructions to program management?

Step S15 Check

Check to make sure you have identified the key system dimensions that will help you illuminate your issue. You should have

❑ Three to five dimensions to serve as the basis for further analysis

❑ A clear, concise question for each dimension

The Big Picture

Systems Path

S15. Identify System Dimensions

S16. Structure the Data for Each Dimension

S17. Identify High Leverage Points

Prework

- Complete customer interviews
- Transcribe interview notes
- Identify system dimensions
- Develop key question for each dimension

Time and Logistics

Individual team members will extract relevant statements for each dimension from transcripts of the interviews they conducted. Allow about 1 – 1½ hours per interview for this work.

Using statements from all the interviews, the team will create one affinity diagram for each dimension. Allow approximately 4 hours for each affinity diagram. It is best to create each affinity diagram in a single meeting and to create all the affinity diagrams in a single week.

Supplies and Equipment

- Copies of verbatim interview transcripts
- Flipchart paper
- 3" x 3" self-stick notes (one color for each dimension)
- Highlighting markers (one color for each dimension)
- Black, red, and blue pens for each participant
- Black flipchart marker
- Tape or pushpins

Outcomes

- One affinity diagram for each dimension
- Approximately 24 of the strongest Level 1 titles from all the dimensions
- A super-affinity-diagram from all the dimensions (optional)

Step S16:

Structure the Data for Each Dimension

Description

In this step you will go back to your interview and observation notes and identify statements that relate to the key questions you identified in the previous step. Then you will create an affinity diagram for each dimension to discover connections among these statements.

Benefits

In this step you will gain a better understanding of the key issues related to each of your dimensions. You will translate the specific statements made by customers in your interviews into broader themes. In the next step, these themes will help you identify a small set of factors that will provide you with the greatest leverage for action.

Getting Your Bearings

In the previous step you wrote a key question for each dimension you decided to explore. Now you will review all the interview transcripts and highlight statements that help answer these questions. In the next step you will look for connections among these statements that provide important insights into your issue.

During this process you will alternate between divergent (broad) and convergent (focused) thinking. For instance, you will start out thinking

S

The statements you highlight in your interview transcripts reflect the customer's voice. In this book the terms voices and statements are used interchangeably.

broadly in order to extract diverse statements from the interview notes; then you narrow the field by selecting only the strongest of those statements. When looking for connections, you again start broadly, looking for as many connections as possible; then you narrow your focus to find the most insightful themes.

You will identify all the relevant statements and then select the strongest for each dimension, one at a time. When you have finished selecting the strongest statements for all the dimensions, you will create an affinity diagram for each dimension. The instructions in this step will take you through one dimension. Substeps C through G will need to be repeated for each remaining dimension.

Two tools, described later in detail, will help you do the work in this step:

1. The Method for Priority Marking™ (MPM) is a useful technique for narrowing down the number of interview statements from potentially several hundred to about two dozen. Your final subset of statements should include the strongest statements that still provide a 360° view of the issue.

2. An affinity diagram is a tool for finding connections among statements. The affinity diagram technique described in this book is designed specifically to help you move slowly up the ladder of abstraction from detailed statements to increasingly broad themes.

How to Structure the Data for Each Dimension

A. Identify relevant statements in interview notes

The first task in understanding your data is to identify the voices of your interviewees that connect to the key dimensions. Read through the verbatim interview notes and highlight any statements that help answer each of the key questions. You should also check for any relevant images or insights from your observation notes.

 To keep the statements separate, it helps to use a different color highlighter for each dimension.

Next, transcribe these statements onto 3" x 3" self-stick notes. This will make them easier to work with during the rest of this process.

 It is ideal for each interview team to work on their own transcripts. Although it is enriching for team member to read all the transcripts, it is not necessary to do so. Later, when creating the affinity diagrams, learnings will be shared.

- Write the statements word for word, as much as possible, putting quotation marks around direct quotes. If the speaker is referring to a previous comment, you may need to add a few words for the statement to make sense. Show any added words with brackets [ ]. If you want to delete irrelevant information from a statement, use three dots (...) to indicate something is missing.

- Print the statements in black, block letters so that everyone will be able to read them. In later stages you will be using different ink colors to indicate more abstract themes, so it is best to use black to represent the lowest level of abstraction.

- Code each note so that you know from which interview it came and from which transcript page. This coding is important for tracking your thinking and decision making back to the Voice of the Customer. You may want to use numerical codes instead of initials for your notes so that you do not introduce bias into the selection process.

If you find many statements from a single interview cover the same issue, you need not transcribe them all. Select the ones that are low on the ladder of abstraction—phrased in the concrete, verifiable language of first-person experience. (In the next substep, you will compare statements across all of the interviews; here, focus on each interview separately.)

 If your transcripts have been entered into a computer you can print your files in 3" columns instead of copying the statements onto self-stick notes. Then cut out the relevant statements and either sort them on a table or tape them to self-stick notes for use on a flipchart.

 If you find you are completely filling the note, you may have multiple statements that should be divided onto separate notes.

 Using different color self-stick notes for each dimension helps keep the notes separate as you continue your work.

The next case study follows the program management team as they search their interview transcripts for relevant statements for each dimension.

Case Study: Program Management (Part 2 of 13)

As a group, the team members agreed on a color-coding scheme for highlighting interview statements related to the three dimensions: process–yellow; policy–green; people–pink. (They chose these colors so they could also match them to their self-stick notes later in the process.) Each team member then went back to the transcripts of the interviews he or she had conducted, and using the appropriate color, highlighted comments that related to each dimension.

An example of a transcript with highlighted statements for each dimension is shown on the next page.

Continued...

Question: What are some examples of things from your experience
that have caused projects to slip?

We try to split the business to our supplier base 60/40, so we limit our
exposure to a single source. On the 49 project, Vendor R made the
critical piece part in one of the circuit cards which was assembled both
by Vendor R and Vendor C. We started seeing piece part delivery
delays from Vendor R to Vendor C, causing C to slip on their delivery
dates. I think, personally, that R wanted all the business themselves.
Even after we got production up, the Field Logistics Support Date
slipped several times due to late technical documentation submission.
Our technical writers and provisioners didn't have information that
was available to engineers and manufacturing.

Policy related

Process related

Question: What are some weaknesses associated with how we conduct
program management?

For starters, we have these cross functional teams. Everyone on the
team comes from a different area and reports to different functional
supervisors. I can arrange for a team meeting, but I can't make the
team members attend. Our contract specialist on the 49 team was
either overworked — or incompetent. When I inquired about the
status of an overdue contract award he responded, "Haven't seen it.
Just work them as I get them." And then, if their supervisor assigns
non-program related priorities, guess what gets worked first.

Policy related

People related

B. Select strongest statements

It is not unusual to identify several hundred statements
in the interview transcripts. Some interviewees will have
made similar statements and many voices may represent
the same issue. Now is the time to review the
statements and eliminate duplication. To extract themes
from all of this data, most people find they must reduce
the number of statements to about two dozen per
dimension. This selection is made by carefully
considering which statements reflect both the depth and
diversity of sentiments expressed in the interviews.

Be careful that in
selecting the strong-
est statements you do
not lose sight of the diverse viewpoints represented. To get a
360° view, sometimes you will
need to include a weak statement that represents a different
perspective. Think of the statements chosen as being symbolic
of others.

It is best to sort all your statements, one dimension at a time, in a single meeting. If you find that a statement assigned to one dimension fits better in another dimension, simply move it. If a statement fits in more than one dimension, copy it onto a second self-stick note and add it to the other dimension(s).

Gather together all statements related to each dimension. If there are more than about two dozen for any one dimension, put all of the ones that sound similar together and pick the strongest from each group. (See "Selecting the Strongest Statements" on page 313.) Set the other data statements aside. Continue this process until you have two dozen or fewer notes.

Strong voices are clear, concise, and specific. They often reflect personal experience. Weak voices are vague and imprecise. People often begin talking at a high level of abstraction, but later in the passage or after a probe make stronger, more detailed statements.

Examples of weak and strong voices

Weak Voice	Stronger Voice
"...size isn't everything."	"...smaller merchants will continue to exist on the basis they have fairly limited shareholder expectations."
"Domestic heating is a serious business and there isn't a serious interface with the people that require it."	"Manufacturers market to the heating industry. Few of us market to the man on the street."

Some team members may have difficulty letting go of so many customer statements. Having done the customer visits, all of the statements may seem important. To help with this, remember to do the following:

- Check back to the key question often

- Recognize that the process will help the team focus on the most important issues without getting lost in a sea of data

- Remember that issues chosen symbolize others that are similar

- Check for omissions to make sure a key issue has not been neglected

Selecting the Strongest Statements

One way to narrow down your statements to a manageable number and, at the same time, sort out the strongest notes is to use the Method for Priority Marking™. This method involves four steps: sorting, unrestrained pickup, focused pickup, and final check.*

Sorting

Start by posting all the notes on one or more sheets of flipchart paper. To find notes representing similar thoughts, you may find it helpful to sort the notes into general categories, using whatever categories come to mind.

Unrestrained Pickup

Next, focus on those notes that seem to best reflect your theme. Working simultaneously, team members should mark a red dot on the lower right corner of notes they think are worth keeping. Individually read through all the notes and look for those that are specific or clearly expressed. Look also for notes that represent or symbolize different perspectives, even though they may not be stated as well as some of the others. The objective is to eventually eliminate notes that are repetitious without losing a 360° view. It is best for everyone to work silently. There are no limits to how many notes may

be marked, but each note should get only one dot. This is not voting; if someone likes a note that already has a dot on it, he or she should simply leave it and move on. When everyone is finished, remove the unmarked notes (but save them in case you need them later to answer any questions).

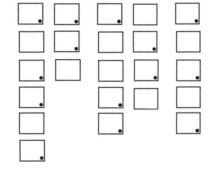

If you have more than 35 to 40 notes left, go through the marking process again, adding a second dot to the notes you want to keep. At the end of this round, remove all notes that have only one dot on them. Continue with additional rounds until you get down to about 35 to 40 notes.

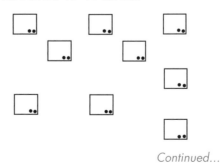

Continued…

---

*See Appendix B for more information on the Method for Priority Marking™.

Focused Pickup

To narrow your choices to roughly 24 notes, divide 24 by the number of people on the team. This is the number of final selections each person gets. If the answer is not a whole number, round up. For instance, if you have a team of seven, each person gets four selections. Each person, in turn, selects one note that he or she thinks is important to keep, reads the note aloud, and explains why it is important. The note is then moved to one side and the next person selects a note, reads it aloud, and explains the selection. The rotations continue until all have completed their specified number of selections.

Final Check

Finally, check to make sure a 360° view has been preserved. Look over the notes that were not selected in the focused pickup and decide if any need to be added. Discuss the notes that have been selected to make sure everyone has a common understanding of their meaning. At this point you should have a workable number of voices that provide clear, strong, and diverse perspectives of your question.

In this illustration, six team members are selecting from notes chosen in unrestrained pickup and placing their selections to the right. Three team members have made three selections each, whereas the other three have made only two selections so far. In the end, each team member will get four selections in this round for a total of 24 notes.

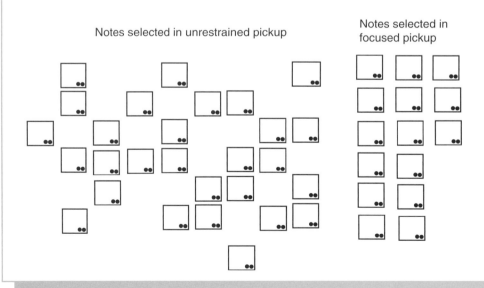

Notes selected in unrestrained pickup

Notes selected in focused pickup

C. Create Level 1 groupings

The categories you used to organize your notes in the MPM™ process created logical groupings. Now you need to look for different types of connections in order to deepen your understanding of the common themes discussed. Considering many alternative groupings allows you to think about your customers' concerns in new ways. (For additional help in creating groups and titles, see "Affinity Diagrams" on page 317.) Complete substeps C through G for each dimension in turn.

- Spread the notes randomly on a flipchart.

- Group the statements into small clusters that reflect a common, yet fairly concrete, theme. Try to keep these themes at a low level of abstraction, only one rung up from the notes themselves. If you started with 24 diverse statements, it should be hard to find a common theme in more than three statements at a time.

> Begin this work of creating groupings silently to avoid interrupting others' train of thought. Toward the end of this activity, however, people may have questions about why notes are being moved, and this discussion can provide new insights.

- Avoid cause-and-effect groupings; these do not have an overlapping common element. Your intent in this part of the process is to gain insight by moving up the ladder of abstraction from the fairly concrete statements to a higher conceptual level. Cause-and-effect relationships will make it difficult to do this.

- Keep moving the notes around until you have approximately 8 to 12 groups.

The first groupings will probably reflect connections you already are aware of or the similarity of words used. To reach new understandings, it is necessary to try new combinations based on different kinds of similarities.

The example on the next page illustrates how the clusters for an affinity diagram to understand the market for digital mammography differed from the broad categories that had been used in the Method for Priority Marking™.

Example of MPM categories vs. affinity diagram clusters

Sample of notes from the MPM process

Resolution of digital images

> With digital you will see glandular tissue in dense breasts

> There is a big question on how much resolution is needed, but people insist on what they are used to.

> People like high contrast images, but radiologists get dumped on for high doses.

Earlier detection

> CAD can save biopsies of $500 to $2000.

> . . . there is a very distinct advantage in detecting small cancers.

Adoption of digital technology

> This will replace film screen like VCR replaced 8mm film

> Full breast digital is at least 3 years away based on recent FDA rulings

> . . . rate of adoption [of soft viewing] will be a function of "Will the doctor rely on soft CRT?"

> Not before turn of the century.

Sample of how notes were reclustered into Level 1 groupings

What these three notes have in common:
Doctors resist trying new technology

> . . . rate of adoption [of soft viewing] will be a function of "Will the doctor rely on soft CRT?" **(Adoption of Digital)**

> This is a sheep market. You must get the leaders to try something new. **(Not shown previously)**

> There is a big question on how much resolution is needed, but people insist on what they are used to. **(Resolution)**

What these two notes have in common:
Digital's improved discrimination allows earlier detection of potential cancer

> . . . there is a very distinct advantage in detecting small cancers. **(Earlier Detection)**

> With digital you will see glandular tissue in dense breasts **(Resolution)**

Affinity Diagrams

An affinity diagram helps you group items so you can see what they have in common.* In the FOCUS process, we recommend that you keep the number of notes in a group relatively small. This should be fairly easy because you have already reduced your number of notes.

Create Level 1 Groupings

Begin by writing the key question in the upper left corner of two flipchart pages taped side by side on a wall. Spread all the statement notes randomly on the paper. Then start grouping the statements, looking for common themes. It is natural to want to group statements into cause-and-effect relationships; that is, one statement is the cause of another. It is better in the long run not to do this. Instead, look for notes that share a common element.

If you start getting groupings larger than two or three notes, you are probably working at too high a level of abstraction. Break the groups apart, looking for the subtle distinctions among them. Sometimes single notes do not relate to any others and will continue to stand alone.

Keep moving the notes around, remembering they can always be moved back. This helps you see connections you might not have noticed

at first. Making and breaking connections is how you will often gain new insights. You should end up with 8 to 12 clusters.

Create Level 1 Titles

Write a summary title sentence that captures the common theme in each group. These titles are critical because they will become the basis for whatever actions you decide are necessary.

Level 1 titles should be fairly specific and are easier to write if you have only 2 or 3 notes in the grouping. If the title is too abstract, it will be difficult to take action later in the process.

A good way to create titles is to start with key words or phrases that reflect what the statements have in common. Then write a sentence that relates the concept reflected in the notes to the key question. When possible, use action verbs in your titles. When the title is complete, print it in red on a self-stick note and place it at the top of the grouping.

Sometimes you may find that one of the notes actually works well as a title. In that case, simply draw a red box around the text to distinguish it from the other notes and move it into position as the title.

Continued...

---

*See Appendix B, Language Processing Method™, for information on a more rigorous method for grouping notes.

Once you have titles for all your groups, check to see if any single notes now fit into one of the groupings. Sometimes having clarified the groupings through titling helps you see how another note is related.

Create Level 2 Groupings

Repeat the clustering steps by looking for ways to group the Level 1 titles into common themes. Stack the groupings so that only the title can be seen on top. This focuses attention on the titles and not the underlying notes.

Again, aim for groupings of 2 or 3 titles. If you start getting larger groupings, you are probably working at too high a level of abstraction. A single note that remained ungrouped might now fit in a Level 2 group.

You will probably still move the groupings around. Sometimes you may find that several groupings can be made from the same set of titles. If you are not sure which is best, check to see which cluster best fits your key question. You should end up with 4 to 8 clusters.

Create Level 2 Titles

Again, write a summary title that captures the common theme in each grouping. These titles are at a higher level of abstraction and will help you capture overall themes that will help you see the big picture. Identifying these themes helps people communicate with managers and others in the organization.

To create Level 2 titles, start with key words or phrases that reflect what the Level 1 titles have in common. Then write a sentence that relates the concept reflected in the titles to the key question. When the title is complete, print it in blue on a self-stick note and place it at the top of the group.

When you have all your Level 2 titles, check to see if any of the remaining single notes or Level 1 clusters now fit into one of the Level 2 groupings. Sometimes having clarified the groupings through titling helps you see how another note is related. If any Level 1 clusters or single notes do not fit into Level 2 groupings, they may remain alone.

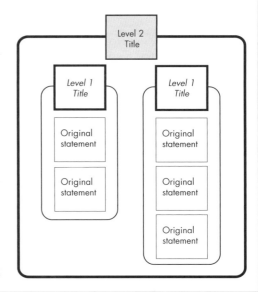

Here is how the program management team created their Level 1 groupings for each dimension.

Case Study: Program Management (Part 3 of 13)

The team identified 350 key statements from the interviews: 150 for the process dimension, 75 for the policy dimension, and 125 for the people dimension. Next they used the Method for Priority Marking™ to select the 24 best statements for each dimension. In the process of doing the MPM, they discovered a few notes that seemed to fit better in another category, so they moved them.

Then they selected only the notes for the process dimension and clustered those statements into related groupings. Initially, the project leader did most of the clustering, but soon everyone was seeing connections and helping form and reform clusters. The following illustration shows some of their final clusters. Later, they would repeat this process for each of the other dimensions.

What are the process-related obstructions to program management?

Sales Department made a strategic decision to close out customer X's account but did not tell the Program Manager	The roll-out schedule for the Trident project changed constantly	It can take over a month to load the actual configuration installed at a customer site into the database
An allowance list assignment for the 49er team was incorrectly routed to the CSS team causing 49ers to miss required due date	The Field Logistics Support date on the 49er project slipped several times due to late technical documentation submission	No allowance was made for the fact the SLED engineering drawings were in Italian
	To attend meetings on the 53 is frustrating because the date changes 3 or 4 times before we actually meet	

D. Write Level 1 titles for groups

Identify what is common in each Level 1 grouping and write a concise summary title. Remember that Level 1 titles should show the connections among the statement notes and will eventually be used to determine where to take action. The more concrete, the better.

The tendency at first is to write titles that simply repeat everything on the original notes. Instead, the title needs to represent the common link between the notes.

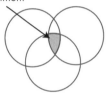

Titles should capture only what the statements have in common.

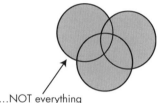

...NOT everything described in the statements.

You may find that it works best for the group to discuss the notes and come up with a single title, or you may prefer to have each person write his or her own title for each cluster. You can then select one that seems best or combine ideas into a single new title.

 Be wary of titles that are too long to fit on a self-stick note or that contain the word "and."

 Avoid cause-and-effect relationships; that is, do not pick a title that is the cause or the result of the statements in the grouping.

 It is easy to spend lots of time trying to perfect the title wording. Sometimes that effort pays off; other times, approximately right is good enough. Use your judgment.

Examples of Level 1 titles

Level 1 Grouping	Possible Level 1 Titles		
...rate of adoption [of soft viewing] will be a function of "Will the doctor rely on soft CRT?"	*Doctors dislike what is unfamiliar and wait for the leaders to try new technology*	*Doctors resist change*	*Doctors resist trying new technology of their own accord*
This is a sheep market. You must get the leaders to try something new.	This title is really not a summary. It is the total of everything written on the notes.	This title is too high on the ladder of abstraction. It encompasses more than what is expressed in the three notes.	This title is best because it captures what the notes have in common at an appropriately specific level of abstraction.
There is a big question on how much resolution is needed, but people insist on what they are used to.			

The next case study follows the program management team as they create titles for their Level 1 groupings.

Case Study: Program Management (Part 4 of 13)

As the team worked together on their Level 1 titles, some titles came fairly easily; others were more of a struggle. Some of their first titles were too high on the ladder of abstraction or described an effect that resulted from the notes in the cluster, but eventually they were worded appropriately. The following illustration shows the titles they wrote for the three clusters shown previously.

Continued...

What are the process-related obstructions to program management?

Necessary information does not always get routed to the Program Manager	*Scheduled events often change*	*Processing of project tasks can take longer than time set to meet required delivery date*
Sales Department made a strategic decision to close out customer X's account but did not tell the Program Manager	The roll-out schedule for the Trident project changed constantly	It can take over a month to load the actual configuration installed at a customer site into the database
An allowance list assignment for the 49er team was incorrectly routed to the CSS team causing 49ers to miss required due date	The Field Logistics Support date on the 49er project slipped several times due to late technical documentation submission	No allowance was made for the fact the SLED engineering drawings were in Italian
	To attend meetings on the 53 is frustrating because the date changes 3 or 4 times before we actually meet	

E. Create Level 2 groupings

Repeat the clustering steps, but this time cluster the Level 1 titles rather than the individual notes. This second round of grouping helps identify larger themes that can provide a broader frame of reference for your thinking.

- Look for groups of two or three titles that have something in common. At this point you can also include single, ungrouped notes in these new clusters. You should end up with four to eight clusters.

 Stack the groupings so that only the title can be seen on top. This focuses attention on the titles and not the underlying notes.

- Once again, avoid cause-and-effect relationships within groupings.

- Begin by working silently. Each team member will probably see different ways to create groupings. Trying to see what others see will help everyone gain a deeper understanding of the issues.

- Sometimes you may find that several groupings can be made from the same set of Level 1 titles. If you are not sure which is best, check to see which cluster best fits your key question.

F. Write Level 2 titles

Repeat the titling steps to find a concise summary title for each Level 2 grouping. These titles should answer your key question. Team members may resist working at this level of abstraction. It may seem that the summaries lose all the power of the customer statements. The affinity diagram will preserve all levels of abstraction—the customer voices and the summaries.

- Identify what is common in each Level 2 grouping.

- Write a title that is only one rung higher on the ladder of abstraction than the Level 1 titles.

- Avoid cause-and-effect relationships.

Write a title as a team or have each person write his or her own title; then either select the best one or combine ideas into a single new title.

The next case study follows the program management team as they create their Level 2 groupings and titles.

Case Study: Program Management (Part 5 of 13)

Having completed the first level of grouping and titling, the program management team was now ready for the second round. To make it easier to focus on only the Level 1 titles, the team stacked the statements in each cluster, with the title on top. Now they were able to move the titles and underlying notes around easily into new clusters, without mixing them up.

Once they had formed their clusters, they needed to write titles again. This time they had each team member write a title for each cluster and then they decided which was best. More often than not, the final title was a combination of two or three ideas. The following illustration shows their Level 2 clusters and titles.

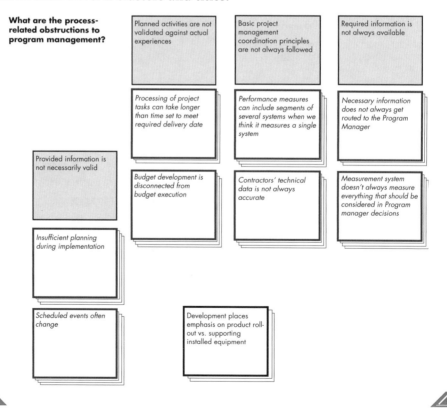

G. Lay out the affinity diagrams

If you placed the self-stick notes on top of each other while you were sorting, spread them out again into the appropriate clusters so that you can see each individual note. If you need more space, add another sheet of flipchart paper.

- Draw black lines around each Level 1 grouping.

- Draw heavy black lines around each Level 2 grouping.

- Tape the notes to the paper to make this a more permanent document.

- Write the date on the final diagram. You may also want to add the name of the team and each team member. Some teams sign their names as a way of acknowledging their consensus.

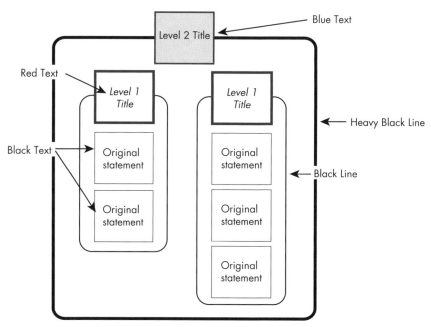

You should complete an affinity diagram for each dimension before proceeding to the next substep.

H. Select the strongest Level 1 titles (if necessary)

In the next step you will be identifying factors related to each of your Level 1 titles and looking for the interactions among factors that will give you the greatest leverage. If you have more than about two dozen Level 1 titles for all your dimensions together, you will find it difficult to identify a small number of high leverage points. To reduce the number of Level 1 titles, and at the same time make sure you preserve those likely to give you the most leverage, use either of the following methods.

Method 1: Voting

Revisit the affinity diagrams and have each team member vote for the top three Level 1 titles on each diagram. An easy way to vote that ensures equal participation is to use a 3-2-1 voting method, described below.

- Each person gets three votes. The top choice gets a score of 3, the second choice a score of 2, and the least favorite a score of 1.

- Working simultaneously, team members write the scores for their top three selections directly on the notes. Single notes that are still not part of a cluster should also be included in the voting.

- Add up the numbers on each note. Some notes may have several votes, whereas others have none.

- Select the top vote-getters from each affinity diagram.

- Select no more than half the Level 1 titles from any one diagram. For example, if an affinity diagram has ten Level 1 titles and eight received votes, select only the top five vote-getters. If an affinity diagram has twelve Level 1 titles but only four got any votes, select all four titles.

Method 2: Multipick*

Use the Method for Priority Marking™ described on page 313 to select the strongest Level 1 titles.

- Copy all Level 1 titles onto new self-stick notes and place them on a flipchart.

- Use the MPM to select no more than 24 titles.

- Check to make sure your final selection of titles covers the diversity of issues in each dimension.

I. Look for connections among Level 1 titles (optional)

Creating a super-affinity-diagram from the Level 1 titles of all your affinity diagrams can help identify common themes that cross the various dimensions of your issue. Although not necessary for completing the Systems Path work, this diagram can provide a deeper understanding of how your dimensions interrelate. Understanding these interrelationships can be valuable because you are trying to understand and explain a complex system.

- Write the Level 1 titles onto self-stick notes. If you reduced the number of Level 1 titles in substep H, use only those titles selected.

- Create an affinity diagram of these titles. Do two rounds of clustering with the Level 1 titles, just as you did with the original interview statements.

*See Appendix B for more information on the Method for Priority Marking™.

The following case study shows how the program management team used a super-affinity-diagram.

Case Study: Program Management (Part 6 of 13)

When the team had completed all three affinity diagrams, they decided to create a super-affinity-diagram in order to deepen their insights into the interrelationships of the different dimensions. They were particularly interested in trying to see how each of the three dimensions might make sense independently, but created problems for the system as a whole when examined together. By regrouping their Level 1 titles, they were able to see how the dimensions interacted to hinder effective program management. Although the team already had a good sense of these difficulties from their interviews and individual affinity diagrams, their understanding was reinforced when they created the super-affinity-diagram.

The super-affinity-diagram was even more valuable when the team brought in their sponsors at the end of the FOCUS process. By starting their presentation with this high-level diagram, they could quickly identify the types of problems they were dealing with. Then they could work backward to show which dimensions were involved in the various groupings, and even some of the individual voices represented. Once they created a frame of reference for their sponsors, they could quickly explain what they would need to do in order to improve the system.

The illustration on the next page shows the team's final super-affinity-diagram.

Continued...

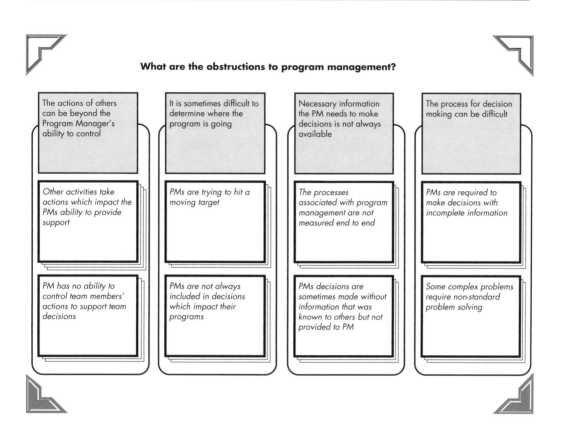

What are the obstructions to program management?

The actions of others can be beyond the Program Manager's ability to control	It is sometimes difficult to determine where the program is going	Necessary information the PM needs to make decisions is not always available	The process for decision making can be difficult
Other activities take actions which impact the PMs ability to provide support	*PMs are trying to hit a moving target*	*The processes associated with program management are not measured end to end*	*PMs are required to make decisions with incomplete information*
PM has no ability to control team members' actions to support team decisions	*PMs are not always included in decisions which impact their programs*	*PMs decisions are sometimes made without information that was known to others but not provided to PM*	*Some complex problems require non-standard problem solving*

Step S16 Check

Check to make sure you understand the key issues in your data. You should have

- ❑ 3 to 5 affinity diagrams, one for each dimension of the issue
- ❑ 24 or fewer of the strongest Level 1 titles from all the dimensions together
- ❑ A super-affinity-diagram of the Level 1 titles from all the dimensions (optional)

The Big Picture

Systems Path
S15. Identify System Dimensions
S16. Structure the Data for Each Dimension
S17. Identify High Leverage Points

Prework
- Create an affinity diagram for each dimension
- Select strongest Level 1 titles
- Create an affinity diagram of Level 1 titles (optional)

Time and Logistics
Identifying high leverage points should be done by the whole group and takes approximately 8 hours. It is best to complete this step in a single day or two consecutive half days in order to stay focused.

Supplies and Equipment
- Copies of affinity diagrams
- Flipchart paper
- Black pens
- Flipchart markers
- White correction tape
- Tape or pushpins
- Straightedge or yardstick

Outcomes
- A factor table
- An influence matrix
- List of high leverage points

Step S17:

Identify High Leverage Points

Description

In this step you will identify key factors, learn how these factors influence one another, and discover which factors can provide you with the greatest leverage for action. The factor table and influence matrix described in this step will help you keep track of all your factors and interactions.

Benefits

At this point you have approximately two dozen Level 1 titles describing areas in which you could take action. Some factors undoubtedly have a greater impact on the system than others, and some factors may have a negative impact on other parts of the system. To maximize the use of your resources, it is important to identify how the factors interact with one another, and which factors have the greatest positive impact on the system as a whole.

Getting Your Bearings

When you structured the data for each dimension, you created several affinity diagrams, each with perhaps three or more Level 2 titles. The Level 2 titles capture the overall themes surrounding your issue, whereas the Level 1 titles identify the main factors you will ultimately address when you take action. However, to identify the high leverage points for action, you need to learn how these factors interact.

The leverage points you identify in this step will show you where you can gain the most influence through your actions. In the next phase of the FOCUS process, you will decide what these actions will be.

How to Identify High Leverage Points

A. Create a factor table

In order to identify the factors in the system where your actions will have the most leverage, you need to translate your Level 1 titles into factors on which you can take action. A factor table is a tool that will help you do this.

Create a table with four columns labeled "Number," "Level 1 Title," "Key Ideas," and "Factor Name."

Sample Factor Table

Number	Level 1 Title	Key Ideas	Factor Name
1	First Level 1 Title		
2	Second Level 1 Title		
3	Third Level 1 Title		
4	Fourth Level 1 Title		

Beginning with your first affinity diagram, number all the Level 1 titles among all your affinity diagrams sequentially. If you narrowed down your Level 1 titles to include only the strongest titles, use only those titles in this step. This numbering will be helpful if you need to refer to the diagrams later for more information or clarification.

If you are working as a team, it is best to create the factor table on a series of flipchart pages taped to the wall. To save meeting time, the factor table can be prepared by one or two people ahead of time.

When the numbering is complete, list the titles in the factor table.

The following case study shows how the program management team constructed their factor table.

Case Study: Program Management (Part 7 of 13)

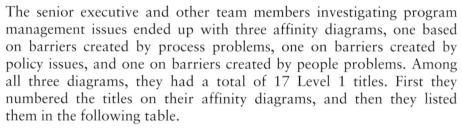

The senior executive and other team members investigating program management issues ended up with three affinity diagrams, one based on barriers created by process problems, one on barriers created by policy issues, and one on barriers created by people problems. Among all three diagrams, they had a total of 17 Level 1 titles. First they numbered the titles on their affinity diagrams, and then they listed them in the following table.

Number	Level 1 Title	Key Ideas	Factor Name
1	Other departments (staff) meet their objectives without concern for program requirements		
2	PM has no control over the field activity inventory assets		
3	Development places emphasis on product roll-out vs. supporting installed equipment		
4	PM has no control over other program team members' priorities that are assigned by higher authority		
5	PM does not have direct influence on actions of other team members		
6	Scheduled events often change		
7	Program requirements change during process		
8	Insufficient planning during implementation		
9	Non-accountable organizations make key decisions PM doesn't have ability to defend		
10	Budget development is disconnected from budget execution		
11	No measuring/monitoring other activities which impact ability to meet delivery dates		
12	Necessary information does not always get routed to PM		
13	After PM makes decision they find out other people had valuable information		
14	Processing of project tasks can take longer than time set to meet required delivery date		
15	Measurement system doesn't always measure everything that could be considered in PM decision		
16	Standard decisions exist for some tasks but not for others		
17	PMs are given problems they can not solve on their own		

B. Identify factor names

Factors are specific aspects of the system that influence its performance, either positively or negatively. Changing one factor in the system is likely to have an affect on other factors. The Level 1 titles on your affinity diagrams describe themes that are important to each of your dimensions. For each Level 1 title, you now need to identify a factor that can be translated into action. To help you name the factors, it may be helpful to identify key ideas, although sometimes the factor name is obvious.

Try to distill each Level 1 title into a few key words or a short phrase that captures the essence of the issue. List these in the Key Ideas column of the factor table. Different people may come up with different key ideas. Try to capture them all. This diversity can help the group come to a better understanding of the issues involved.

> *If you are struggling with key ideas, you may want to go back and read the original notes on the affinity diagram.*

Developing factor names can be difficult. The following guidelines may help you.

- Phrase the factor name so that increasing the factor is better. This will be important when you start looking at interactions. When trying to phrase the factor name, it helps to ask, "What is better?" and "More is better for what outcome?" Do not include the word "more" in the name.

- Phrase the factor so that someone can take action on it. This does not mean that it needs to be within the control of the group. Many important factors may be outside your direct control. However, factor names should still be phrased in such a way that they can result in action.

- Phrase the factor so that you identify the part of the system with which you are concerned and the aspect of that part of the system which you want to increase. For instance, in the factor name "Installation ease," "installation" is the area of concern and "ease" is the aspect to increase. This factor name could also be written "Ease of installation."

- If you have an "and" in your factor name, make sure that you do not really have two factors.

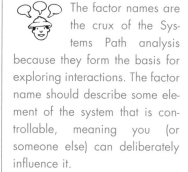

The factor names are the crux of the Systems Path analysis because they form the basis for exploring interactions. The factor name should describe some element of the system that is controllable, meaning you (or someone else) can deliberately influence it.

The following factors are all phrased so that more is better for the system being explored. They are all factors on which action can be taken, although they are not necessarily areas where the team itself, or even the company involved, can take action alone.

Examples of how to write factor names

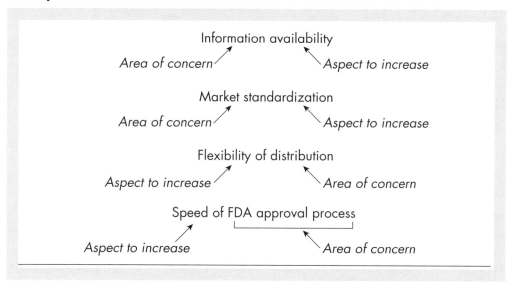

The following examples represent several different projects. Each row of the table shows how the team went from a Level 1 title to a factor name. Key ideas were frequently useful, but not always necessary.

Example of a factor table

Number	Level 1 Title	Key Ideas	Factor Name
1	Significant niche markets are emerging.	small target populations new areas for growth	Market segmentation
2	End users expect higher performance from systems.		Systems performance
3	Government increasingly regulates environmental responsibility.	Green Politics	Support of systems to meet environmental regulations
4	Current digital performance has not yet demonstrated enough superiority to be an acceptable alternative solution.		Performance of digital technology
5	Competitors are branching into new markets through acquisitions.	Growth Niche markets	Acquisition of niche players

The same factor name may sometimes seem appropriate for more than one Level 1 title. You may use the same factor name more than once; in fact, understanding that two issues have the same factor may be a valuable insight. Do not struggle to find a new way to say basically the same thing. However, if you find that the same few factor names keep repeating themselves throughout the table, you are probably working too high on the ladder of abstraction. Try to rename the factors with more specific language.

Sometimes one factor may turn out to be included in another factor. For instance, Age Segmentation is one form of Market Segmentation. Sometimes this additional detail can be valuable, whereas at other times the factors may be redundant. If you are not sure about a factor's value, keep it until it becomes clear that you will not gain anything from it. You can always cross it off later in the process.

The next case study follows the program management team as they construct their factor table.

Case Study: Program Management (Part 8 of 13)

The first Level 1 title listed in the team's factor table was, "Other departments (staff) meet their objectives without concern for program requirements."

After some discussion, the team decided the core issue was that other people—quite naturally—put their objectives first because no incentive existed for them to do otherwise. The team entered "Others' objectives first" in the Key Ideas column.

Then they asked themselves, "With regard to this issue, what would we like more of in order to do our work in less time and at less cost?" Their initial answers included:

- "More priority for our projects"

- "More control over decisions that affect us"

Next, they looked at how they could shape these ideas as a factor that could be translated into action. Eventually, they settled on Program Requirement Precedence.

Their concern was with their own program requirements, and they wanted precedence for these program requirements to increase. Increasing the precedence of program requirements would improve program managers' ability to control their budgets and resources.

Number	Level 1 Title	Key Ideas	Factor Name
1	Other departments (staff) meet their objectives without concern for program requirements	Others' objectives first	Program rqmt precedence

The team followed the same procedure for the rest of the Level 1 titles. Their completed factor table follows. When they got to Title 5, they realized that their key ideas were very similar to the key ideas for Title 2. Someone suggested that both titles were influenced by the same factor; therefore, they decided they did not need a new factor name for

Continued...

Title 5. They also decided Titles 12 and 13 were both related to how much information was available to program managers as they planned and monitored their projects, so they created only one factor for both titles.

Number	Level 1 Title	Key Ideas	Factor Name
1	Other departments (staff) meet their objectives without concern for program requirements	Others' objectives first	Program rqmt precedence
2	PM has no control over the field activity inventory assets	No control over field	Management control
3	Development places emphasis on product roll-out vs. supporting installed equipment	Emphasis not on life cycle	Life cycle support importance
4	PM has no control over other program team members' priorities that are assigned by higher authority	Control over team resources	Resource control
5	PM does not have direct influence on actions of other team members	No control over others	Same as #2
6	Scheduled events often change	Schedule changes	Schedule adherence
7	Program requirements change during process	Changing requirements	Requirement stability
8	Insufficient planning during implementation	Not enough planning	Planning thoroughness
9	Non-accountable organizations make key decisions PM doesn't have ability to defend	Ability to defend decisions	Decision defense
10	Budget development is disconnected from budget execution	Execution of developed budget	Budget execution
11	No measuring/monitoring other activities which impact ability to meet delivery dates	Monitoring other activities	Performance monitoring
12	Necessary information does not always get routed to PM	Necessary information availability	Information availability
13	After PM makes decision they find out other people had valuable information	Necessary information availability	Same as #12
14	Processing of project tasks can take longer than time set to meet required delivery date	Process time delays	Process timeliness
15	Measurement system doesn't always measure everything that could be considered in PM decision	Measurement system omissions	Measurement system completeness
16	Standard decisions exist for some tasks but not for others	Non-standard tasks	Task standardization
17	PMs are given problems they can not solve on their own	Assistance from others	Independent problem solving

C. Construct an influence matrix

The purpose of an influence matrix is to help you keep track of how the factors influence one another. As you work through the matrix, the team will be building a common understanding of the system. Once you have completed the matrix, identifying which factors will provide you with the greatest leverage is relatively easy.

- Draw a matrix that has one more row than there are factor names and two more columns than there are factor names. The first row and the first column will be used for labels, the second column will remain blank until later. If you have the same factor identified for more than one Level 1 title, you only need to list it once on the matrix.
  - If you have 12 Level 1 titles and each factor name is unique, you should have 13 rows and 14 columns
  - If you have 18 Level 1 titles and 15 different factor names (3 were used twice), you should have 16 rows and 17 columns

- List the factor numbers and names in the first column. When you come to a factor name that was used more than once, include the numbers for all of the associated Level 1 titles.

- Leave the second column empty for now; then enter the factors across the top of the matrix. To save time and space, you can list only the factor numbers across the top. When you come to a factor name that was used more than once, include the numbers for all of the appropriate Level 1 titles.

- Label the left side "Influencing Factors" and the top "Affected Factors."

For ease of reference, shade the cells where a factor intersects itself.

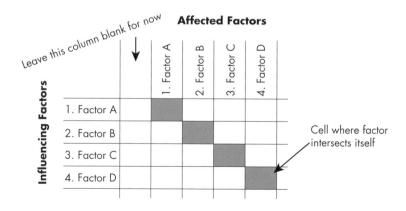

The next case study shows how the program management team constructed their influence matrix.

Case Study: Program Management (Part 9 of 13)

The team had 17 Level 1 titles but only 15 factor names because two were used twice. Therefore, they constructed a matrix with 16 rows and 17 columns. In the top row they only numbered the factors, but along the side they included the full factor names. They left the second column blank for later use.

Affected Factors

	Factor Name		1	2/5	3	4	6	7	8	9	10	11	12/13	14	15	16	17
1	Program requirement precedence		■														
2/5	Management control			■													
3	Life cycle support importance				■												
4	Resource control					■											
6	Schedule adherence						■										
7	Requirement stability							■									
8	Planning thoroughness								■								
9	Decision defense									■							
10	Budget execution										■						
11	Performance monitoring											■					
12/13	Information availability												■				
14	Process timeliness													■			
15	Measurement system completeness														■		
16	Task standardization															■	
17	Independent problem solving																■

Influencing Factors

D. Identify factor interactions

Now that you have identified the major factors of your system, you need to determine which of these will provide you with the most leverage. Trying to act on all the factors could be an overwhelming task. To decide where your actions can have the greatest impact, you need to learn how the factors interact with one another. The first step in this process is to determine whether an interaction exists between two factors, and, if so, whether it is positive or negative.

 Remember that you want to know what influence the factors along the side (Influencing Factors) have on the factors across the top (Affected Factors). Sometimes you may see a positive relationship and want to put a plus sign in the cell when it is actually the Affected Factor that would cause an increase in the Influencing Factor. Be careful to pay attention to the direction of the influence.

- Work down the column of influencing factors (on the left side of the matrix), starting with the first row and going across cell by cell. For each cell ask, "If I increase the factor on the left, will the factor at the top be affected?" If you think there will be an effect, ask if increasing the left factor will cause the top factor to increase or decrease.

  - If the affected factor will increase, put a plus sign in the cell.
  - If the affected factor will decrease, put a minus sign in the cell.
  - If no interaction exists, leave the cell blank.

- Continue this process for all of the cells.

 If you are working with a group and have trouble agreeing on an interaction, have each member vote—thumbs up for a positive interaction, thumbs down for a negative interaction, and thumbs to the side for no interaction.

If one factor might affect another, a weak and/or indirect link probably exists between the two factors. For instance, A affects D because A affects B, and B affects C, and C affects D. If you have identified the right factors, you will probably find at least some of the intermediate links, which will be stronger and more direct. If you have to look hard to find a possible interaction, you are usually better off leaving the interaction cell blank. Remember that you are looking for a few high leverage points here.

At this point your factor matrix should look something like this:

Affected Factors

Influencing Factors		1. Factor A	2. Factor B	3. Factor C	4. Factor D
	1. Factor A		+		−
	2. Factor B				
	3. Factor C	+			+
	4. Factor D		+	−	

The next case study follows the program management team as they identify and label factor interactions.

Case Study: Program Management (Part 10 of 13)

Starting with Factor 1 and working across the table, the team asked themselves whether an increase in Program Requirement Precedence would cause each of the other factors to increase. If Factor 1 would cause a factor across the top to increase, they entered a plus sign in the appropriate column; if it would result in a decrease, they entered a minus sign. When they finished looking at how Program Requirement Precedence would affect each of the other factors, they moved down a row and repeated the process for Management Control.

In some cases the group was not sure what to write down. Occasionally, one or two people saw connections others failed to notice. The team also realized all interactions were not equal. Some were clear and definite; others were indirect or only possible. By discussing the factor interactions, everyone gained a better understanding of the system as a whole.

Continued...

342   © 2005 Center for Quality of Management

The following illustration shows selected rows of the completed matrix. As you can see, Factors 2/5, 8, 11, and 12/13 each had many positive interactions. For instance, increasing Management Control (Factor 2/5) would have a positive affect on Program Requirement Precedence (Factor 1) because if managers had more control, they could make sure program requirements were satisfied before other, less important activities were completed. On the other hand, the same increase in Management Control would reduce people's ability to be flexible and operate independently, so a negative interaction was indicated between Management Control and Independent Problem Solving (Factor 17).

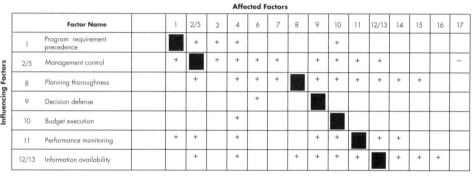

E. Assess type of influence

You now have a matrix with a lot of plus signs and probably a few minus signs. You most likely sense that all of these interactions are not the same. Some have a direct influence on the affected factor; others have an indirect influence (that is, there are intervening factors). Because you want to find a few high leverage points, you want to identify factors that have direct interactions.

For each interaction in the matrix (negative as well as positive) ask, "How many steps before the effect is felt?"

- If the effect will be immediate, put a D in the box. Direct effects will provide you with the most leverage.

Do not be tempted to hurry through this sub-step. Taking time to discuss the nature of the interactions, especially the indirect interactions, will help everyone in the group develop a richer understanding of the system.

- If there will be several intervening steps before the effect will be felt, put an I in the box. Indirect effects are part of a chain of interacting forces. They may have a lot of influence, but acting on a factor with an indirect effect will also impact all of the intervening factors.

Your factor matrix should look something like this:

Affected Factors

	1. Factor A	2. Factor B	3. Factor C	4. Factor D
1. Factor A		+ D		– I
2. Factor B				
3. Factor C	+ D			+ D
4. Factor D		+ I	– D	

Influencing Factors

When you have identified the type of influence for each interaction, you should perform two checks.

Having more than three Ds in a single row is only a signal to further examine the interactions. In some cases you may, in fact, have a factor with more than three direct influences.

- Count up the number of Ds in each row. Few factors have a direct influence on more than two or three other factors. Therefore, if you have more than three Ds in a single row, you may have labeled an indirect interaction (I) as direct (D).

- Look over your matrix and see if you have omitted any interactions. Your discussions of direct and indirect interactions can lead you to interactions you missed the first time through. Add these new interactions to the chart. You will want to recalculate the number of Ds for that particular row.

The following case study shows the program management team's assessment of how their factors influenced one another.

Case Study: Program Management (Part 11 of 13)

After the team had identified the direction of each factor interaction (positive or negative), they went back to the top of the matrix and decided whether each interaction was direct (D) or indirect (I).

Affected Factors

Influencing Factors

	Factor Name		1	2/5	3	4	6	7	8	9	10	11	12/13	14	15	16	17
2/5	Management control		+D	■	+I	+D	+I	+I		+I	+I	+I	+D				-D
8	Planning thoroughness			+D		+I	+I	+D	■	+I	+I	+I	+D	+I	+I		
9	Decision defense						+I			■							
10	Budget execution					+I					■						
11	Performance monitoring		+I	+D		+I				+I	+I	■	+I	+I			
12/13	Information availability			+I		+I			+I	+D	+I	+I	■	+D	+D	+I	

Planning Thoroughness (Factor 8) has a direct effect on Management Control (Factor 2/5) because increasing the thoroughness of management's planning would directly increase their ability to control projects. However, Management Control has an indirect effect on Decision Defense (Factor 9). Increasing Management Control would improve the availability of information on planning and tracking projects (Factor 12/13), and this in turn would improve the ability of program managers to defend their decisions (Factor 9). If you follow the chain of interactions, you will see that Factor 2/5 has a direct influence on Factor 12/13, which in turn has a direct influence on Factor 9; thus Factor 2/5 has an indirect influence on Factor 9.

Process Changes Versus Behavioral Changes

There are two basic ways to make changes: you can change the way a process works or you can change the way a person behaves.

As you can see from the table below, it is usually easier to make process changes than to make behavioral changes, although in some situations process changes can also be difficult to make. Process changes represent changes to physical things and, thus, they tend to be less personal. Behavioral changes require a person to act differently.

Changing our own behaviors (eating less, exercising more, not being so quick to judge others, delegating more responsibilities, etc.) is difficult enough; changing someone else's behavior is almost impossible unless 1) you have a lot of influence over the person (e.g., their job is on the line) or 2) you can convince them that the change is in their own best interest.

Assessing whether a behavioral change has been successfully implemented can also be difficult.

Processes, on the other hand, are usually the result of a series of decisions made by several people over a period of time. Changing them based on customer data and systematic analysis minimizes the potential for emotional or political resistance. If you transfer the responsibility for making customer adjustments from the Accounting Department to the Sales Department, for instance, some people may feel a loss of power or prestige, but this process change is likely to be accepted eventually, especially if it is supported by customer data and systematic analysis. A process change may also require some behavioral changes, but these will be the outcome of the process change, not the focus of change.

Examples of process versus behavioral changes

Process Changes	Behavioral Changes
• Changing a manufacturing line	• Changing the way an individual thinks about making decisions
• Changing the way information flows	• Changing the way an individual communicates with others
• Changing where decisions are made	• Changing an individual's need to be in control

F. Identify nature of the change required

You now know which factors have a direct influence on the system, but you probably still have more factors than you can reasonably affect. The best way to narrow the field further is to identify those factors that you are most likely to be able to change.

Read through the list of influencing factors and ask yourself whether changing each factor requires changing a process or changing an individual's behavior.

- If the factor requires a process change, put a P in the blank column to the right of the factor name.

- If it requires a behavioral change, put a B in the column.

 Some factors may involve both process change and behavioral change. If the behavioral change is minimal, put a P in the column. However, if the behavioral change is significant or unknown, then put a B. Remember that you are trying to find the factors with the greatest impact. If the behavioral changes are great enough that you cannot clearly select a P, you will probably be better off not trying to change this factor initially.

Affected Factors

Influencing Factors	P or B	1. Factor A	2. Factor B	3. Factor C	4. Factor D
1. Factor A	P		+ D		– I
2. Factor B	B				
3. Factor C	B	+ D			+ D
4. Factor D	P		+ I	– D	

Changing a process is easier than changing an individual's behavior; therefore, you can leverage your efforts by focusing on those factors labeled P.

The next case study shows how the program management team labeled the type of change needed to influence their factors.

Case Study: Program Management (Part 12 of 13)

To focus their efforts on those factors where they were most likely to be able to effect a change, the team labeled each factor as requiring either a process change (P) or a behavioral change (B). Their first factor, Program Requirement Precedence, related to the problems that occurred when managers gave priority to activities unrelated to program requirements. Getting managers to change the way they prioritized their work would require getting them to change their behavior, so the team wrote a B in the empty column for Factor 1.

After some discussion, the team decided the next five factors also required behavioral changes. Although changing Factor 6, Schedule Adherence, and Factor 7, Requirement Stability, would involve some process changes, most of the changes would be behavioral, so they also put a B in the empty column for these factors.

Finally, when they looked at Factor 8: Planning Thoroughness, the team decided this factor could be increased primarily through process changes. Instead of considering only the issues under their direct control during planning, the team would change their processes to also identify and incorporate more factors outside their control during the planning stage. They also decided that Factors 10, 11, 12/13, 14, 15, and 16 all required process changes.

	Factor Name	P or B	1	2/5	3	4	6	7	8	9	10	11	12/13	14	15	16	17
1	Program requirement precedence	B	■	+I	+I	+I					+I						
2/5	Management control	B	+D	■	+I	+D	+I	+I		+I	+I	+I	+D				-D
6	Schedule adherence	B		+I		+I	■		+D		+I		+I	+D			
7	Requirement stability	B		+I			+D	■		+I	+I		+I	+I		+I	
8	Planning thoroughness	P		+D		+I	+I	+D	■	+I	+I	+I	+D	+I	+I		
12/13	Information availability	P		+I		+I			+I	+D	+I	+I	■	+D	+D	+I	

When the team looked at their matrix, they saw that approximately half of their factors would require behavioral changes and half would require process changes. Their high leverage points would have to come from this latter group.

G. Determine the smallest set of high leverage points

High leverage points are factors that have a great deal of influence and can be affected through process changes. At this point you want to find the smallest number of factors that will influence all of the other factors. Identifying these factors allows you to leverage your time and resources for the greatest possible impact on the system.

- Highlight the influencing factor that has the most direct influences (most Ds across a row) and can be altered through process changes (P in the second column).

- Locate the first D in that row and put a star (or other mark) at the top of the column where the D is located. Continue for all other Ds in that row. This procedure helps you keep track of which factors across the top of the matrix are affected by the influencing factor.

Affected Factors

	Factor Name	P or B	1	★ 2/5	3	4	6	★ 7	8	9	10	11	★ 12/13	14	15	16	17
2/5	Management control	B	+D	■	+I	+D	+I	+I		+I	+I	+I	+D				–D
8	Planning thoroughness	P		+D		+I	+I	+D	■	+I	+I	+I	+D	+I	+I		

Influencing Factors

- Now highlight the influencing factor that has the second highest number of direct influences and can be altered by process changes. Move across the row, again putting a star at the top of any column where a D appears.

 If two or more factors have an equal number of Ds and a P in the second column, highlight first the one that affects the most factors not already affected by a previously selected influencing factor.

- When you have completed the second round, look across the top of your matrix and identify any factors that have not yet been affected directly. If all of the columns have been marked, you do not need to go further.

  - If there are a large number of unmarked columns, continue the process, moving on to the factor that has the next highest number of Ds across the row and a P in the second column.

– If there are only a few unmarked columns, determine whether they are affected indirectly by the influencing factors you have selected. Put a different mark (such as a square or circle) at the top of each column where a selected factor has an indirect influence. If you still have a lot of unmarked columns, you may want to add a third and perhaps fourth leverage point.

- When you have selected your leverage points, you need to look for negative influences. A negative influence is a constraint on the system. If you ignore a negative influence, you will cause one part of the system to increase while another part decreases, which is like using the brake and the gas pedal at the same time.

- Understanding where negative interactions occur allows you to deal with them in your solutions. You need to find solutions that will neutralize or balance the constraint, rather than simply pushing harder on the positive interactions.

	Factor Name	P or B	1	2/5	3	4	6	7	8	9	10	11	12/13	14	15	16	17
			❑	★		❑	❑	★	❑	★	❑	★	★	★	★	❑	
2/5	Management control	B	+D	■	+I	+D	+I	+I		+I	+I	+I	+D				-D
6	Schedule adherence	B		+I		+I	■		+D		+I		+I	+D			
8	Planning thoroughness	P		+D		+I	+I	+D	■	+I	+I	+I	+D	+I	+I		
12/13	Information availability	P		+I		+I			+I	+D	+I	+I	■	+D	+D	+I	
15	Measurement system completeness	P	+I	+I		+I	+I		+I	+I	+I	+D		+I	■		
17	Independent problem solving	B		+I			+D		+I								■

Negative interaction

↑
Influences on Mgt. control

– In the preceding example, Management Control (Factor 2/5) has a negative influence on Independent Problem Solving (Factor 17). If you increase Management Control, you will decrease Independent Problem Solving, but you want to increase both of these factors.

- A negative influence on Independent Problem Solving not only affects that one factor, it also affects all of the factors that Independent Problem Solving influences. For example, a decrease in Independent Problem Solving will also decrease Schedule Adherence.

- You need to look at which leverage points (Factors 8, 12/13, and 15) will cause an increase in Management Control. In this case all three have an influence and Planning Thoroughness has a direct influence. When you get to the point of creating solutions you need to take into account that although you want more Management Control, you also need to find ways to minimize the negative influence so there is still room for Independent Problem Solving.

In this next case study, the program management team completes their analysis of factors and identifies their leverage points.

Case Study: Program Management (Part 13 of 13)

In their completed influence matrix, the team found three rows with three or more Ds: Factors 2/5, 8, and 12/13. Factor 2/5, Management Control, required a behavioral change though, so they focused on Factor 8, Planning Thoroughness, and Factor 12/13, Information Availability.

Because both factors had three Ds, it didn't really matter which one of these they evaluated first. The team chose to start with Factor 12/13. Moving across the row, the team put a star at the top of the column for Factor 9, Decision Defense (the first factor directly influenced by Factor 12/13). Continuing across the row, the team also put stars at the top of the columns for Factors 14 and 15 (the remaining two factors directly influenced by Factor 12/13).

	Factor Name	P or B	1	2/5	3	4	6	7	8	9 ★	10	11	12/13	14 ★	15 ★	16	17
12/13	Information availability	P		+I		+I			+I	+D	+I	+I	■	+D	+D	+I	

Continued...

Because many factors remained that were not being influenced, the team followed the same procedure for Factor 8 and added stars above columns 2/5, 7, and 12/13. By changing Information Availability (Factor 12/13) and Planning Thoroughness (Factor 8), the team could directly influence six of the 15 factors.

				★				★		★			★	★	★		
	Factor Name	**P or B**	1	2/5	3	4	6	7	8	9	10	11	12/13	14	15	16	17
8	Planning thoroughness	P		+D		+I	+I	+D	■	+I	+I	+I	+D	+I	+I		
12/13	Information availability	P		+I		+I			+I	+D	+I	+I	■	+D	+D	+I	

Next, the team looked for ways they could influence the rest of their factors. Few direct interactions were left that were influenced by process changes. Therefore, they looked to see which factors their current leverage points would influence indirectly and marked the columns for Factors 4, 6, 8, 10, 11, and 16 with boxes.

Because Factor 1, Program Requirement Precedence, and Factor 3, Life Cycle Support Importance, did not have any direct influences, the team decided these factors were peripheral to the core issues of the project and did not give them further consideration.

In evaluating the status of the influences, the team decided that a complete solution would need to have a direct influence on Factor 11 (Performance Monitoring), and therefore they added Factor 15 to their list of high leverage points. With this addition they could change the box at the top of the column for Factor 11 to a star.

				❏	★		❏	❏	★	❏	★	❏	★	★	★	★	❏
	Factor Name	**P or B**	1	2/5	3	4	6	7	8	9	10	11	12/13	14	15	16	17
8	Planning thoroughness	P		+D		+I	+I	+D	■	+I	+I	+I	+D	+I	+I		
12/13	Information availability	P		+I		+I			+I	+D	+I	+I	■	+D	+D	+I	
15	Measurement system completeness	P	+I	+I		+I	+I		+I	+I	+I	+D		+I	■		

Continued…

Finally, they looked for negative influences and discovered that the only influence on Factor 17, Independent Problem Solving, was a negative direct influence from Factor 2/5, Management Control. They chose not to address Independent Problem Solving directly because it is primarily behavioral; but they realized that the more they increased Management Control, the more they would discourage Independent Problem Solving. There was an obvious conflict here, but they believed that by focusing on Planning Thoroughness, Information Availability, and Measurement System Completeness they would be able to enhance an individual's ability to solve problems independently while still providing management monitoring capability if problems arose. Whatever solutions they eventually put into place would have to address this constraint.

When their analysis was complete, the team had identified three factors to target as high leverage points. Factor 8, Planning Thoroughness; Factor 12/13, Information Availability; and Factor 15, Measurement System Completeness. Changes to these leverage points would allow the team to affect 13 of their 15 factors. They had also identified a potential constraint on the system in terms of the negative interaction between Individual Problem Solving and Management Control. This conflict would need to be taken into consideration in the next stage of work.

The following diagram shows the rows of their final influence matrix that contain the three high leverage points.

Continued...

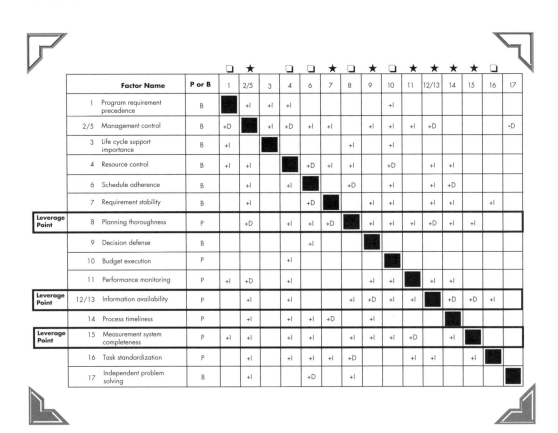

	Factor Name	P or B	1 ☐	2/5 ★	3 ☐	4 ☐	6 ★	7 ☐	8 ★	9 ☐	10 ★	11	12/13 ★	14 ★	15 ★	16 ★	17 ☐
1	Program requirement precedence	B	■	+I	+I	+I					+I						
2/5	Management control	B	+D	■	+I	+D	+I	+I		+I	+I	+I	+D				-D
3	Life cycle support importance	B	+I		■				+I		+I						
4	Resource control	B	+I	+I		■	+D	+I	+I		+D			+I	+I		
6	Schedule adherence	B		+I		+I	■		+D		+I			+I	+D		
7	Requirement stability	B		+I			+D	■		+I	+I			+I	+I		+I
Leverage Point 8	Planning thoroughness	P		+D		+I	+I	+D	■	+I	+I	+I	+D	+I	+I		
9	Decision defense	B					+I			■							
10	Budget execution	P				+I					■						
11	Performance monitoring	P	+I	+D		+I				+I	+I	■		+I	+I		
Leverage Point 12/13	Information availability	P		+I		+I			+I	+D	+I	+I	■	+D	+D	+I	
14	Process timeliness	P		+I		+I	+I	+D		+I				■			
Leverage Point 15	Measurement system completeness	P	+I	+I		+I	+I		+I	+I	+I	+D		+I	■		
16	Task standardization	P		+I		+I	+I	+I	+D		+I	+I			+I	■	
17	Independent problem solving	B		+I			+D		+I								■

Step S17 Check

Check to make sure your leverage points will have the maximum positive impact on your system. You should have

- ☐ A list of key factors that influence your system
- ☐ An understanding of how the factors influence one another
- ☐ A small set of high leverage points that will allow you to influence the entire system

Section Summary

You have now worked through the Systems Path of Understand the Voices. You should have completed the following:

❏ Selected appropriate dimensions for analysis

❏ Developed a key question for each dimension to focus your analysis of the interview data

❏ Identified relevant statements in the interview notes

❏ Created an affinity diagram showing what your strongest customer statements had in common

❏ Created a factor table to identify the factors in the system where your actions will have the most leverage

❏ Constructed an influence matrix to help you understand how the factors influence one another

❏ Identified whether the change required is process or behavioral

❏ Determined the smallest set of high leverage points

Looking ahead...

The final phase of the FOCUS process, Select Action, provides steps on how to translate your learnings into a complete solution, as well as some background on the creation of an action plan. Many teams at this point have gained so much insight into their issue that their next steps are clear. Other teams have only to make a report of their learnings to their sponsor or management. Review Select Action to see how these steps can best be used to meet your team's requirements.

S

Out of FOCUS

A company was developing a new product. The marketing department met with customers and discussed their needs. They met with lead users to learn where the field was headed. Then they handed off their research to a development team. Because they had not been involved in the initial research, the development team failed to see the importance of the work done by the marketing group. They considered themselves to be experts in the field and to have a good grasp on customer needs. Although they all read through many of the interviews, they never worked together to get a 360° view of their customers' world, or to gain a common perspective on customer needs.

When the team got together to brainstorm possible solutions, many wonderful ideas emerged. During a week of daylong meetings they pieced together each of their favorite ideas into an exciting product idea. However, they had no way to evaluate the value of either their individual ideas or their unified product concept for their customers. They could only judge it against what they thought was "good."

Nine months later the team tested a final prototype with several focus groups. The product bombed. No one wanted it. People thought it was beautiful and very well made, but it didn't meet their needs. For some it was too complex; for others it was overpriced; and for some it was just the wrong idea at the wrong time. Maybe a couple of years ago they could have used it, but not now.

Faced with the choice between entirely redesigning the product or simply scrapping it, the company chose to scrap it. Nine months' efforts by the entire development team went down the tubes.

SELECT
Action

SECTION CONTENTS

SELECT

F

FRAME THE PROJECT
1. Determine Purpose
2. Review Existing Data
3. Create Customer Profile Matrix
4. Create Interview Guide

O

ORGANIZE RESOURCES
5. Estimate Project Requirements
6. Meet With Sponsors
7. Negotiate Scope, Schedule, and Resources
8. Schedule Interviews

C

COLLECT DATA
9. Prepare for Visits
10. Polish Your Skills
11. Finalize Preparations
12. Conduct Interviews
13. Follow Up

U

UNDERSTAND THE VOICES
14. Check Your Direction
15. Focus Your Data Analysis
16. Structure the Data
17. Determine Key Areas to Address

S

SELECT ACTION
18. Generate Ideas
19. Evaluate Ideas and Create a Complete Solution
20. Develop an Action Plan

SELECT

Overview

In Understand the Voices, you had a choice of three paths for analysis. If you chose the Targeted Path, you identified the key themes that represent the greatest opportunities related to your issue. If the Requirements Path was most appropriate for your project, you identified performance requirements for a product, service, process, or policy. If the Systems Path best fit your needs, you identified several high leverage points that will have the greatest influence on the system as a whole.

Before beginning the work of Select Action, review the expectations and parameters that you outlined in Frame the Project. Being clear about the boundaries for the project will help you stay on target while going forward with Select Action.

Exploration of your issue through interviews and analysis has led you to a deeper, richer understanding of your customers' needs. In Select Action you translate this understanding into action.

SELECT

What You Gain by Selecting Action

- A variety of creative solutions or alternative actions to address your issue

- Selected actions based on customer input

- A basic plan in place to implement your actions

Questions You Will Be Answering

- What are all of the alternative ideas/actions/solutions to respond to what has been identified in the analysis of our interview data?

- How will we evaluate the alternatives?

- What actions will be taken?

- How will the actions be implemented?

Logistics

Much of the work in Select Action will be done by the group as a whole. The amount of time it will take will vary according to whether you are working with key themes, requirement statements, or high leverage points.

If you followed either the Targeted Path or the Systems Path, Step 18, Generate Ideas, is likely to take 2 – 4 hours. If you followed the Requirements Path this work could take several days and is best done in 2 – 4 half-day sessions. To maintain your focus, try to hold the sessions on sequential days rather than spreading them out.

> The group should generate and evaluate ideas to create a complete solution. However, it is not necessary to involve everyone in developing an action plan. This work can best be done by one person or a small group with input from others as needed.

Regardless of which path you took through Understand the Voices, Step 19, Evaluate Ideas and Create a Complete Solution, will take 4 – 8 hours.

If necessary, Step 20, Develop an Action Plan, can be completed by a subset of the team or the team leader. The time needed for this work will vary depending on the level of detail needed.

The following table shows how long this work typically takes.

Step	Estimated Time
Step 18: Generate Ideas	2 – 4 hours for themes or leverage points 2 – 4 half-day sessions for customer requirements
Step 19: Evaluate Ideas and Create a Complete Solution	4 – 8 hours
Step 20: Develop an Action Plan	2 – 4 hours to become familiar with the planning process 2 – 4 days to create a detailed implementation plan

SELECT

The Big Picture

18. Generate Ideas

19. Evaluate Ideas and Create a Complete Solution

20. Develop an Action Plan

Prework

- Determine project purpose
- Negotiate project scope, schedule, and resources
- Complete customer interviews
- Identify main themes, requirements, or leverage points

Time and Logistics

If you are generating ideas to address key themes or to capitalize on high leverage points, allow 2 – 4 hours for this work. If you are working with customer requirements, allow 2 – 4 half days.

Supplies and Equipment

- Flipchart or roll of white craft paper
- 3" x 3" self-stick notes
- Black, red, and blue pens for each participant
- Tape or pushpins

Outcomes

- Many possible ideas for action
- A tree diagram

SELECT

Step 18:

Generate Ideas

Description

Having learned what is important to your customers, it is now time to find ways to address the concerns or opportunities you have discovered. As in other steps of the FOCUS process, some iteration is built into the generation of ideas. You will alternate between divergent thinking to generate ideas and convergent thinking to narrow down the possibilities and build on the strengths of selected ideas.

Benefits

One of the most powerful outcomes of the FOCUS process is that a team of people who began a project with their own thoughts and ideas about the issue at hand share a common understanding by the time they are ready to select action. Collectively, they can focus their thoughtful, creative capacity on generating ideas to respond to that understanding.

Getting Your Bearings

You have just completed your analysis of the interview information. The synergy that results from the experience of analysis energizes the team to respond creatively to the findings. The ideas generated in this step will become pieces of a complete solution.

SELECT

How to Generate Ideas

A. Do background research (if needed)

At this point, teams often look to additional sources to expand their store of possible solutions or actions. Talking to organizations with similar processes can also spark ideas. Potential sources that you may find relevant include

- Internal or external experts
- Research, technical, or trade journals
- Related literature
- Databases
- Networking with other organizations
- Benchmark studies
- Patent searches
- Ideas suggested by your interviewees

B. Structure the process

Before plunging into the generation of ideas, structuring the process will optimize your creative output. Regardless of which path you followed in Understand the Voices, the work you do in these steps will be very similar. However, the structure you follow will vary somewhat.

If you followed either the Targeted Path or Systems Path, you will have a small set of key themes or high leverage points. Write each key theme or leverage point on a separate piece of flipchart paper. Complete substeps C through I for one theme or leverage point at a time. At the end of Step 18 you will have one tree diagram for each theme or leverage point.

If you followed the Requirements Path, you will have a set of Level 1 requirement titles. Write each Level 1 title on a separate piece of flipchart paper. Below each Level 1 title add the original requirement statements in that cluster. Next, complete the work of substeps C and D for each Level 1 title in turn. It is easier to generate a full set of ideas for one requirement before progressing to the next. When you have generated ideas for all the requirements, then you go back through each Level 1 requirement for substeps E and F. Finally, you will complete Step 18 by combining your best ideas into a single tree diagram.

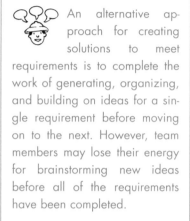 An alternative approach for creating solutions to meet requirements is to complete the work of generating, organizing, and building on ideas for a single requirement before moving on to the next. However, team members may lose their energy for brainstorming new ideas before all of the requirements have been completed.

C. Generate blue sky ideas

For whichever path you are following, brainstorm a multitude of blue sky ideas that address your Level 1 key theme, requirement, or high leverage point.

The purpose of generating blue sky ideas is for the group to think as broadly as possible. The ideas brainstormed here do not have to be practical. The goal is to break out of old patterns of thinking. Ideas and solutions have to start somewhere.

Brainstorm ideas from multiple perspectives. Try to think like

- A customer
- A competitor
- A five-year-old
- A science fiction writer
- A mad scientist
- An athlete, etc.

SELECT

The following examples show blue sky ideas for three different projects. Although most of the examples in this book use words to describe an idea, some people may find it easier to draw pictures.

Examples of blue sky ideas

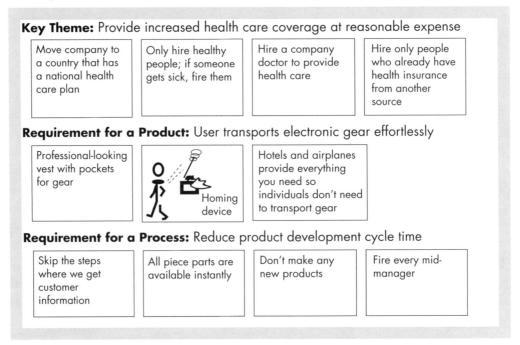

Key Theme: Provide increased health care coverage at reasonable expense

Move company to a country that has a national health care plan	Only hire healthy people; if someone gets sick, fire them	Hire a company doctor to provide health care	Hire only people who already have health insurance from another source

Requirement for a Product: User transports electronic gear effortlessly

Professional-looking vest with pockets for gear	Homing device	Hotels and airplanes provide everything you need so individuals don't need to transport gear

Requirement for a Process: Reduce product development cycle time

Skip the steps where we get customer information	All piece parts are available instantly	Don't make any new products	Fire every mid-manager

Blue sky ideas usually test the limits of any or all of the following:

- Market constraints—ideas you think customers would not like

- Organizational constraints—ideas so counter to organizational policies or procedures that they could get you fired

- Technology constraints—ideas beyond the levels of current technology; something you would have to be a magician to accomplish

You are more likely to find an innovative idea or solution if you have a large number to evaluate, so do not hold back. Print or draw each idea in black on a self-stick note and place it on the flipchart.

Brainstorming Checklist

The following guidelines will help your team use their brainstorming time most effectively:

- ❏ Start with silent thinking time (at least a minute or two)

- ❏ Freewheel—do not hold back

- ❏ Do not allow discussion during the brainstorming

- ❏ Do not criticize any idea—not even with a groan or grimace!

- ❏ Hitchhike—build on others' ideas

- ❏ Write down all ideas

The following case study shows how one company brainstormed blue sky ideas related to their customer requirements.*

Case Study: Web Site Development (Part 1 of 7)

A company decided it needed to create a World Wide Web site to meet its customers' expectations for using this technology and to reach out to prospective customers. The president decided to use the FOCUS process because Web site development was new to the company and no one knew what was important to their customers who used the Internet. When the Web site development team began the Select Action phase of the FOCUS process, they had ten Level 1 requirement titles.

- Users access pages quickly

- Users navigate site easily

- Site attracts users visually

- Site works effectively regardless of computer configurations

Continued...

*See Appendix B, *The Team® Handbook Second Edition,* for more information on brainstorming.

SELECT

- Targeted users value information found at site
- Site contains accurate information
- Users access company easily through various means
- Search engines identify site frequently
- Users place orders through site easily
- Users download information easily

For each Level 1 requirement, the team brainstormed ideas for solutions. They started out with blue sky ideas—ones that were unlikely to be selected but that might provide seeds for other ideas. For their first requirement, they generated the following ideas that would create faster access for users.

Users access pages quickly

Simple line graphics	Government provides everyone with ISDN lines
One word pages	Send entire page in a single chunk
Install fiber optics to all users	No graphics

D. Generate mainstream ideas

Blue sky ideas alone are not likely to get you to the point of creating a solution. Now pull back into the realm of more traditional, mainstream ideas. Write or draw your ideas in black on self-stick notes. Place these on the flipchart along with your blue sky ideas. You may also come up with additional blue sky ideas that can be added to the group.

The following examples illustrate mainstream ideas for the same three projects shown previously.

Examples of mainstream ideas

Key Theme: Provide increased health care coverage at reasonable expense

Move to a managed care plan	Build on-site health club	Free memberships at local health clubs	Provide multiple plans to choose from

Requirement for a Product: User transports electronic gear effortlessly

Use a sturdy but lightweight fabric	Add external pocket sized for cell phone	Professional-looking backpack design	Install "roller blade" wheels in the bottom

Requirement for a Process: Reduce product development cycle time

Get customer information on an ongoing basis so we don't start from scratch with each new project	Design to minimize piece parts	Design to minimize assembly steps	Get customer information earlier

SELECT

Here is the second round of ideas generated by the Web site development team.

 Case Study: Web Site Development (Part 2 of 7)

Still working with their first customer requirement, "Users access pages quickly," the team brainstormed the following mainstream ideas for solutions.

Use graphic server for graphics	Relatively small graphics
Keep background simple	Use width and height tags for graphics
Interleave graphics	Use image previews for large graphics

If you are working with requirements, cycle back to substep C for the next Level 1 requirement. Complete all Level 1 requirements before continuing. For key themes and high leverage points, complete the rest of Step 18 before cycling back for the next key theme or high leverage point.

E. Organize the ideas (optional)

If you have more than 30 ideas on any single flipchart, consider clustering the notes into subsets to make the following work more manageable. Clustering allows you to step back from the detail of generating ideas and see the big picture. Cluster notes by similarities or categories of how to do something. You may find it helpful to write broad titles to help you categorize the ideas. You are not, however, creating an affinity diagram. You can have any number of notes in a cluster and you can use any titles that seem to make sense. Once the notes have been clustered, take time to do a quick check for any aspects of the issue that have not been addressed yet.

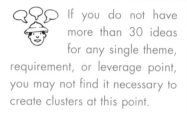

If you do not have more than 30 ideas for any single theme, requirement, or leverage point, you may not find it necessary to create clusters at this point.

F. Build on strengths of previous ideas

The ideas you have generated are pieces of what will become a total solution. Brainstorming allows for creativity and the inclusion of all ideas. You now want to see if any of those ideas can be improved upon.

On flipchart paper create one continuum for each theme, requirement, or leverage point. If you subdivided a set of ideas into clusters, create a separate continuum for each cluster. You will find it difficult to work with more than about 30 notes on a single continuum.

Draw a horizontal line on the paper and divide it into five levels of acceptability, as shown below.

| Far-fetched idea | Kernel of something useful | Threshold of acceptability | Good idea—could implement | Perfect idea |

Place each idea where you think it belongs along the continuum, as shown in the example on the following page. The ideas to the right of the threshold of acceptability are ones you might implement as part of a solution. However, even the ideas to the left of the threshold line, no matter how wacky or outrageous, usually have some merit. Try now to build on those strengths in order to move less acceptable ideas over the threshold of acceptability.

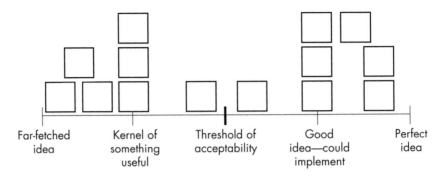

Starting on the left side of the continuum, evaluate each idea by asking, "What's the strength of this idea? How can we improve it?" Now try to build on that strength and generate another idea that falls further to the right on the continuum. Write this new idea on a self-stick note and place it where you think it falls on the continuum, as shown below.

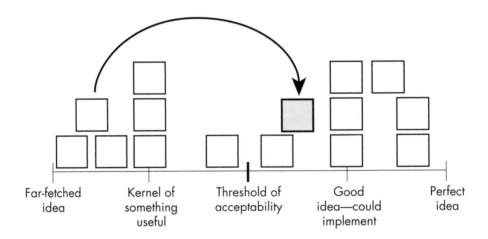

It is possible for one original idea to lead to multiple new ideas. You may also come up with unrelated ideas that can be added to the continuum at any time.

SELECT

The following illustration shows how ideas to the left of the threshold of acceptability can be built on to create new, more feasible ideas. The first example is laid out on the continuum; the rest illustrate how the principle might work.

Examples of ideas built on other ideas

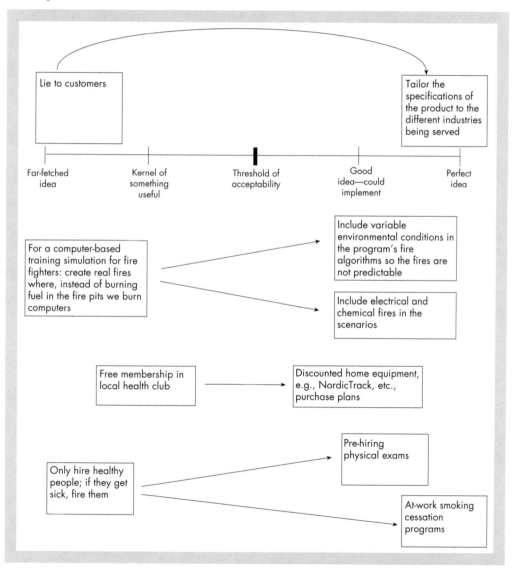

Here is how the Web site team created a continuum for their first customer requirement.

Case Study: Web Site Development (Part 3 of 7)

Because the team had only generated 24 ideas for their first requirement, they did not divide these ideas into clusters. Instead, their first continuum contained all of their initial ideas around accessing pages quickly. As the team laid out their ideas on a continuum, they discussed the merits of each. They identified some ideas that would never fly. For instance, ISDN lines and fiber optics were far-fetched ideas because the team could not control when users would have access to these technologies.

Some ideas, however, did have strengths on which the team could build. For instance, the idea of using simple line graphics led to two new ideas: "Limit colors as appropriate" and "Use minimum graphic complexity needed to convey message." They knew customers wanted a visually appealing site, but complex graphics slow down accessing pages. By limiting color and complexity, they could use graphics that were visually appealing and compatible with quick access.

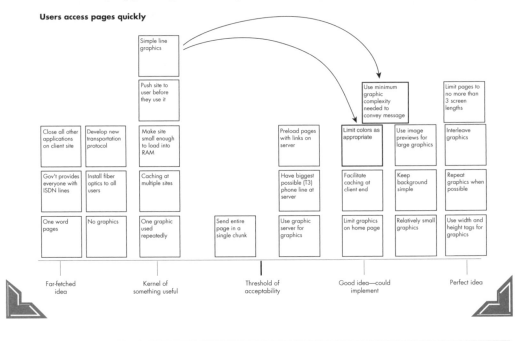

If you are working with requirements, cycle back to substep E for the next Level 1 requirement. Complete the process of organizing and building on ideas for each Level 1 requirement before continuing. For key themes and high leverage points, proceed with the rest of Step 18 before cycling back to substep C for the next theme or leverage point.

G. Choose best ideas

The ideas you have generated so far are only fragments of a total solution. In order to identify a complete solution, you will organize these ideas into one or more tree diagrams to create a cohesive whole. But first you should review the ideas and select those you think are best to carry forward.

If you are working with requirements, you will combine all of your ideas into a single solution. To do this, consider all ideas that made it past the threshold of acceptability on each requirement continuum. Then identify no more than 40 of the best ideas to use in the tree diagram.*

If you are working with key themes or high leverage points, you will create a solution for each one. Combine the ideas that made it past the threshold of acceptability on each cluster's continuum; then identify no more than 40 of the best ideas to use in each tree diagram.

A useful technique for choosing the vital few from the useful many is the Method for Priority Marking™.** Working simultaneously, each team member should mark a red dot on the lower right corner of the ideas they consider to be the best of the group. If someone likes a note that already has a dot on it, he or she should simply leave it and move on. When everyone is finished, remove the unmarked ideas (but save them for possible future reference). If you have more than 40 notes left, go through the marking process again, adding a second dot to the notes you want to keep. At the end of this round remove all of the notes that have only one dot on them. Continue with additional rounds until you get down to 40 ideas. (For further details on the MPM process, see p. 217 in Understand the Voices.)

*See Appendix B for more information on tree diagrams.
**See Appendix B for more information on the Method for Priority Marking™.

SELECT

Here is how the Web site team identified their strongest customer voices.

Case Study: Web Site Development (Part 4 of 7)

After the team had brainstormed solutions and identified the most feasible ideas on a continuum for each of their requirements, they realized that they had many more ideas than they could possibly address. Their next step was to identify the 40 strongest from the 300+ ideas that had passed the threshold of acceptability.

They posted their continuums for each requirement, or cluster, around the room and team members marked any ideas they thought valuable with a red dot. After the first round they still had more than 40 notes, so they gathered together all of the notes with red dots. Then they went through another round of selection, adding a second red dot to the most important ideas. Reducing the number of notes was not as difficult as they expected. They found that some ideas had been repeated for several requirements, so they selected the one that was worded best. At the end of the second round they discovered that they were down to 39 notes.

H. Structure the ideas

You now have a manageable number of ideas, but they are still only that—individual ideas. Now you need to understand how these ideas fit together to create a clear solution on which you can take action. Identifying these relationships is the first step in creating a tree diagram.

Although these steps resemble an affinity diagram, there are some differences. In this case, you *are* looking for cause-and-effect relationships. The title for each cluster should be the *effect* which the individual ideas in the cluster would *cause*.

- In the upper left corner of a piece of flipchart paper, identify the problem you are trying to solve. A useful format is to begin your questions with

  – "How do we address _____?"
  – "How do we solve _____?"
  – "How do we fix _____?"
  – "How do we impact _____ ?"
  – "How do we design _____?"

SELECT

If you are working with requirements, you should have one question for whatever it is you are trying to create or redesign. If you are working with themes or leverage points, you should have one question related to each.

- Review each selected idea to make sure it can be translated into action and is low on the ladder of abstraction. If necessary, rephrase the idea and write a new note. Since these notes will become the basis of your action plan, it is important to word them as actions.

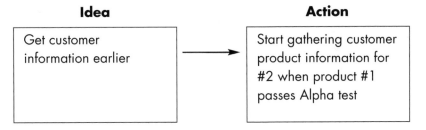

Idea	**Action**
Get customer information earlier	Start gathering customer product information for #2 when product #1 passes Alpha test

- Next, group the notes according to common purpose; each group should be solving the same issue. You should have no more than four notes in a group.

- For each cluster of notes, write a title that is action-oriented and describes what the group of notes will accomplish. To write a title, it may be helpful for the team to ask, "If we do all of these things, what will we accomplish?" Print your title in red on a self-stick note.

- Gather the original notes for each cluster and place them under their red Level 1 titles so that only the titles show.

- Group these Level 1 titles according to common purpose and write Level 2 titles for the new clusters in blue on self-stick notes. If you have more than five Level 2 clusters, continue the clustering and titling process until there are five or fewer groups. For each new level of titles, select a different pen color to more easily differentiate the levels later in the tree diagram. These multiple levels of clusters and titles will help the team see the big picture when creating a complete solution.

SELECT

The following examples show clusters and Level 1 titles for three different projects. The first cluster, on the left, is for a training simulator for fire fighters. The second cluster is for an alternative to the traditional briefcase that can incorporate the electronic gear many people need to carry today. And the two clusters on the right are both for ways to provide increased health care coverage at reasonable expense.

Examples of clusters

Simulate different types of fires	Integrate some electronic gear as part of whole product	Promote healthier lifestyle	Research alternative health care providers
Include electrical fires in the scenarios	Put pocket for phone on outside	Free membership in local health club	Identify area HMO's
Include chemical fires in the scenarios	Include a cell phone	Discounted home exercise equipment	Develop tiered offerings
Provide a variety of scenarios in different settings	Include a built-in battery recharger	At-work smoking cessation programs	Create matrix of alternative providers vs. services provided
Include the possibility of buildings containing hazardous materials			

SELECT

Here is how the Web site team sorted their ideas into clusters and wrote Level 1 titles.

Case Study: Web Site Development (Part 5 of 7)

Next, the team sorted their ideas into small clusters of no more than four notes each. As with the affinity diagram in their data analysis, people moved notes around for awhile. Gradually, they started discussing why they felt notes belonged in certain groups, and eventually they settled on 16 clusters.

Then, for each cluster they asked, "If we do these things, what will we accomplish?" The answer became the title, which they wrote in red and placed above the cluster. For instance, if they could redirect automatically for old or expired links, create frequently changing information dynamically from an updatable database, and assign a Web site "owner" to manage updates, they would be able to keep the site up-to-date and accurate. This then became the Level 1 title for the cluster (see third Level 1 cluster from the left in the illustration on the following page).

When the team was finished titling the Level 1 groupings, they stacked the clusters, with only the Level 1 titles showing. Then they clustered Level 1 titles until they had only five Level 2 titles, which they wrote in blue. The following illustration shows two of their five Level 2 clusters. The notes have been spread out to show the complete clusters.

Continued...

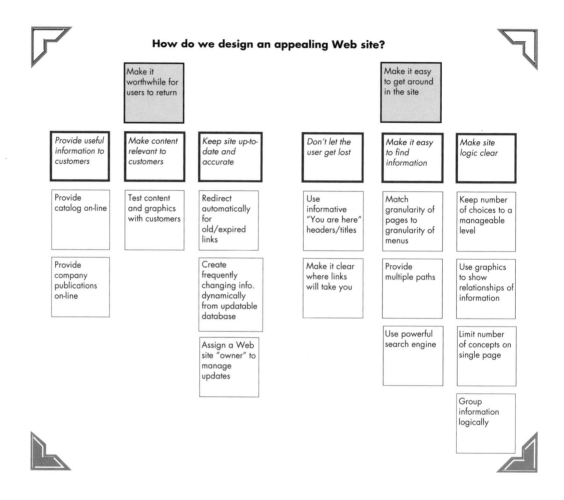

How do we design an appealing Web site?

I. Lay out tree diagram

You will now lay out the groupings and titles in a tree diagram, which will show how your individual ideas for actions relate to an overall solution. If you are working with requirements you will create a single tree; if you are working with themes or leverage points you will create one tree for each.

- Tape multiple sheets of flipchart paper together on the walls, allowing enough space for all of your original notes to lie side by side in a single horizontal line (approximately ten feet).

   Instead of taping flipchart paper together you may prefer using rolls of white craft paper, available at most art supply stores.

- Start at the left side of the paper and follow down one branch at a time by placing the first top level title toward the top of the paper. Eventually these top level titles will spread across the full width of the paper.

- For each top level title, place the next level titles that are part of the cluster below it. Check to see if the lower level titles are sufficient to accomplish the higher level title. Is anything missing? If so, add another note at this level and then create all of the lower levels that are necessary components to achieve the action of this new title. Don't worry if you have more titles than are necessary. Your action plan will not have to include every idea; at this point you are more concerned with making sure you have not left anything out that might be needed later for a complete solution.

- Continue laying out the titles and clusters, checking at each level to make sure nothing is missing to accomplish the action described in the title.

- Once you are satisfied that your tree diagram is complete, draw connecting lines to show the relationships among the notes.

Example of sequence for layout of the tree

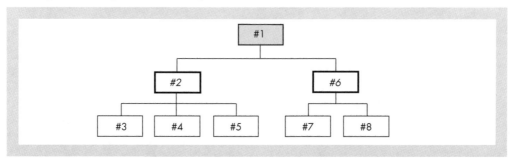

After completing your tree diagram, you should have at least three levels of notes: the original notes across the bottom, the red Level 1 titles in the middle, and the blue Level 2 titles at the top. If you have additional levels these would continue up the paper.

SELECT

The following case study shows how the Web site development team laid out their tree diagram.

Case Study: Web Site Development (Part 6 of 7)

To begin laying out their tree diagram, the team spread their Level 2 titles across four sheets of flipchart paper taped together. Then they checked to see if their solution was complete. When they were satisfied that nothing was missing, they laid out each of the Level 1 titles under the Level 2 titles. Then they checked to make sure the Level 1 titles were sufficient to accomplish the Level 2 titles. Finally, they laid out all of the original notes in a straight line under the Level 1 titles. Because they had to move clusters around to get all of the notes to fit, they were glad they had not started drawing lines yet. When the diagram was complete, they drew lines to show the relationships.

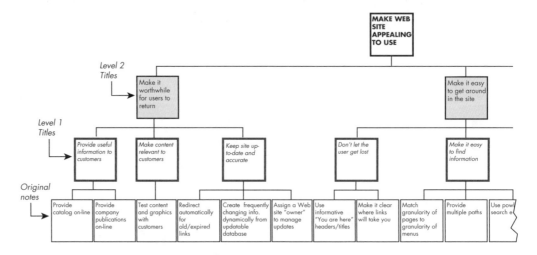

Step 18 Check

Check to make sure your ideas completely address your issue. You should have

- ❑ Diverse ideas that address the themes, leverage points, or requirements

- ❑ A tree diagram showing the components of a comprehensive solution

SELECT

The Big Picture

18. Generate Ideas
19. **Evaluate Ideas and Create a Complete Solution**
20. Develop an Action Plan

Prework

- Create one tree diagram for all requirements or one tree diagram for each theme or leverage point

Time and Logistics

Evaluating ideas and creating a complete solution will take 4 – 8 hours. This is best done in one meeting devoted specifically to this work.

Supplies and Equipment

- Copy of tree diagram(s)
- Flipchart or roll of white craft paper
- Flipchart markers
- Straightedge or yardstick
- Tape or pushpins
- 3" x 3" self-stick notes
- Black, red, and blue pens

Outcomes

- Evaluation matrix
- Criteria to evaluate ideas
- Identification of the best solution(s)
- Meeting with sponsors to present your learnings and solution

Step 19:

Evaluate Ideas and Create a Complete Solution

Description

In this step you will objectively evaluate all of the alternative solution components, based on effectiveness, feasibility, and thoroughness in addressing themes, requirements, or leverage points. You will then choose and refine a complete solution.

Benefits

At this point you probably have many more ideas than can be included in your solution, and some may even contradict one another. Evaluating the effectiveness and feasibility of the ideas will help you select the best components of a complete solution.

Getting Your Bearings

In Step 18 you generated and organized a host of ideas to address your issue at hand. However, some of those ideas are more important than others, some are more effective than others, and some are easier to implement than others. You will now impartially evaluate each idea on the bottom level of your tree diagram to determine which are the best to implement. The ideas you select here form the basis for your action plan.

SELECT

How to Evaluate Ideas and Create a Complete Solution

A. Determine evaluation criteria

To decide on what actions to take, the team needs to evaluate the selected ideas. Two main criteria to consider are effectiveness and feasibility.

- Effectiveness indicates how much improvement or change you would see if a particular idea were implemented. For some organizations, effectiveness might be a change in a measurable indicator (such as time, defects, errors, or quality). For others, it might mean a more qualitative change (such as employee perceptions that something is easier).

- Feasibility indicates how easy an idea would be to implement. Typical factors that influence feasibility are the amount and type of change required, time and cost required, level of investment needed, whether training is called for, and so on.

Effectiveness and feasibility are key evaluative criteria against which to check your possible solutions. If an idea is not effective, it may not be worth spending energy trying to make it work. An effective idea may not be feasible at this point in time.

Prior to rating the ideas, the group may want to briefly discuss and define what effectiveness and feasibility mean in the context of your issue. The following questions can be used as a guide for this discussion.

SELECT

Examples of evaluation criteria

Effectiveness	Feasibility
• How directly will this idea address the concern behind the customers' requirement?	• How compatible is the idea with existing capabilities or competencies?
• Does it substantively enhance a high leverage point?	• Does the solution support or conflict with other ongoing
• Does it help to neutralize or balance a system constraint indicated by a negative interaction?	• Does the solution require changes in behavior?
	• How much will it cost to implement the idea?
	• How much time will be needed to implement the idea?
	• Are the necessary resources available, such as equipment, supplies, staffing?
	• How much training will be needed?

B. Construct an evaluation matrix

Each tree diagram you constructed will now become the top part of an evaluation matrix. You will likely need to add sheets of flipchart paper below the tree diagram to construct the evaluation matrix. You need enough paper to add one row each for effectiveness, feasibility, and a rating summary. If you are working with requirements, you will need additional space to list each requirement on its own row. You need as many columns as you have bottom level notes to evaluate plus one additional on the far left side of your matrix to write in the names of the rows. Your evaluation matrix should look similar to the example on the next page.

SELECT

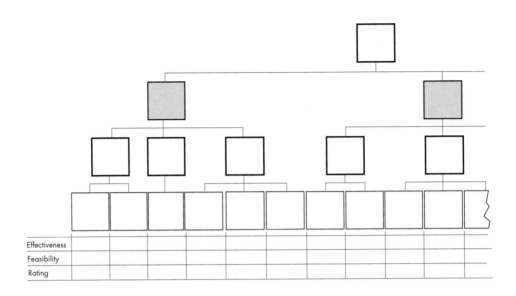

Effectiveness										
Feasibility										
Rating										

C. Evaluate the ideas

Use a visual evaluation system, such as the following, to assess each note for effectiveness and feasibility.

⊙ strong

◯ moderate

△ weak

When voting, team members can use the signs of thumbs up, sideways, or down to indicate strong, moderate, or weak, respectively. Evaluate the ideas (bottom level notes) one at a time, first for effectiveness and then for feasibility.

D. Rate the ideas

Compare your evaluations with the symbol combinations below and indicate in the rating row of your evaluation matrix the appropriate number. A rating of 1 indicates a very strong solution component, and a rating of 9 indicates a solution component not likely worth pursuing.

Effectiveness	◉	◉	◯	◯	◉	△	◯	△	△
Feasibility	◉	◯	◉	◯	△	◉	△	◯	△
Rating	1	2	3	4	5	6	7	8	9

This rating scheme is weighted to recognize that effectiveness is more important than feasibility—if an idea is not effective, its feasibility is not all that important.

Some of your ideas will be rated 1, 2, or 3. These are strong candidates to become part of your complete solution. Some ideas may be rated 7, 8, or 9. These are strong candidates to ignore. Review the mid-range ratings. Some ideas may receive a strong rating in one category, but a moderate or weak rating in another. For instance, an idea may have a low feasibility rating and a high effectiveness rating. If some people think the idea is essential to implement, the group may want to think of a new idea—a similar way to solve the issue that is more feasible. If you generate a new idea, add it to the matrix and then rate it. However, the group may decide to simply change the rating of the idea. In this case, write the new rating in a different color ink on the matrix.

 If the group identifies ideas that are crucial but require additional resources, you may want to talk with your sponsors about the possibility of securing the additional resources needed.

SELECT

E. Check matrix for complete coverage of issue (Requirements only)

Check to make sure that the ideas you generated collectively address all of your requirements. You particularly want to make sure you have addressed those requirements that received high importance ratings on your customer survey. Begin with the ideas that received a rating of 1 and place a check mark in the corresponding cell at each requirement it addresses. It is possible that a strong idea will address more than one requirement. After you have worked through the ideas that received a rating of 1, then go on to those with a rating of 2, then 3, and so forth.

> Ideally your complete solution will address all of your requirements. However, if feasibility or resource limitations constrain you, the feedback from the customer survey will help you identify which requirements are most critical to fulfill.

The following case study follows the Web site team as they complete their evaluation matrix.

Case Study: Web Site Development (Part 7 of 7)

Although the team felt confident that they had not left out any ideas in their tree diagram, they knew they had more than they needed. In fact, some of their ideas were mutually exclusive or at least needed to be balanced against one another. For instance, using frames in the Web site design might make navigation easier, but it would not work on older browsers. Frames would also make it more difficult for users to directly access specific pages through bookmarks. One possible solution would be to create two mirror sites, one with frames and the other without. Graphics were another area that would require balancing. Customers liked visually appealing sites that loaded quickly.

First, the team evaluated each idea for effectiveness and feasibility. Next, they rated each idea. Then, they listed their requirements and checked to see whether they were still all addressed. In areas where they would have to make trade-offs, they could see which ideas satisfied the most requirements. They focused primarily on items with ratings of 4 or lower.

Continued...

SELECT

A portion of the team's evaluation matrix is shown below.

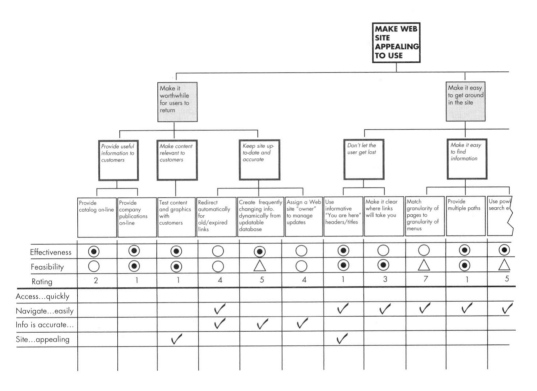

Two of the items with the moderate score of 5 still seemed as if they would be valuable additions to the Web site: "Create frequently changing information dynamically from updatable database" and "Use powerful search engine." These had both received high ratings for effectiveness and low ratings for feasibility. When the team discussed why they had scored them low in feasibility, they realized that in both cases special expertise was necessary to accomplish the tasks. They decided to go to their sponsors to try to get funding to pursue these ideas.

F. Create solution

All the work of the FOCUS process culminates in a recommendation for a solution that will completely address the issue under exploration. The completed matrix, or matrices, should serve as an aid to your decision making, not a substitute for it. The decision you make at this point is crucial.

In most cases, the solution to be implemented is a combination of ideas. If in the process of creating the complete solution you come up with additional ideas, add more notes to the solution tree and rate the new proposals for effectiveness and feasibility, as you did the other ideas.

When you have all of the alternatives laid out, make your choice based on everything you know, not only on what is captured in the matrix:

- In your best judgment, does the matrix capture the best possible solution components?

- Which solution components seem best when you look at the ratings?

- Do the final ratings match what your experience tells you is true?

- Does your choice reflect all of the ideas, issues, and concerns you have generated, as well as the discussions that occurred during your analysis?

- Is anything missing?

Revise and refine the solution components as needed until you feel comfortable with the complete solution chosen for implementation.

G. Document solution

Now that you have determined the solution to your issue, or decided how to address your key themes, high leverage points, or requirements, it is important to document this solution. Depending on the project, your documentation could be a drawing, flowchart, or a written report highlighting the significant points of the solution. Whatever method of documentation you choose, it is important to tie the solution back to the customers and how it meets their needs. You will use this documentation when you meet with your sponsors to present your learnings and proposed solution.

You may choose to check your solution with some of the interviewees and include their feedback in the documentation. In performing this check, not only will you receive feedback on the proposed solution, but also your customer relationships will be enhanced by this confirmation that the interviews provided useful information.

SELECT

H. Meet with sponsor

In this critical meeting with your sponsor, you will present your learnings from the customer interviews and the team's proposed solution for dealing with the issue at hand. The documentation created in the previous substep can serve as the foundation for this presentation. This meeting also allows management the opportunity to review your proposed solution and ensure that it meets the organization's requirements.

If you are expected to provide more information than simply your findings and a recommended solution, you may want to take some time to review Step 20, Develop an Action Plan. This step contains some common planning tools used to create an implementation plan. Reviewing Step 20 can also help you anticipate and prepare for questions the sponsors may ask.

It is important for each team member to be present and to have a role in this meeting. This participation will foster a sense of ownership and allow everyone to share in the credit for the work done.

This meeting may signal the end of the team's work. Depending on the structure of your organization, a new group may be formed to develop a detailed implementation plan and assume responsibility for carrying out the solution.

Step 19 Check

Check to make sure you have a complete solution that can be implemented. You should have

- ❑ An evaluation matrix rating each idea for effectiveness and feasibility

- ❑ A solution that addresses the key issues

- ❑ Documentation of your solution

- ❑ Met with your sponsor to present your learnings and solution

SELECT

The Big Picture

18. Generate Ideas
19. Evaluate Ideas and Create a Complete Solution
20. **Develop an Action Plan**

Prework
- Select one or more solutions for implementation
- Meet with sponsor, if necessary

Time and Logistics

If you are using this step for preliminary planning, the work is likely to take 2 – 4 hours. However, if you are using this step as a springboard for a more detailed plan, allow 2 – 4 days to create the plan. In the interest of time and efficiency, this work may be done by the team leader or a small subset of the team, with input from other team members as needed.

Supplies and Equipment
- Copy of documentation of solution(s)

Outcomes
- A plan for implementation of your solution

SELECT

Step 20:

Develop an Action Plan

Description

This step will help you determine the actions needed to implement the selected solution. The material presented here does not include everything you need to develop a detailed action plan. However, the outline of the basic steps will shape your thinking and provide an overview of some helpful tools.

Benefits

The development of an action plan forces the team to think through the necessary steps for successful implementation of the solution. The planning process will also help you identify possible obstacles and allow you to develop contingency plans.

Getting Your Bearings

Having evaluated all possible ideas and identified the best solution to address the learnings from the interviews, your team's work may be over. However, for other teams it is now time to develop an action plan to implement the solution.

The people who will be responsible for implementing the solution may not be the same people who did the work of the FOCUS process. It is important that whoever will be responsible for implementing the action plan be part of developing the plan. If the implementation team does not include any members of the FOCUS process team, the documentation that was created at the end of Step 19 will be a key resource to this new team of people.

SELECT

How to Develop an Action Plan

A. Identify and sequence implementation steps

Identifying the implementation steps can be accomplished in a variety of ways. Here are two possible approaches. Your organization may use others.

- Brainstorm a list of possible actions; then sort them into steps and substeps arranged in chronological sequence.

- Start from the beginning and walk through the implementation process step-by-step.

 Writing the steps on self-stick notes will allow for resequencing steps as your plan evolves. You could also use a computer program that will number, renumber, and then sort steps as you make changes.

At first you probably will not identify every step necessary for implementation. As you arrange the steps in chronological sequence, ask yourself, "Can I move directly from step to step, or are some actions missing?" If so, identify and include those actions. Performing this check for each step will move the group closer to identifying all of the steps. However, do not be surprised if your sponsors are able to identify additional gaps. People outside the team often see things differently and ask valuable "What about?" or "What if?" questions.*

B. Develop sketch of steps and schedule

It is helpful to display the identified steps or tasks in a flowchart. This process captures the basic flow of steps and allows people to look at the information in a different way. Looking at the information in a flowchart also provides the opportunity for identifying gaps between steps or overlooked areas. Many types of flowcharts can be used, but either a basic flowchart or a deployment flowchart is most useful for this purpose.

It is also helpful to develop and display a project schedule. By having this available from the start, you will be able to see how missing deadlines shifts the entire project schedule. Also, the schedule is a good point of discussion if project resources change.

*See Appendix B for more information on the 9-Step Project Planning System.

SELECT

Guide to Common Planning Tools

Basic flowchart

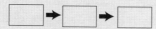

Visually displays the basic flow of steps. Captures the overall picture. Easy to construct.

Deployment flowchart

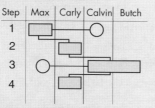

Shows who does what, when. Good tool for team members to work from. Extremely useful when there are many handoffs between people or groups.

PERT chart

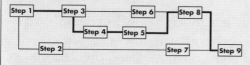

Shows how a plan is put together. Useful for showing the interrelationship of steps. Identifies the critical path where efforts should be concentrated.

Gantt chart

STEP	WEEK		
	Nov 1	Nov 8	Nov 15
Purchase equipment	▬		
Develop training	▬		
Training session		▬	
Pilot test			▬

Communicates progress and expectations. Visually shows the timing and duration of steps. Good tool for team members to work from. Some software planning tools combine the PERT chart and Gantt chart into a single diagram.

Resource allocation chart

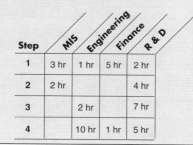

Step	MIS	Engineering	Finance	R & D
1	3 hr	1 hr	5 hr	2 hr
2	2 hr			4 hr
3		2 hr		7 hr
4		10 hr	1 hr	5 hr

Shows how much time each step will require from the various functions. Useful for determining the needed resource levels and for developing overall timeline.

SELECT

C. Complete a planning or implementation worksheet

Once you have identified the steps needed to implement the solution, you may want to begin thinking about the resources necessary to do the work and the timeline for making it happen. The following planning worksheet documents six categories of information:

1. Summary Task: As you identified your steps, you probably found that you had several large steps, each made up of several substeps. The larger steps are the summary tasks that need to be accomplished to implement the solution. The number of summary tasks will vary, depending on the complexity of the project.

2. Step/Task: These are the substeps or individual tasks that must be accomplished to meet each summary task.

3. Prerequisites: These identify what has to happen before work on a given step or task can be initiated or completed. It is important to distinguish between initiated and completed. At times, steps may be carried out simultaneously, but there may be steps that cannot be completed until another step is finished.

4. Resources: These people, departments, equipment, etc. are necessary for the completion of the step or task.

5. Duration: This is an indication of how much time will be needed from the person or function to complete the step or task.

6. Start/Finish: This reflects the elapsed time from the beginning of the work on the step or task to the completion of the work.

Planning Worksheet

Summary Task	Step/Task	Prerequisites	Resources	Duration	Start/Finish

If you need to develop your project plan in greater detail, you may want to complete an implementation worksheet similar to the following sample. It includes measures of progress, target values, and scheduled review dates. Such a worksheet will help you determine if the project is staying on track to meet its deadlines.

Implementation Worksheet

Summary Task (& Owner)	Step/Task (& Owner)	Measure of Progress	Target Value (& Actual)	Scheduled Completion (& Actual)	Scheduled Review Date

The next case study shows how one team completed their implementation worksheet.

Case Study: Performance Indicators (Part 1 of 1)

A team studying departmental conflicts identified the lack of common performance indicators as a key barrier to progress. The implementation worksheet on the following page shows the first steps the team planned to take in order to develop a set of common measures for the entire division.

Step 1, identifying implementation team members, will be done by the department managers. The measure of progress for this step is the number of people identified, and the target value is eight people—one from each department. This task should be completed by January 1.

Step 2 involves identifying six process measures for each of four functional areas. The measure of progress is the number of measures, and the target value is 24 (six measures multiplied by four areas). This task cannot begin until the first task is completed because the team is responsible for the work in this step.

Continued...

SELECT

Step 3, operationally defining measures, will take several weeks to complete. Depending on what the next step is, it may be possible to start work on Step 4 before Step 3 is completed. Some steps may be interrelated without being dependent on the completion of one before another begins.

On February 1, progress on all three steps will be reviewed. However, it is important to keep close track of progress throughout the work. If Step 1 is not completed on schedule, the rest of the steps will also be late.

Implementation Worksheet for
Performance Indicators Team

Summary Task (& Owner)	Step/Task (& Owner)	Measure of Progress	Target Value (& Actual)	Scheduled Completion (& Actual)	Scheduled Review Date
Develop divisional performance indicators	1. Identify team members (department mgrs)	number of people	8	Jan 1	Feb 1
	2. Identify 6 process measures for each functional area (team)	number of measures	24	Jan 8	Feb 1
	3. Operationally define measures (team)	number of agreed-on definitions	24	Jan 22	Feb 1

D. Complete plans and identify contingencies

To complete your plans, pull together your evaluation matrix and all of the documentation generated in this step, including any flowcharts, worksheets, or other planning tools. Review these plans and identify any assumptions you have built into the plans. Now think about contingency plans for each assumption—what would you do to keep your plan moving forward if a key assumption were changed?

The following examples show some assumptions and possible contingencies.

Examples of various contingencies

Type of Assumption	Possible Contingency
Resources (especially budget or people)	If the budget is squeezed, we will have to defer part of the implementation until next quarter
Schedule	If needed staff are unavailable, the time frame may expand by two months or we will need to hire additional people.
Marketplace trends	If consumer buying behavior changes, we will continue to monitor the marketplace and assess how changes impact other assumptions.
Dependencies on other events or processes	If HR plans are not completed by May 15, we can deploy one staff person for two hours a week to help finish work.

E. Plan for progress updates

As you are building your plan, think about how and with whom you will communicate the progress of your plan. Some of your planning documents, such as the implementation worksheet, can serve as visual updates for people. Also think of written communications you may need to prepare. Finally, you will want to build into your plan routine progress checks to update your sponsors.

SELECT

Step 20 Check

Check to make sure you understand the basic components of an implementation plan. You will need to have

- ❏ The sequence of the individual steps necessary to complete your project
- ❏ The resources required to complete each step
- ❏ An understanding of the relationships among the steps
- ❏ A way to monitor progress
- ❏ Contingency plans for key assumptions
- ❏ Routine progress checks with your sponsor

SELECT

Section Summary

You have now worked through the final phase of the FOCUS process, Select Action. You should have completed the following:

- ❏ Generated ideas

- ❏ Laid out the best ideas in a tree diagram

- ❏ Evaluated the ideas

- ❏ Created a solution

- ❏ Documented the solution

- ❏ Met with sponsors

- ❏ Developed an action plan

Looking ahead...

The team that was assembled at the beginning of this FOCUS process has now reached its destination—you know how to address your customers' needs. It is now time to move from exploration to implementation, which may well be the work of a new team.

Before your team disbands, take time to pull together your project documentation and reflect on the FOCUS process. You may also want to share what you have learned about the process with others in your organization.

Reflect,
Acknowledge,
Celebrate the team's work!

SELECT

Case In Point

In FOCUS: The Health Alliance of Greater Cincinnati

Four very different hospitals were merging to form the Health Alliance of Greater Cincinnati. The leadership of the new Alliance decided that for the integration of some functions, such as laundry service, changes would be made on the basis of cost, customer service, and quality. For the more people-oriented functions, such as laboratory and pharmacy services, they wanted to involve hospital staff in determining the redesign of the merged services.

"This effort involves the merging of six pharmacies from four hospitals, employing the equivalent of 203 full-time pharmacists and pharmacist technicians. Over the course of the next three to four years, 15 pharmacy technician positions will be reduced through a policy of attrition, and six pharmacists will be redeployed to clinical positions which will focus on reducing the costs of medications. An annual operating budget of $50 million will be reduced by $6 million per year (12%) by becoming more efficient in the use and ordering of drugs from vendors, and insisting on a rational use of drugs as part of a patient's overall treatment program.

"Although the team may not have broken new ground in their redesign of the pharmacy systems, we believe the way we packaged the program is a significant improvement over what we would have done without the FOCUS process. For example,

- We knew that we needed to improve services to outpatients because of the increase in ambulatory care, but through our interviews we learned what customers would need in order for the transition from inpatient to outpatient care to be seamless.

- We knew that we would make changes to the way medications were dispensed on the hospital floor, but we learned that nurses' preferences were different than what we had anticipated.

- We knew that pharmacists wanted to "get out of the dungeon," as they often referred to their sense of isolation, but we had not expected the degree to which doctors and nurses also wanted pharmacist involvement with patients.

"Using the FOCUS process provided the team with a template to direct our course of action. A team of people, who potentially came into the project with private agendas aimed at protecting their world as they knew it, were forced to redesign services that best met the customers' needs: doctors, nurses, vendors, hospital staff, patients, and their families. The level of consensus that was achieved, and the conviction behind the decisions made, is incredible. There is less resistance to the consolidation because it is widely recognized that we used a comprehensive, thought-out process to make our decisions, and these are not independent or casual ideas.

"Use of the FOCUS process is also making the necessary transitions easier. Without it, the team would not have had the level of consensus from senior managers which has helped to smooth the way for the changes.

"And although the switch will still be difficult for many people on the staff, they understand that this was not an independent or casual approach because we received repeated feedback throughout the process. The changes do not represent the whims of one person, or even of the team. They represent the needs of the customers.

"This project is seen throughout the Health Alliance of Greater Cincinnati as a very successful consolidation effort, and I believe that because we talked to our customers, we were able to integrate a lot of components into a much better program than if we had used our traditional methods for approaching redesign efforts."

Dick Seim, Vice President
Health Alliance of Greater Cincinnati

Appendix A

At-A-Glance View of the FOCUS Process

	Step	Outcomes	Tools Used
FRAME THE PROJECT	**1: Determine Purpose** 1 – 3 hours See page 23	A purpose statement that describes the goals of the project; clearly articulated statements of what you hope to learn; and confirmation that the project fits with your organization's goals.	Ladder of abstraction
	2: Review Existing Data Several hours to several days, spread over time See page 41	List of sources of relevant information and a plan for gathering data. Reviewing data will be ongoing work throughout the FOCUS process.	None
	3: Create Customer Profile Matrix 1 – 4 hours See page 47	A matrix of types of people to visit that provides a 360° view of your issue.	Customer profile matrix
	4: Create Interview Guide 1 – 2 hours See page 63	A standard introduction for the interviews, one or more interview guides, and an observation guide, if necessary.	None
ORGANIZE RESOURCES	**5: Estimate Project Requirements** 1 hour or less See page 87	An estimate of the team members' available time to work on this project; an estimate of time needed to complete the project; and an estimate of the resources needed to complete the project.	Project requirements worksheet
	6: Meet With Sponsors 1 – 2 hours See page 95	Agreement on organizational fit; agreement on scope, schedule, and resources; and a schedule of future meetings with sponsors.	Scope, schedule, & resources grid
	7: Negotiate Scope, Schedule, & Resources 30 minutes or less See page 103	Agreement on how to balance scope, schedule, and resources.	Scope, schedule, & resources grid
	8: Schedule Interviews Up to 8 hours See page 113	Names, addresses, and phone numbers of interviewees; complete schedule of interviews; and assignment of interview teams.	Customer profile matrix

Step	Outcomes	Tools Used	
9: Prepare for Visits Approximately 2 hours See page 137	Interview roles determined; common understanding of ground rules for customer visits; and confirmed schedule and travel plans.	None	
10: Polish Your Skills Approximately 4 hours See page 147	Team members have practiced listening, probing, notetaking, observation, and debriefing skills.	Interview practice exercise; Observation practice exercise; Interview guide; Observation guide	
11: Finalize Preparations Approximately 1 hour See page 161	Interviewees have received agenda and topics of discussion; customer background information has been reviewed; and there is a complete set of interview supplies and equipment.	None	**COLLECT DATA**
12: Conduct Interviews 2 – 3 hours per interview + travel & observation time See page 167	Set of verbatim notes and observation notes for all interviews.	Interview guide; Observation guide; Quick reference guides	
13: Follow Up 15 – 20 minutes per interview + 30 minutes See page 183	Team members reflect on their experience with customer visits, and follow-up thank-you letters are sent to interviewees.	None	
14: Check Your Direction 1 hour or less See page 195	Agreement on which analytical path to take and a review of your scope, schedule, and resources.	Path for analysis table	
T15: Develop Key Question Approximately 30 minutes See page 205	A clear, concise question to focus the analysis.	Ladder of abstraction	**UNDERSTAND TARGETED PATH**
T16: Structure the Data 1 hour per interview + 4 hours See page 211	A completed affinity diagram showing relationships among the customer statements.	Method for Priority Marking™; Affinity diagram	
T17: Identify Key Themes 1 hour or less See page 235	Identification of no more than three Level 1 titles from the affinity diagram to target for action.	Affinity diagram	

	Step	Outcomes	Tools Used
UNDERSTAND REQUIREMENTS PATH	**14: Check Your Direction** 1 hour or less See page 195	Agreement on which analytical path to take and a review of your scope, schedule, and resources.	Path for analysis table
	R15: Identify Key Customer Concerns 1 hour per interview See page 245	Identification of customer voices representing key ideas, needs, problems, concerns, and solutions from all of the interviews.	Method for Priority Marking™
	R16: Construct Requirement Statements At least 8 hours See page 255	A list of key requirements derived from the customers' stated ideas, needs, problems, concerns, and solutions.	Translation worksheet
	R17: Assess Requirement Priorities 5 hours + time to get surveys back See page 273	The identification of two dozen or fewer high priority requirements; a relative priority ranking of key requirements based on customer feedback.	Method for Priority Marking™; Affinity diagram; Importance questionnaire (or other survey tool)
UNDERSTAND SYSTEMS PATH	**14: Check Your Direction** 1 hour or less See page 195	Agreement on which analytical path to take and a review of your scope, schedule, and resources.	Path for analysis table
	S15: Identify System Dimensions 1 – 3 hours See page 299	The identification of three to five key dimensions of your system; key questions for each dimension to guide your analysis.	Ladder of abstraction
	S16: Structure the Data for Each Dimension 1 – 1½ hours per interview + 4 hours per dimension See page 307	An affinity diagram for each dimension to help identify the key issues; an understanding of common themes across all of the dimensions (optional).	Method for Priority Marking™; Affinity diagram
	S17: Identify High Leverage Points Approximately 8 hours See page 331	The identification of key factors and the relationships between them; identification of a small set of high leverage points that influence the system as a whole.	Factor table; Influence matrix

Step	Outcomes	Tools Used
18: Generate Ideas 2 – 4 hours or 2 – 4 half days, depending on path See page 363	Many possible ideas for action organized in one or more tree diagrams.	Brainstorming; Strength continuum; Method for Priority Marking™; Tree diagram
19: Evaluate Ideas & Create a Complete Solution 4 – 8 hours See page 385	The identification of a solution based on evaluation criteria; presentation to sponsors of the learnings and proposed solutions.	Evaluation matrix
20: Develop an Action Plan 2 – 4 hours for overview 2 – 4 days to create plan See page 397	Implementation plan for the identified solution; method for ongoing communication with sponsors.	Flowcharts; PERT chart; Gantt chart; Resource allocation chart; Planning worksheet; Implementation worksheet

SELECT ACTION

Appendix B

Additional Resources From CQM and Oriel

Supplemental Tools and Methodologies

The FOCUS method described in *Voices into Choices* can be widely applied, as you have seen. However, there is also a rich array of complementary methods available, some of which are referenced in this book. These methodologies are compatible with the FOCUS process in tools and language and offer additional capability. In combination, these techniques offer an integrated management system to address today's business challenges.

7-Step Problem Solving Method
The Voice of the Customer provides important data that can focus improvement efforts. When it comes to tackling the problem itself, a 7-Step problem-solving method offers a standardized, disciplined approach to explore a problem, gather data, understand root causes, and implement solutions that stick. In fact, some 7-Step teams use the FOCUS process to help them generate ideas for solutions. The 7-Step method can be deployed throughout an organization to maximize continuous improvement efforts. It is designed to help everyone resolve problems that impact progress and profits. (Available from CQM and Oriel)

9-Step Project Planning System
For an effective method for project planning that is complementary to the FOCUS process, you may want to consider the 9-Step Project Planning System. It is widely used by individuals and groups to plan and execute cross-functional or complex projects. It offers a systematic way to identify and coordinate components of your project planning system, including key project considerations, a clear set of steps by which to proceed, problems that can impact the project, and necessary countermeasures. (Available from CQM)

Concept Engineering™
This proven, best-in-class method is used in the early stages of new product or service development to anticipate and define customer requirements and effectively translate them into product and service concepts. A more rigorous approach than the FOCUS process, Concept Engineering excels in its use of contextual imagery to discover latent requirements. This step-by-step methodology leads the team to develop metrics for measuring the product's or service's performance in meeting customer requirements. (Available from CQM)

Interactive Planning

While the FOCUS process helps you gain insight into strategic issues, it is not a comprehensive strategic planning methodology. Interactive Planning is Professor Russell Ackoff's world-class strategic planning method which CQM has integrated with the operational strength of TQM. Interactive Planning's Mess, Design, and Means Planning modules offer companies a method to design or redesign their strategic plan and cascade it into their operational planning system. In addition, Interactive Planning has been used effectively to redesign a process or a product. (Available from CQM)

Language Processing Method™

The Language Processing Method offers a similar but much more powerful approach to using language data than the affinity diagram. The LP Method includes problem-solving principles and semantic techniques taught by internationally recognized behaviorists, linguists, and quality management thought leaders. Executives, managers, new product teams, and workers use the LP Method to understand, analyze, and use language to gain new insights, generate new ideas, come to consensus, and make decisions. (Available from CQM)

Method for Priority Marking™

The Method for Priority Marking is an effective way to manage language data and reduce statements from the "valuable many" to the "vital few." Described briefly in *Voices into Choices*, the MPM is fully described in one of CQM's ToolKit manual series. (Available from CQM)

Plain & Simple® Series

Understanding data related to your issue is important to your Voice of the Customer effort. *Plain & Simple®* is a series of books designed to teach people appropriate methods of data collection and how to analyze and interpret data through the use of basic statistical tools. These easy-to-use guides can be implemented at all levels of an organization. (Available from Oriel)

The Team® Handbook Second Edition

Employ sound team practices as you focus on the Voice of the Customer. *The Team® Handbook Third Edition* is a widely used, comprehensive resource for teams needing to develop the fundamentals of problem solving, conflict resolution, meeting skills, decision making methods, brainstorming techniques, and team roles and responsibilities. (Available from Oriel)

The Team® Memory Jogger™

Skilled interviewers listen to understand and know how to listen effectively. *The Team® Memory Jogger* is a handy reference for team members to refresh their listening and other team-related skills. (Available from Oriel)

Tree Diagram Technique

This is a powerful technique to help groups or individuals organize, evaluate, and prioritize. Described briefly in *Voices into Choices*, the tree diagram is fully described in one of CQM's ToolKit manual series. (Available from CQM)

Other CQM Products and Services

A New American TQM: Four Practical Revolutions in Management, by Shoji Shiba, Alan Graham, and David Walden, examines four practical revolutions in management thinking: customer focus, continuous improvement, total participation, and societal networking.

A New American TQM (video series). This series is designed to accompany *A New American TQM: Four Practical Revolutions in Management* and can be used to help launch TQM initiatives. The series includes 12 videotapes, textbooks, and facilitator guides.

The CQM Journal. This journal offers insights into new and improved management practices and provides guidance on how to implement them. Prominent industry and academic leaders contribute to the *Journal*, which is published quarterly.

The Quality Improvement ToolKits. This set of eight manuals is based on the work of Dr. Shoji Shiba, with contributions from hundreds of practitioners from CQM member companies. The kit offers up-to-date information on CQM's most successful problem-solving methods and includes worksheets, checklists, models, and hints on how to use the most effective quality improvement tools. The set of eight includes:

The 7-Step Problem-Solving Method
The 9-Step Project Planning System
Concept Engineering™
Diagnosing Teamwork through the Quality Improvement (QI) Story
The Language Processing Method™
Managing Teams
The Method for Priority Marking™
Tree Diagrams

Seminars and Training Programs. The Center for Quality of Management offers both public and on-site courses and provides advising services to help companies develop skill. These services include the following topics:

7-Step Problem Solving Method
9-Step Project Planning System
Concept Engineering™
Conversation for Action
Conversational Competence to Build High Performance Organizations
Hoshin Planning
Interactive Planning
Language Processing Method™
Mobilizing Quality Improvement Teams
Practical Benchmarking for Problem Solving
Process Discovery
Strategic Planning
Succeeding with Teams
Tools for Teams
Total Quality Management for Senior Executives: Planning and Implementation
Understanding Variation
Voice of the Customer: The FOCUS Method

Quick Reference Cards. User-friendly cards that contain comprehensive definitions, examples, and graphics of the tools and steps taught in courses.

Center for Quality of Management

One Alewife Center, Suite 450
Cambridge MA 02140
☎ 617-873-8950
✆ 617-873-8980
E-mail: CQM_Mail@cqm.org
www.cqm.org

Other Joiner Products and Services

Fourth Generation Management: The New Business Consciousness, by Brian L. Joiner, describes how a new synthesis of management principles can create rapid, sustained improvement. This book covers everything from developing a customer focus, to using data, to rethinking performance appraisal.

Fundamentals of Fourth Generation Management. An 8-module video program that explores the basic principles of customer focus, the scientific approach, and working together as a team. The program mixes video instruction with real-time exercises that emphasize key points and skills.

Guiding Successful Projects. A set of reference cards based on the proven Joiner 7 Step Method™. These cards help readers know the right questions to ask, when to ask them, and what is expected at each phase of the project.

Joiner 7 Step Method™ Notebook. A structured approach to problem solving that helps you develop effective solutions to get the necessary results, and maintain the gains.

Joiner 7 Step Method™ Storyboard. A user-friendly, ready made format on disk to help teams document their progress and present the results of their improvement effort in a polished, professional presentation.

Plain & Simple® Series. A set of 10 guides that teach users how to decide what tools to use in a situation, how to collect the right kind of data, create the charts, interpret the information, and put it to use. The books can be used for self-study, as a resource, or in training sessions. The set of 10 includes:

Introduction to the Tools
Data Collection   *How to Graph*
Flowcharts   *Pareto Charts*
Time Plots   *Individuals Charts*
Frequency Plots   *Scatter Plots*
Cause-and-Effect Diagrams

The Team® Handbook Second Edition. This book covers the fundamental skills necessary for teams to be successful, such as conflict resolution, problem solving, discussion management, sponsor and management responsibilities, and more. A set of 212 color overhead transparencies is also available.

The Team® Memory Jogger™. A handy pocket guide written from the team member's point of view. This reference is valuable for improving team effectiveness, providing practical tips on feedback skills, having effective meetings, dealing with common team problems, and more.

Running Effective Meetings. Learn how to get much more out of meetings. This 4-hour instructional program is designed to help any kind of group learn and practice effective meetings skills.

Training Services. Joiner offers public and on-site seminars, workshops, and training programs featuring hands-on learning in skills such as problem solving, tools, teams, change, facilitation, and leadership.

Consulting Services. Our experienced consultants specialize in helping customers understand current needs and opportunities, make significant improvement in key business objectives, and implement organization-wide changes. They work with all levels of organizations, from senior executives to shop floor employees, in a breadth of industries encompassing services, manufacturing, education, and government.

Oriel®
3800 Regent Street
Madison WI 53705-0445
☎ 800-669-TEAM   608-238-8134
✆ 608-238-2908
E-mail: sales@orielinc.com
www.oriel.com

Index

In the spirit of mutual learning, we encourage you to share your stories and experiences using the FOCUS process. You may write, fax, e-mail, or call

> Center for Quality of Management
> Attn: Communications Manager
> One Alewife Center, Suite 450
> Cambridge, MA 02140
> 617-873-8950 (phone)
> 617-873-8980 (fax)
> CQM_Mail@cqm.org

The information you share will be held confidential and will not be used in any part without your written permission.

About the Authors

Gary Burchill has a B.S. in Engineering from Duke University, an M.B.A. with Distinction from Harvard University, and a Ph.D. in Operations Management from the Massachusetts Institute of Technology. He has published articles, lectured, and developed courses on product development and process improvement for industry and university settings. A member of the Center for Quality of Management's Opportunity Discovery Board, he has been associated with CQM since its founding in 1990. He has 20 years service as a Naval Officer involved in logistics support and sustainment for both the submarine and surface ships. He has developed, designed, patented, and licensed products related to his outdoor hobbies.

Christina Hepner Brodie is a consultant in the area of new product development process and has been an associate of the Center for Quality of Management since 1994. She has introduced executives, senior managers, and new product developers to Voice of the Customer methodologies at over forty corporations and organizations across the U.S. and in Europe, including ADAC Laboratories, the Health Alliance of Greater Cincinnati, Hewlett-Packard, Honeywell, L.L. Bean, Nike, Titleist, and Volvo. Christina's work in teaching, consulting, coaching, and professional speaking is grounded by her B.A. in Education from Capital University and M.A. in Counseling from Ohio State University. These degrees, combined with years of experience, provide the foundation for her approach to enabling people to develop the means to achieve their professional and personal goals.